THE FABRIC OF THIS WORLD

The Fabric of This World

* * *

INQUIRIES INTO CALLING, CAREER CHOICE, and the DESIGN OF HUMAN WORK

by

Lee Hardy

WILLIAM B. EERDMANS PUBLISHING COMPANY
GRAND RAPIDS, MICHIGAN

255 Jefferson Ave. S.E., Grand Rapids, Mich. 49503

Printed in the United States of America

Reprinted 1995

Library of Congress Cataloging-in-Publication Data

Hardy, Lee, 1950-

The fabric of this world: inquiries into calling, career choice, and the design of human work / by Lee Hardy.

p. cm.

Includes bibliographical references.

ISBN 0-8028-0298-2

1. Vocation. 2. Work—Religious aspects—Christianity. 3. Vocational guidance. I. Title.

BV4740.H37 1990

261.8′5—dc20 90-32758

CIP

To my parents,
Pat and Anne Hardy,
for their support, their confidence,
and their example

But they tend to the fabric of this world,
and their prayer is in the practice of their trade.

Ecclesiasticus 38:34

* * *

Contents

Preface x

Introduction xiv

PART ONE: ***Expositions***

1. Work: Divine Prerogative or the Burden of the Beast? 3
   - *The Greek Solution* 6
   - *The Medieval Continuation* 16
   - *The Renaissance Reversal* 26
   - *Marx: Self-Realization Through Work* 29
   - *Freud: Work as a Form of Self-Denial* 38
   - *Summary and Transition: The Promise of the Concept of Vocation* 43

2. Our Work, God's Providence: The Christian Concept of Vocation 44
   - *Luther: God's Providential Presence in the Work of our Hands* 45

The Calvinist Elaboration: Work and the Organic Structure of Social Life 54
The Calvinist Modification: The Call to Reform Fallen Structures 63
Ecumenical Convergence: The Contemporary Catholic Position 67

PART TWO: *Applications*

3. Work, Life, and Vocational Choice: Investing Yourself in the Divine Economy 79
Making the Match: Career Choice 80
Finding the Fit: Job Placement 93
Changing the System: Conflict and Strategy 107
Balancing Commitments: Work and Vocation 111
Reformed Monasticism: The Work of Prayer 119
Summary and Transition: From Career Choice to Job Design 122

4. The Shaping of Human Work: Management Theory and Job Design 124
Frederick W. Taylor: The Imposition of Science and the Brutalization of Work 128
Elton Mayo: The Hawthorne Experiment and the Discovery of the Human Dimension of Work 140
Chris Argyris: Conflicts Between Organizational Structure and Human Self-Realization 145
Frederick Herzberg: Human Needs, Motivation and Hygiene 151
Douglas McGregor: Theory X, Theory Y, and Management by Integration 155

Peter F. Drucker: Respect for Persons, Management by Objectives, and Responsible Work 160

Robert Levering: The Ethics of Trust and the Politics of Fair Play in Great Workplaces 167

The Bottom Line: Must We Choose Between People and Profits? 174

Live Options for Job Design: Restoring a Sense of Vocation to Work 178

Bibliography 186

Index of Names 209

Index of Subjects 211

* * *

Preface

MY FATHER WAS a pharmacist. So was my grandfather. Drugs, you might say, ran in the family. Besides being pharmacists, my immediate forebears were also entrepreneurs in the best tradition of American independent shopkeepers. The owner of his own drugstore before the days of mass-produced grooming aids, my grandfather once concocted a red liquid which he bottled and sold under the name "Hardy's Hair Stay-Down." It looked suspiciously like cough syrup. But evidently it did the trick: he had repeat customers. Later, when men's hairstyles shifted in the direction of the crewcut and flattop, he came out with a yellow paste—the chief ingredient of which, as I recall, was beeswax. He dubbed the successor product "Hardy's Hair Stay-Up." Its net effect on one's appearance, however, was less tidy than "Hardy's Hair Stay-Down." I can remember putting some of the stuff on the front of my flattop as a kid. During the summer it would melt, making a greasy mess of my forehead.

In 1952 my father took over the family business. And as soon as I was able bodied, I became a regular fixture in the drugstore—dusting shelves, marking stock, mopping floors, and generally applying myself to a variety of semiskilled tasks. One afternoon after school, while soaking labels off bottles in the back room, I chanced to look up and noticed a number of discolored cotton wads stuck to the ceiling. Curious, I called to my father at the prescription counter and asked him how they got there. He came back and explained, with some embarrassment, that when he was a kid soaking labels off bottles in the back room, he had invented a chemical solution which, when put in a narrow-necked bottle followed by a cotton ball and shaken, could propel soggy wads of cotton to a considerable height. Success was sticking one to the ceiling.

My father refused to give me the formula for that liquid propellant. Some of the things he did as a boy were not the kinds of things he wanted his own son to do. Still, I admired him for his early ingenuity. It made sense that later, as a student at the University of Southern California just before World War II, he had intended to be a chemical engineer. The war, however, changed his plans.

Beyond my childlike admiration for my father, I also felt at that moment an identification with him, an identification borne by the tradition of work in our family. Some thirty years before my father was just like me, I suddenly realized, working for his father in the same back room, performing the same tasks—albeit with more inventiveness.

In spite of that identification I did not grow up to be a pharmacist. Nor did I go into business on my own. But I did acquire in my youth a feeling for the centrality of work in human life. Work is indeed a "fundamental dimension of human existence," as Pope John Paul II said, though at the time I would hardly have articulated my feeling in those words. Along with a sense for work I also as a youth acquired a decidedly philosophical bent of mind. Perhaps that was largely a result of growing up in the 1960s, which, for all its misplaced idealism, was at least a time when ideas were taken seriously. At any rate, that bent of mind was eventually to carry me through the rigors of graduate school as a philosophy student.

My early sense of the centrality of work in human life and my later passion for philosophical reflection came together in an unexpected way when I turned to teaching. When I was hired at Calvin College as an instructor in philosophy, I was told that besides teaching regular semester courses I should also be prepared to teach an Interim course, the proposal for which was two months overdue. Not having much time to think about a course topic, I recalled an Interim course taught by a former professor of mine, Dr. Maarten Vrieze, on the philosophy of labor. Although I never took that course, the subject intrigued me. I decided to try something similar, later realizing how this course would serve as an ideal occasion for integrating my philosophical proclivities with my personal history and, as it turned out, my religious convictions as well.

The book before you is largely a product of that Interim course, taught several times by me and later by an interdisciplinary team under the title "Christian Perspectives on Work and Vocation." The approach I take to work in this book is also interdisciplinary. It draws upon such diverse disciplines as theology, sociology, psychology, philosophy, history, and economics. Since I am qualified in at most only one of these disciplines, I have necessarily incurred a number of debts in developing this book. I should like to thank, first of all, the members of the interdisciplinary research team on work and vocation which met for two successive summers at Calvin—Shirley Roels, Dale Cooper, Glen van Andel, Dick Karpinnen, and Steve Simpson. I benefitted greatly from their input and encouragement. Second, I should like to thank my colleagues in the philosophy department at Calvin College, past and present. Early drafts of several chapters went through the dreaded Tuesday Philosophy Department Colloquium. Criticisms of these chapters were to the point, usually helpful, and always delivered in a spirit of trust and friendship. Nick Wolterstorff, Rich Mouw, Clif Orlebeke, Pete de Vos, Ken Konyndyk, John Cooper, Greg Mellema, Del Ratzsch, Steve Wykstra, Mary Stewart van Leeuwen, Lambert Zuidervaart, Mark Talbot, David Snyder, Arvin Vos, and Tom Kennedy—thanks. Third, my thanks to a number of outside readers and respondents: Arthur Holmes, John Vander Stelt, John Schneider, Eugene Dykema, George Monsma, David Lyon, Karen de Vos, Gene Klaasen, Mike McGervey, and Calvin P. van Reken. Fourth, to the people I interviewed for information included in several segments of the third chapter: Marty Weirick, John Roels, Rolf Bouma, and Dr. Robert Bulten. Fifth, to my student assistants: Nancy de Wolde, Houston Smit, Dwayne Mulder, Lisa de Boer, Gloria Banas, and Keith Wyma. Sixth, to Calvin College for a research leave of absence during interim 1987 and its support in the administration of a CAPHE grant funding the interdisciplinary summer faculty seminars on work and vocation. Seventh, to my students for their many and varied responses to my ideas—even their incomprehension was at times instructive. Eighth, to my pastor at Eastern Avenue Christian Reformed Church, Leonard Vander Zee. His spiritual guidance both from the pulpit and in personal conversation has been of great help to me. I trust that he may detect some of his influence in my work. Ninth, to the good people at Eerdmans—Jon Pott, Phil Apol, and Ina Vondiziano. And last, but by no means least, to my wife Judy, a professional copy editor who went over my entire manuscript free of charge.

* * *

Introduction

IN THEIR BEST-SELLING analysis of American society, *Habits of the Heart,* Robert N. Bellah and his associates claim that at the heart of any recovery of our common life, of our "social ecology," there must be "a change in the meaning of work."[1] The meaning of work must change, they insist, because it has been too long informed by the spirit of modern individualism, a spirit which promotes the idea of work as a means of private advancement rather than public contribution—a spirit which will rend the social fabric of our society and erode our democratic institutions if allowed to have full sway in American life.

According to the cultural taxonomy developed in *Habits of the Heart,* modern American individualism comes in two forms: utilitarian and expressivist. The utilitarian individualists among us locate the meaning of their lives in the public world of work. They turn to work in pursuit of personal success, which is often measured financially. They are hard working, highly competitive, and willing to sacrifice their private lives for the sake of career advancement. Expressive individualists, on the other hand, typically turn away from the harsh realities of the world of work and seek meaning in private life—personal rela-

1. Robert N. Bellah, Richard Madsen, William M. Sullivan, Ann Swidler, and Steven M. Tipton, *Habits of the Heart: Individualism and Commitment in American Life* (New York: Harper & Row, 1986), p. 289.

tionships, leisure activities, and "life-style enclaves." They have decided to bow out of the rat race for the sake of a more humane and sensitive existence. Both kinds of individualists, however, live primarily for self. One seeks self-fulfillment on the job; the other seeks it off the job. Neither approaches work with the primary intention of serving others in it, of making a contribution to the common good. But this is precisely the meaning that work must come to have, the Bellah group claims, if American society is to regain its social solidarity and face the challenges of the future as a house undivided.

The understanding of work as service to one's neighbor, however, is by no means foreign to American soil. Within the now dominant cultural tradition of modern individualism lie the strands of two other cultural traditions which reach further back into American history: the republican and the biblical. And within the biblical tradition's understanding of social life, as articulated by the English Calvinists who founded the Massachusetts Bay Colony, is a strong emphasis on work as a form of mutual service, as a vocation. Indeed, the Bellah group argues, it is precisely this concept of vocation, embedded in our own cultural heritage, which must be made to live again and walk among us. If our troubled and fragmented social world is to be reconstituted, we need a "reappropriation of the idea of vocation or calling, a return in a new way to the idea of work as a contribution to the good of all and not merely as a means to one's own advancement."[2]

The Fabric of This World might be read as an attempt to help revitalize the concept of work as vocation—or calling—at least within the professing Christian community, where it should have some force. My primary intent is to flesh out the concept of vocation, to delineate its historical background, to mark out its place in the array of possible attitudes towards the meaning of work in human life, to illuminate its full religious content, and to explore its practical implications, both personal and social.

2. Ibid., pp. 287-88.

A glance at the table of contents will reveal that my work on the concept of vocation is divided into two parts—expository and applicatory. In the first part I begin with a representation of the history of Western attitudes towards work. The scheme I employ in this representation draws its inspiration from a theme in Reformed theology. John Calvin stated in the opening sections of his *Institutes* that our self-knowledge depends upon our knowledge of God. In the first chapter of my work I generalize on this formula and convert it into a method of exposition: we understand ourselves—and the place of work in our lives—in terms of our understanding of the divine. Traditionally, Western thinkers have pictured humankind as occupying a place in the cosmic scheme of things somewhere between the divine and the animal. Something about us is god-like; but equally, something about us is animal-like. Furthermore, most Western thinkers agree that human beings must emphasize, cultivate, and reinforce what is god-like about us, and downplay, ignore, and even repress what is animal-like about us. Despite this formal agreement, opinions range widely as to the nature of the divine. Hence there is disagreement as to what is god-like about us and what kind of lives we should live. In the first chapter I indicate how Western attitudes towards work have been directly and decisively shaped by our self-understandings as they follow from our understanding of God. Work has sometimes been seen as activity which demotes us to the level of animal existence, sometimes as activity which exalts us to the status of divine beings. Attitudes towards work have been accordingly either negative or positive.

Against the background of these polarized attitudes towards work I set forth in the second chapter the concept of work as vocation as inaugurated by the Protestant Reformers. In a certain sense the Reformed concept of work as vocation steers a middle path between the vilification and the glorification of work. The concept of vocation, as we shall see, claims it is in our work that we bear within us God's image as Creator. Indeed, it claims more than that. Reformed thought claims that through the work we are called to do God himself carries on his creative activity in this world. But precisely for this reason work does not make us into gods, although it does relate to what is god-like about us. Rather, work makes us into God's representatives on earth, his stewards, entrusted with the task of developing the rich resources of the earth for the benefit of the human community. Although work does not make us into gods, it does not reduce us to the level of animals either. It relates to what is specifically human about us.

In the second part of the book I make two practical applications of the Christian concept of vocation—one to the personal issue of career choice, and one to the social issue of job design. The Christian understanding of work and its relation to career choice has been discussed in a number of recent books by evangelical authors. I think this is a good indication that many American Christians are concerned about the relation between their faith and their lives on the job. It bespeaks a commendable desire for integrating faith and life and for religious consistency. But the practical advice offered in most of these books rarely goes beyond the personal issue of career choice. Rarely does it raise the question of how best to pursue one's chosen career within the given social structure of work; and hardly ever does it take up the question of the social structure of work itself. In this regard evangelical reflection on work remains in the grips of modern individualism—not that it promotes or even condones self-seeking in work, but rather that it poses the issue of work strictly from the vantage point of the individual. It seeks only to guide the individual through the given structures of the world of work, but never to examine or challenge those structures themselves. Near the end of chapter 3 and in the whole of chapter 4 I attempt to examine critically the social and structural dimension of work in light of the practical implications of the concept of vocation. I am convinced that such examination is essential, and that any individualistic treatment of the problem of work is incomplete. For our work can count as a vocation only if it occurs in the kind of social structures that make it a genuine service to others through the responsible use of our talents and abilities.

I have written this book mindful of college students preparing themselves for careers. But I think it can be read with profit by any educated person concerned about the meaning of work, regardless of that person's stage or status in life. A word of advice, however, for the general reader: Chapter 4, on management theory, was written especially for those intending to go into—or already in—management. Unsuspecting general readers may find the treatment of the development of American management theory overly technical and personally unrewarding. Such readers may lay down the book at the end of chapter 3 and still have a "complete reading experience." I hope, however, that the flow of the argument will sweep them into chapter 4 and carry them through to the end, as this chapter sheds some light on the motive ideas behind the structure of the work world today—a world with which we all must contend to one degree or another.

Finally, a note to scholars: this book is not a scholarly treatise on work, although it does have a scholarly basis. For the aid and comfort of my readers I have tried to keep the qualifications and digressions to a minimum. These I have tucked away in the footnotes, and the scholars among us are hereby referred to them. Some will no doubt notice in my work the conspicuous absence of any reference to or discussion of the dreaded "Weber Thesis." Weber's claim that the fervent economic activity associated with the inception of capitalism in northern Europe should be understood as an attempt on the part of Protestants to relieve the religious anxiety induced by the Calvinist doctrine of election has been roundly and well criticized in other volumes.[3] As much ink has already been spilled over this topic, I feel little obligation to add any. Nor do I want my discussion of the Protestant concept of vocation to be dominated by a speculative thesis which, in my estimation, has rightly lost its credibility.

3. Cf. Robert W. Green, ed., *Protestantism, Capitalism, and Social Science: The Weber Thesis Controversy*. 2nd ed. (Lexington, MA: Heath, 1973), and Robert M. Mitchell, *Calvin's and the Puritan's View of the Protestant Ethic* (Washington, DC: University Press of America, 1979).

PART ONE

* * *

Expositions

CHAPTER ONE

* * *

Work: Divine Prerogative or the Burden of the Beast?

I SUPPOSE MOST students enter colleges and universities with the idea of preparing themselves for a career. To help finance that educational venture, many will no doubt hold an odd assortment of summer jobs. But if these jobs turn out anything like the jobs I had as a college student, they will be tolerable only because they are guaranteed to last no longer than three months at a time.

I can recall rearranging clods of dirt with a rusty rake in a housing development on the outskirts of Pittsburgh. That was my first summer as a graduate student. As I bent over the barren ground, coughing in the dust, my boss pulled up on his vintage Ford tractor and gleefully informed me that I was now a genuine landscaper. Before that job I had always associated landscaping with the fitting design and artful care of flora about the human habitat. In my case, I seemed to be doing something decidedly less satisfying than that—"landscraping," perhaps, but not landscaping.

I also have some unpleasantly distinct recollections of hosing particles of cow flesh off the bandsaws of a supermarket butcher department somewhere in the southwest suburbs of Chicago. That was during my second year of college. According to the personnel manager's book of job descriptions, I was at that time an "environmental engineer." But somehow that sanitized title failed to capture the full essence of my work.

I have equally fond memories of pitching watermelons out of the stuffy, straw-laden trailers down at the produce docks of Los Angeles. I was just out of high school. Perhaps I was a "pre-packaged perishable goods redistribution facilitator." I never did find out the official title of that job. The regular union dock workers, who refused to touch uncrated produce, called us "swampers"—an obviously derogatory term, but, given the nature of the job, entirely appropriate.

In the light of my early forays into the barren foothills of paid employment, it would hardly surprise me to find out that going to college, university, or a vocational training center is largely an attempt to avoid being saddled for life with precisely these kinds of jobs. They are unpleasant, uninteresting, and not terribly lucrative. Most of us are greatly concerned about the kind of work we do, or will be doing, especially in these days of relatively high unemployment, downward mobility, unforeseen shifts in the job market, and economic uncertainty. We want good jobs. And we are willing to spend a lot of time, money, and effort equipping ourselves with the "marketable skills" we need to get them.

What I do find surprising, given the level of our concern about work, is that we rarely pause to reflect on work itself — its nature, history, present shape, and proper place within our lives. For those of us employed full time, roughly half of our adult waking life will be spent on the job. We will spend more time at work than doing anything else, aside from sleeping. More time at work than at home—unless we work at home; more time at work than at church—unless we work at church; more time at work than at the arts—unless we work at the arts. To what end is all this time and energy being spent?

One obvious answer is this: we work to make a living, as we must. But is work just a matter of making a living? Or is there something more to it? Is work in itself a good thing for human beings? Should we count it among our blessings? Does it fill our lives with meaning, purpose, and direction? Does it offer the occasion for accomplishment, satisfaction, and self-fulfillment? Is it something we would be glad to do even if we didn't have to?

Or does work represent a curse upon human life? Is it, at best, a necessary evil? Does it consign us to a dull, narrow, and unadventurous existence? Does it condemn us to a life of self-denial for the sake of mere survival? Does it put us at the mercy of impersonal market forces, robbing us of our freedom and autonomy? Would a person in his right mind work if he didn't have to?

Moreover, should we as a society strive toward the goal of full employment, and dedicate ourselves to making all jobs as rich and as rewarding as possible? Or should we admit that work is and always will be a "disutility," try to minimize the need for work through advanced technology, and convert to a leisure-based society?

If we were to embark on such considerations, we would quickly come across a certain ambivalence in our attitude toward work. Most of us would not hesitate to contrast work with play. After all, work is no fun. This would seem to be one of the fundamental axioms of life. If the interviews conducted in Studs Terkel's book, *Working,* are a representative sample, the vast majority of Americans loath their daily occupations, or, at least, find them exceedingly tedious. Moreover, if the boredom and banality of the weekday routine were not compensated by a little excitement on the weekends, most employees would find their work unbearable. This holds not only for those with "blue-collar" jobs; it is the unhappy experience of many office workers and professionals too. For them, work offers very few, if any, intrinsic rewards. They work because they have to. It's a matter of financial necessity. If they didn't have to work, chances are they would be off pursuing their favorite leisure activity.

On the other hand, no one really wants to be out of work either. And that's not just because of the money. The devastating psychological effects of unemployment indicate that we do indeed value work for more than its monetary reward. Wrapped up in our jobs is also our self-esteem and our sense of identity and purpose in life. At work we find out what we can do. Our talents are identified, and our skills put to use. At work we acquire a sense of where we fit into the scheme of things and what we are supposed to be doing on a day-to-day basis. In fact, a significant number of people find their work far from boring or tedious. Rather they are positively challenged by their jobs. And when they perform, they receive a bracing round of recognition by their peers as well as their superiors. Often these people are so hooked on the rewards of their work—the stimulation and the recognition—that they can hardly stop working. They can't think of anything else they would rather do. Retirement is for them a form of death. And if the weekend didn't come as a period of enforced relaxation, most of them would burn out after five years of full-time employment.

The institution of work is undeniably one of the chief integrators of persons in our society. It orients our lives; it organizes our time; it puts us in touch with people. To be unemployed is to be afflicted with a kind of social leprosy. Few of us want to be out of work. And yet we are not entirely sure if work is, in itself, a good thing. Some of us work only in order to live; some of us live only to work. But most of us are somewhere in between. And our attitude toward work is divided accordingly. A nationwide survey of a cross section of Americans found that although the vast majority defined work as necessary, done for the sake of money and in itself unenjoyable, over three-fourths would continue working even if they were to receive enough money to live comfortably for the rest of their lives.[1]

The Greek Solution

To gain some perspective on the paradox of our own attitude toward work, it may be helpful to review the history of the way the meaning of work in human life has been construed in the West. For human beings have not always maintained such an ambivalent attitude toward work. Take the ancient Greeks. Compared to our attitude toward work, theirs was admirably

1. Robert L. Kahn, "On the Meaning of Work," *Journal of Occupational Medicine* 16 (November 1974): 716.

straightforward and uncomplicated: "To the Greeks," as Adriano Tilgher puts it, "work was a curse and nothing else."[2] In their world, work was an unmitigated evil to be avoided at all costs. It had no redeeming features or compensating factors. Unemployment, on the other hand, was a positive social virtue.[3] In fact, unemployment was one of the primary qualifications for full participation in society and a necessary condition for the possibility of a genuinely worthwhile life.[4] In ancient Greek society, to be out of work was a piece of singular good fortune.

Why this wholly negative attitude toward work? Granted, work has its share of drawbacks. But why couldn't the Greeks appreciate its good points as well and thus maintain a healthy, well-balanced ambivalance toward work as we do? The answers to these questions will probably seem implausible from our own cultural standpoint. To understand them, we must first exercise our historical imaginations and try to "live into" the Greek experience and organization of work.

The ancient Greeks associated work with that endless cycle of activity forced upon us by embodied existence. For bodies—both animal and human—are not self-sufficient. If we fail to regularly feed, clothe, and protect them from the elements, they expire. Thus hunting, farming, cooking, spinning, weaving, sewing, construction, plumbing, roadwork, and the like were all seen as various activities in which our existence is bound over to the biological order of necessity. If we are to survive, we must work.

But to spend our entire lives working is to sweat and toil and eventually die like animals, passing into oblivion without having left a mark or made a difference in this world. Through work we may have managed to stay alive for a while, but to what end? We did nothing to distinguish ourselves from the brutes. They too spend their whole life ministering to the daily recur-

2. Adriano Tilgher, *Work: What It Has Meant to Men Through the Ages* (New York: Arno Press, 1977), p. 3.

3. Aristotle, *Politics*, I.viii.9.

4. Aristotle, *Nicomachean Ethics*, X.7.

rent needs of the body. A life dominated by such work is a life condemned to animal futility: we work into order to eat, and eat in order to work, until our bodies wear down, die and disintegrate, leaving nothing behind but the dust from which they came. Eventually forgotten by subsequent generations, our existence, ruled by the grinding necessity of labor, will have signified nothing.

Yet, the Greek experience of the vanity of a life ruled by labor is not exclusively Greek, but a common and universal human experience. One can find poetic expression given to this sense of futility by the teacher in the book of Ecclesiastes:

> What does man gain from all his labor
> at which he toils under the sun? . . .
> What has been will be again,
> what has been done will be done again;
> there is nothing new under the sun. . . .
> There is no remembrance of men of old,
> and even those who are yet to come
> will not be remembered by those who follow. . . .
> What a heavy burden God has laid on men!
> I have seen all the things that are done under the sun;
> all of them are meaningless, a chasing after the wind. . . .
> Man's fate is like that of the animals;
> the same fate awaits them both:
> As one dies, so dies the other. . . .
> All go to the same place;
> all come from dust, and to dust all return.
> (Eccl. 1:3, 9, 11, 13, 14; 3:19, 20)

What is particularly Greek is not the recognition of the futility of work, but the response to it. Whereas the teacher of Ecclesiastes concludes that nothing is better than that a man enjoy his work and find satisfaction in his toil while revering God, whose works last forever (Eccl. 3:13, 22), the Greeks sought to escape the necessity of work altogether and to live in a way that takes part in the immortality of the gods. The trick was to come into a position whereby one would not have to engage in the work necessary for survival, but rather be free to pursue worthwhile activities —"practical" activities, such as great deeds in the political realm, or courageous acts in military conflict.

Besides their intrinsic worth, such feats performed before the public eye may win one a measure of immortality by virtue of living on in the memory of future generations. All mortals must die, but the names and reputations of a fortunate few will live on forever. Solon, Pericles, Alexander the Great, Julius Caesar, Mark Anthony, Constantine, Charlemagne, George Washington, Thomas Jefferson, Napoleon, Bismarck, Winston Churchill, and Franklin Delano Roosevelt—these radiant and enduring figures tower like Olympian gods over the nameless and obscure masses that scurry about in the shadowy underbrush of history. "By their capacity for the immortal deed, by their ability to leave imperishable traces behind," Hannah Arendt writes, such

> men, their individual mortality notwithstanding, attain an immortality of their own and prove themselves to be of a 'divine' nature. The distinction between man and animal runs right through the human species itself: only the best *(aristoi),* who constantly prove themselves to be the best . . . and who prefer 'immortal fame to mortal things,' are really human; the others, content with whatever pleasures nature will yield them, live and die like animals.[5]

But, we might ask, given the necessity of work in order to meet the daily recurrent needs of the human body, how could we ever find enough time to pursue an unpaid career in public life? How could we possibly avoid having all of our available time swallowed up by the activities demanded of us by natural necessity? For most of us, just making ends meet is a full-time job. The answer that ancient Greek society gave to this question can be summarized in a word: slavery. If a man were wealthy

5. Hannah Arendt, *The Human Condition* (Chicago: University of Chicago Press, 1958), p. 19.

enough to own slaves, then they could take care of all necessary work, leaving him free to pursue the life of honor through the accomplishment of some great and noble deed.

We moderns, committed to the idea of universal human rights, no doubt find this ancient solution to the problem of work repugnant. But the Greek philosopher Aristotle held that this answer was squarely rooted in the order of nature itself. Some people are just cut out to be slaves. Who are they? Those who, to put it delicately, have an underdeveloped capacity for rational thought and deliberation. In other words, the dumb ones. Especially the dumb ones with big, slightly stooped bodies. These people Aristotle called "natural slaves."[6] They were to engage in the productive work within the private realm of the household, thereby making it possible for the independently wealthy members of the leisure class to engage in political activity within the public space of the *polis.*

The Greek solution to the futility of mortal life was by no means a wholly democratic one. Only the rich and the powerful were to be released from the necessity of work; the rest were condemned to it by force. Since "men were dominated by the necessities of life," Hannah Arendt explains, "they could win their freedom only through the domination of those whom they subjected to necessity by force. The slaves' degradation was a blow of fate worse than death, because it carried with it a metamorphosis of man into something akin to a tame ani-

6. Aristotle, *Politics,* I.v.8. It should be pointed out that Aristotle was not defending the institution of slavery against its detractors. The institution was rarely, if ever, questioned in the ancient world. Rather, Aristotle was concerned with the question of *why* slavery is justified, not *if* it was justified. There were those in Athens who held that slavery was a matter of convention. All men are equal; but some men have had the singular misfortune of being made slaves by force. (Prisoners of war were often brought home and sold as slaves). In opposition to this "might-makes-right" position, Aristotle held that slavery is justified because some men are slaves by nature. That is, some human beings are less than fully human. It follows from this that not all those who are actually slaves ought to be slaves. For inconsistencies in Aristotle's concept of the natural slave, see R. G. Mulgan, *Aristotle's Political Theory* (Oxford: Oxford University Press, 1977), pp. 40-44.

mal."[7] The immortality of a few was to be won at the expense of the humanity of the many.

The Greek philosophers Plato and Aristotle agreed that the life of practical activity in the political domain is decidedly superior to the life of productive work in the economy. But they held that there was an even higher way of life, a way of life in which the noblest of human potentials could be realized: the contemplative life of the mind. Through the contemplative life, not the practical, we come closest to the true form of divine life and thereby achieve the highest possible degree of human happiness.

But what, we might ask, did they find so irresistibly attractive about the prospect of a life spent in sedentary contemplation? What good could come of such idleness? Why not spend one's leisure time waterskiing on the blue Aegean, or sunbathing on the bright and balmy beaches of Mykonos? Indeed, according to Aristotle, that is the question: the proper use of one's leisure. Waterskiing and sunbathing might suggest themselves to modern pleasure seekers. But Plato and Aristotle didn't consider the pursuit of pleasure worthy of a human being. The pursuit of pleasure and the avoidance of pain are fine as principles of animal behavior, but not human behavior. For the highest and therefore defining characteristic of the human soul is not the mere capacity for pleasurable sensations, but the capacity for knowledge. The human being is, after all, a "rational animal"—that is, a living being with the capacity for thought and speech. Hence, the activity most appropriate for a human being in the absence of external compulsion is thinking. Those who choose a life in the pursuit of pleasure, in Aristotle's opinion, live a life designed for "grazing animals."[8] "They look down always with their heads bent to the ground like cattle," Plato writes, less generously, and "at the banquet tables they feed, fatten, and fornicate."[9] A life worthy of a human being would be

7. Arendt, *Human Condition*, p. 84.
8. Aristotle, *Nicomachean Ethics*, I.5.
9. Plato, *Republic*, 586a.

spent rather in the high-minded and disciplined pursuit of philosophical knowledge.

Not only is thinking the activity by which we distinguish ourselves from the animals; by it we most liken ourselves to the gods. Aristotle conceived of the gods not as the swashbuckling adventurers of popular Greek mythology—fighting, loving, hating, conniving, avenging — continually engaged in actions spurred by the passions. Rather, he thought of them as pure, self-contained mental substances, fixed in the distant heavens above — calm, silent, contemplating all truth for eternity. Complete within themselves, lacking in nothing, the gods have no need to interact with other persons. The practical life is far from them.[10] Rather, the gods specialize in contemplative thought. Accordingly, reason, by which we are able to contemplate truth, is the highest and most divine-like element within us. And we ought, Aristotle says, to go "to all lengths to live a life that expresses our supreme element."[11] As he states in his *Politics,* we ought to "prefer the activity of the part [of the soul] which is in its nature the higher."[12] To the degree and at the time we engage in contemplative thought, we become like the gods and participate in their serene and self-sufficient state of beatitude.

Compared to the contemplative life, the practical life of political engagement comes in a distant second. Although superior to the productive life, it is itself deeply flawed in certain respects. The good that it would achieve—fame, honor, and glory— is too dependent upon the fickle and changing opinions of the crowds. Perhaps this was the lesson the Greeks learned during the turbulent period immediately following the Peloponnesian Wars, when the sudden reversal of individual political fortunes was almost a daily occurrence.[13] We do not have complete control over our reputations; and after we die, we are

10. Aristotle, *Nicomachean Ethics,* X.8.

11. Ibid., X.7.

12. Aristotle, *Politics,* VII.xiv.13.

13. See Friedrich Solmsen, "Greek Ideas About Leisure," in *The Wingspread Lectures in the Humanities* (Racine, WI: The Johnson Foundation, 1966), p. 28.

powerless to defend them. Furthermore, the life spent in the proud pursuit of honor requires more by way of external goods—more wealth, more friends, more power, more beauty—than the humble life of the philosopher. Upon reflection, it appears that the practical life is overly dependent upon factors which are largely beyond our control.[14] Tomorrow we could lose our fortune on the stock market, or be horribly disfigured in a car accident. The philosophical life excels because it is less vulnerable, less dependent upon external circumstances for the achievement of its goal. Thus in the philosophical life we come closest to the self-sufficiency of the gods. And, "that human activity that is most akin to the gods' will, more than any others, have the character of happiness."[15]

Yet in this life there will always remain a significant difference between us and the gods: we are burdened with bodies, whereas they are not. As rarified, immaterial substances, the gods are wholly self-sufficient. Unlike us, they need never trouble themselves about having enough food to eat, winter clothing, or the rising cost of utilities. Furthermore, they need never go outside of themselves to find things to think about, for their minds have the power to provide themselves with all possible objects of thought. Our minds, on the other hand, are vastly inferior to the gods'. We mortals start out largely ignorant, and knowledge of the first principles by which we can grasp all things comes only after a long and arduous series of mental operations are performed on the body's sense experience.

For this work it is fortunate we have bodies, for they supply our minds with the requisite raw material to produce knowledge. But the body is also a hindrance to the mind. For the body is not at all self-sufficient, and regularly interrupts us in our attempts to achieve contemplative bliss. No sooner do we sit down to think than we get hungry, cold, or sleepy. Not only is our contemplative project interrupted to meet the needs of the body, we must also dedicate a substantial amount of time and

14. Aristotle, *Nicomachean Ethics,* X.8.
15. Ibid.

energy to work in order to provide regularly for such needs. Moreover, since we are not self-sufficient, our work necessarily takes place within human society. We must work on nature to get what we need. But we must also work with other people. And dealing with other people can be thoroughly exasperating. Thus, if the philosophical life is a genuine possibility, it requires not only the work of slaves to take care of the needs of the body, but also the activity of the politicians to take care of the needs of the body politic. Only when the philosopher is surrounded by the protective walls of enforced labor and social stability, shielding him from the intrusions of both natural and political necessity, can he turn his mind, undisturbed, to matters of eternal import.

What Aristotle had in mind then, as the ideal organization of human life, was a social hierarchy of an elitist sort: the work of the slaves makes possible the activity of the men of public affairs, while the activity of the men of public affairs makes possible the leisurely contemplation of the philosophers. Thought is the most god-like of human activities, work the most animal-like, fit only for natural slaves, the most animal-like of human beings. The whole of human society is to be organized so that a few men can actualize the highest of human potentials. In ancient Greek society, as Adriano Tilgher points out, the hard work for basic needs was performed by the majority, "in order that the minority, the elite, might engage in the exercise of the mind."[16]

Plato was in essential agreement with Aristotle in his low estimation of work, his high estimation of the contemplative life, and the need for a hierarchically-structured society in order to make the latter possible.[17] But he came to these positions on the basis of somewhat different reasons, reasons derived from a different understanding of the human soul and its relation to the body.

16. Tilgher, *Work*, p. 5.

17. We find the superiority of the contemplative life, Hannah Arendt points out, "in Plato's political philosophy, where the whole utopian reorganization of *polis* life is not only directed by the superior insight of the philosopher but has no other aim than to make possible the philosopher's way of life." Arendt, *Human Condition*, p. 14.

For Aristotle, the human soul was not itself a substance distinct from the body, but the "form" of the body. As the form of a statue is not distinct from the statue but makes that statue what it is, so the soul is not a substance separate from the body but makes the human body what it is—a *human* body. As the form of the body, the soul so organizes the body that it is capable of certain kinds of activities and thus makes it the kind of body that it is. All living things have a soul, which is just the vital principle which enables them to perform certain functions. Plants are animated by a "vegetative" soul, animals by an "appetitive" soul, and humans by a "rational" soul. The rational soul, being only the form of the body, is dependent upon the body for its proper operations. Thinking must always start from sense experience provided through the bodily organs of perception. Thus body and soul cooperate in the production of knowledge. Whether the rational soul survives the demise of the body was not entirely clear in Aristotle's account.

For Plato, the relation between the body and the soul was marked more by conflict than cooperation. By his account, the human soul was a substance separate and distinct in kind from the body. It was not the form of the body. Rather, it inhabited the body, like a prisoner inhabits a cell. As a nonmaterial substance, the soul is incorruptible and therefore immortal. In fact, it is not only immortal, but eternal. Not only does it survive death, it also existed before birth. Drawing inspiration from the teachings of the mystery religions of the day, Plato held that before physical birth, the soul inhabited an invisible realm where it enjoyed the unobstructed vision of the essence or forms of all things—what he called the "ideas." Here the rational soul existed in a blissful state of pure knowledge. At birth the soul falls from this ethereal domain into the material body below, suffering amnesia as a result of the concussion. The soul, now ignorant, is presented with the images of visible things through the agency of the body's sensory apparatus. These things, however, are not the proper objects of knowledge. For they are unstable in all their ways and keep changing. To gain genuine knowledge, the soul must turn away from sensory things and attend to the things of the mind.

This reorientation of the soul, however, is now contrary to its natural inclination. For through its experience of the pleasures and pains associated with the body, the soul's attention has now been firmly riveted on the material world.[18] Only through the diligent practice of philosophy can the soul remove itself from the distracting influence of the body and begin to make real progress in the pursuit of knowledge.[19] Thus in his chosen discipline the philosopher anticipates death as the release of the immortal soul from the prison house of the corruptible body.[20] For at death the soul purified by philosophy rises to the intelligible realm where it finds complete blessedness in the pure and undisturbed contemplation of the truth in the company of the gods.[21] The body then is seen only as an impediment to the fulfillment of human life, and work done for the needs of the body is a diversion from the true vocation of the soul. "The body keeps us busy in a thousand ways because of its need for nurture," Socrates laments in Plato's dialogue, the *Phaedo;* "it is the body and the care of it, to which we are enslaved, which makes us too busy to practice philosophy. Worst of all, if we do get some respite from it and turn to some investigation, everywhere in our investigation the body is present and makes for confusion and fear, so that it prevents us from seeing truth."[22]

The Medieval Continuation

The basic Greek attitude toward work and its place in human life was largely preserved in both the thought and practice of the Christian church during the Middle Ages. Not until the Reformation were some of the basic Greek assumptions about human nature, the purpose of human life, and the meaning of

18. Plato, *Phaedo,* 83d; see also Plato's *Republic,* 519a.
19. Plato, *Phaedo,* 79c-d, 83d.
20. Ibid., 64a.
21. Ibid., 69c, 81a.
22. Ibid., 66b-d.

work effectively overthrown. But this should come as no surprise. The gospel, after all, was initially proclaimed to a culture dominated by the world and life view of the Greeks. And many of the church fathers, having been brought up on Greek philosophy, interpreted the gospel by the basic framework of Greek thought. They often gave the impression, for instance, that the Good News of the kingdom of heaven amounts to little more than the promise of an eternally disembodied life spent in the undisturbed contemplation of the highest possible object of thought (i.e., God). St. Augustine, for instance, maintains in his work on the Trinity that "the contemplation of God is promised us as the goal of all our actions and the eternal perfection of happiness."[23] Meanwhile, perseverance in the faith during this life will yield sporadic victories over the sensuous desires of the flesh so that the mind can catch a fleeting glimpse of God as a foretaste of the life to come.

The Greek definition of the human being as a rational animal was also retained by the Christian thinkers of the Middle Ages. It was generally agreed that the highest of human activities is the activity of the mind. For this reason salvation, as the fulfillment of human life, was primarily understood in intellectual terms—it was to culminate in the "beatific vision," the direct and immediate knowledge of God in the afterlife, unhampered by the distracting demands of the body. The preeminent theologian of the thirteenth century, St. Thomas Aquinas, states in his *Summa Theologica* that, "the contemplation of divine truth . . . is the goal of the whole of human life."[24] This is because "the contemplative life is according to that which is most proper to man, namely his intellect."[25] Productive work, which meets the needs of this temporal bodily life, is therefore in itself of no lasting religious significance. For the most part it hinders the individual's relation to God, which can be cultivated only in the leisure of contemplation.

23. St. Augustine, *On The Trinity,* I, 8.

24. St. Thomas Aquinas, *Summa Theologica,* II, 2nd, Q. 180, art. 4.

25. Ibid., II, 2nd, Q. 182, art. 1; see also Aquinas, *Summa Contra Gentiles,* bk. III, chap. 37.

Not only the life of productive work, but even the practical or "active" life, consisting of virtuous activity directed toward one's neighbor, was seen by many medievals as an impediment to the true goals of the religious life. "Except a man shall say in his heart 'I alone and God are in the world,'" counsels the desert father, Abbot Allois, "he shall not find peace."[26] Meditation requires quiet. The life of the contemplative is best lived in complete social isolation.

This religiously motivated turn away from one's neighbor is strikingly expressed in Thomas Aquinas's comments on the summary Jesus gave of the requirements of the Old Testament law: to love God, and to love your neighbor as yourself. To love God, Aquinas states, is to desire to think about him. The love of God thus leads to the solitary life of the contemplative. The love of one's neighbor, on the other hand, leads to the active life, the life spent in the service of others.[27] But if we were to put ourselves in the service of others we would no longer enjoy the tranquil solitude necessary for sustained progress in the contemplative life. The demands for action in response to others' needs would constantly interrupt our religious project. "In a sense it is evident that the active life impedes the contemplative, because it is impossible for anyone to be involved in external works and at the same time give himself to divine contemplation."[28] Thus the two requirements of the law seem to draw a person in opposite directions. The love of God bids us to come out of the world and spend time alone with God in prayer and meditation; the love of neighbor draws us into the world and into a life of active service. Divine contemplation or service to one's neighbor: to which type of activity should I give precedence? Aquinas's answer: the contemplative, for it better accords with our nature and ends as rational animals. Although some might be required to pursue the active life, given the cir-

26. As quoted in C. H. Lawrence, *Medieval Monasticism* (London: Longman, 1984), p. 6.

27. Aquinas, *Summa Theologica*, II, 2nd, Q. 182.

28. Ibid., art. 3.

cumstances of this earthly life, a man could give no more eloquent proof of his love for God, Aquinas maintains, than by renouncing everything which belongs to this life and giving himself entirely over to divine contemplation.[29]

The Thomistic position on the relative merits of the active and contemplative life was generally held by the church fathers as well. Only the "obligations of charity make us undertake virtuous activity," wrote St. Augustine in the early fifth century, but "if no one lays this burden upon us, we should give ourselves over in leisure to study and contemplation."[30] The need for the active life is temporary, while the contemplation of God shall continue on into the life hereafter. It alone is of eternal significance. Thus, in the judgment of the sixth century pope, St. Gregory the Great, "The contemplative life is greater in merit than the active, which labors in the exercise of present work, while the other already tastes with inward savor the rest that is to come. Although the active life is good, the contemplative is better."[31]

The Christian ideal of the contemplative life found its concrete manifestation in the medieval institution of the monastery. Renouncing marriage, property, and related worldly entanglements, the monks abandoned their earthly occupations, withdrew to the cloister and committed themselves to the mortification of desires and the discipline of the mind, hoping that such a regimen would lead them to a mystical union with God. For it was only in the solitude of the monastery, C. H. Lawrence points out in his study of medieval monasticism, that "a man might achieve that detachment from created things that prepared him for the supreme encounter with God."[32]

The goal of the monastic life, then, was the mystical union with God through prayer and meditation. But the path to that goal was a difficult one. Sin had set our desires in disarray and

29. Ibid., art. 1 & 2.
30. St. Augustine, *City of God,* XIX, 19.
31. St. Gregory the Great, *Homilies in Ezech.,* I, 39.
32. Lawrence, *Monasticism,* p. 3.

our mind in darkness. Only through an intense regimen of inward self-discipline could the soul approach the spiritual perfection required to achieve unification with God.

Although we moderns have much to learn from the monastics about the spiritual disciplines, it should be noted that during the Middle Ages progress in the spiritual life was seen as a matter of justification, not sanctification. The disciplines of the devout life were engaged in not so much as a grateful response to God's grace freely available in Christ, but as a sure method of becoming worthy of his benefits. The practice of prayer was not to draw close to God on the basis of his prior acceptance, but to draw close to God in order to attain his acceptance. The Prologue to the Rule of St. Benedict, which formed the backbone of monastic culture during the medieval period, says we are separated from God because of laziness and disobedience; we must now approach God through the labor of our obedience.[33] Moreover, it is only through our own "good conduct" that we can expect to find shelter in the kingdom of God.[34] The various commands of our Lord are the "conditions for living in his Kingdom, . . . but we shall live there only if we fulfill these conditions."[35]

Thus the practice of the spiritual disciplines at that time was incorporated into a specifically medieval understanding of the economy of salvation. As if they were part of an elaborate commercial system, divine punishments and rewards were dealt out to persons on the basis of their individual accounts of moral debits and merits. Upon baptism, an infant starts out with a clean slate, in a state of innocence. Every sin committed thereafter must be dealt with individually: one must be overcome by a feeling of contrition, and perform acts of confession and penance to render satisfaction for that sin and thereby avoid punishment. Obliged to see to the salvation of its charges, the

33. *The Rule of St. Benedict,* trans. by Anthony C. Meisel and M. L. del Mastro (Garden City: Doubleday, 1975), p. 43.

34. Ibid., p. 44.

35. Ibid., p. 45.

medieval church had developed a detailed and standardized list of penance for every imaginable sin. If, for example, a priest or deacon were to vomit due to drunkenness, forty days of penance were required; if a layperson were to commit the same indiscretion, fifteen days would suffice.[36] If one's spiritual account was in arrears at the time of death, one would have to do remedial work in purgatory before being released to paradise.

On the other hand, for the good works that one performs above and beyond the call of duty—in acts of "supererogation"—one can accumulate a store of merit. Unlike the debits that accrue to one's individual account due to sin, merits can be shared. Christ the Son of God, the Blessed Virgin Mary, the apostles, and the saints have accumulated much more merit than was required for their own salvation. Thus a vast treasury of merit—the *thesaurus meritorum*—was built up in the church with the passage of time. Under the supervision of church officials, this merit could be transferred to individual accounts in a variety of ways. The merits of the saints, for instance, were usually dispensed to others upon the veneration of their relics. During the latter part of the Middle Ages, Pope Leo X decreed that every relic of the saints in Halle had the power to reduce a person's time in purgatory by four thousand years.[37]

Given the salutary effects of such relics, each church was anxious to build its collection of them. They were the basis of spiritual prestige as well as its ecclesiastical clout. Frederick the Wise, elector of Saxony, was an enthusiastic supporter of the Castle Church at Wittenberg. By 1520 he had developed an impressive collection of relics, including a thorn from the crown of Christ, a tooth from St. Jerome, four hairs from the head of Our Lady, a piece of the bread eaten at the Last Supper, and a suitably charred twig from the burning bush of Moses. In addition, the collection of holy bones numbered 19,013. In that particular

36. According to the 7th century Penitential attributed to Archbishop Theodore of Canterbury. See Lawrence, *Monasticism*, p. 62.

37. Roland Bainton, *Here I Stand: A Life of Martin Luther* (New York: Abingdon, 1950), p. 47.

year Pope Leo X had declared that all who viewed these relics on the Eve of All Saints Day—and made certain financial contributions to the church—could have time in purgatory reduced by 1,902,202 years and 270 days.[38]

One could make withdrawals from the treasury of merit through acts of piety other than the veneration of relics. Again, one could, through the performance of these acts, cause the corresponding merit to be credited to the accounts of other persons, living or dead. In Rome, in front of the Church of St. John, were the "Scala Sancta"—the stairs which ostensibly stood before the palace of Pontius Pilate. A soul would be released from purgatory every time a person crawled up them on his hands and knees, repeating the Lord's Prayer at each of its twenty-eight steps.[39]

Toward the latter part of the Middle Ages, a person could also bank on the store of merit through the purchase of an indulgence. An indulgence excused one from certain forms of canonical penance in order to make satisfaction for sin. Originally granted on behalf of those who had given their lives in the Crusades, indulgences were later extended to those who could not participate in the Crusades but made substantial financial contributions to them. Realizing their potential as fundraisers, the church eventually sold indulgences widely, using the money to finance a number of ambitious building projects. Again, the spiritual benefits of an indulgence were transferable. It was not unusual for people to purchase an indulgence in order to shorten a deceased relative's stay in purgatory.

The monks by their monastic vows were also contributing to the spiritual capital of the day. Those who were not able to renounce the world and engage in the monastic rigors of self-denial could secure their own salvation through vicarious participation in the work of the monks. According to the institution of "confraternity," a lay patron could be made eligible for the spiritual

38. Ibid., p. 71.
39. Ibid., p. 48.

benefits of the monastery which received his financial support.[40] The common understanding of the agreement by which temporal benefits were exchanged for eternal rewards is reflected in the preamble to the charter by which the Cluny monastery was founded in the year 909 by Duke William II of Aquitaine.

> Desiring to provide for my own salvation while I am still able, I have considered it advisable, indeed most necessary, that from the temporal goods which have been conferred upon me I should give some little portion for the gain of my soul. . . . And this is my trust, this is my hope, in deed, that although I myself am unable to despise all things, nevertheless by receiving those who do despise the world, whom I believe to be righteous, I may receive the reward of the righteous.[41]

It is important to point out that the medieval attitude toward work was not wholly negative. Although most of the early monastic communities found work necessary in order to be self-supporting, work was valued, as Tilgher points out, as "a means of purification."[42] As an ascetic discipline designed to foster humility and deny desire, work could be made to contribute to the ends of the contemplative life. But "since the primary goal was union with God, the material results of his work were less important to the monk than the growth in virtue that accompanied them."[43] St. Benedict stipulates in his rule that the monks should engage in manual labor not because they might become a burden on society if they didn't, but because "idleness is an enemy of the soul."[44]

During the late Middle Ages, however, the major monastic orders became increasingly dependent upon the work of others. The lay patrons of the monasteries had strongly en-

40. R. W. Southern, *The Making of the Middle Ages* (New Haven: Yale University Press, 1953); see also Lawrence, *Monasticism*, p. 88.

41. Lawrence, *Monasticism*, p. 63.

42. Tilgher, *Work*, p. 41.

43. *St. Benedict*, Intro., p. 10.

44. Ibid., chap. 48.

couraged augmenting spiritual capital through a dramatic increase in daily liturgical practices of the monks.[45] It was, after all, a matter of getting the best return on their investment.[46] When King Edgar founded a new monastery at Winchester in 966, his hope was that the community of devout monks would be pleasing to God and "intercede for us without ceasing."[47] Since the lion's share of the choir monk's time was now taken up with readings, recitations, and prayers, there was little time left over for manual labor—no matter how valuable such labor might be as an ascetic discipline. The tenant farmers tended the fields on the monastery's property, as usual. But there was a growing reliance on the work of the "lay brothers." An adult convert to the monastic way of life, the lay brother also took the monastic vows of chastity, poverty, and obedience. But he did not wear the distinctive cowl, nor did he participate in the recitations of the choral offices. A second-class citizen of the monastery, he took care of the manual labor and business transactions necessary for the support of the order, leaving the choir monks with leisure sufficient for their devotional practices.[48] By the high to late Middle Ages the religious elite within the major monastic orders relied almost entirely upon the work of others.

Throughout the medieval period the common assumption, as Lawrence puts it, was "that the Christian life could only be lived fully in the cloister and that a serious religious commitment meant becoming a monk."[49] Those who remained outside the cloister, who remained involved in the world, may be Christian, but they were less than fully Christian. Parallel to this two-tiered spirituality, the church had made, quite early in its career, a distinction between the "precepts" and the "counsels" of the gospel. The precepts of the gospel were obligatory. They bound

45. Southern, *Middle Ages*, p. 159.

46. Oxford historian R. W. Southern, in his treatment of the monasteries and their relation to the lay patrons, writes, "It is scarcely putting it too strongly that their benefactors expected value for their money." Ibid., p. 155.

47. Ibid., p. 161.

48. Lawrence, *Monasticism*, p. 149.

49. Ibid., pp. 154-55.

all who would call themselves Christian. One must not kill, steal, commit adultery, or tell lies. The counsels of evangelical perfection, however, were optional. To sell all that one owns and give to the poor, to forego the married state—these were suggestions Jesus handed out to those who wanted to distinguish themselves from the common herd of believers, entangled as they were in the mundane occupations of this life. Those who were not given the grace to take the monastic vows remained profane; those who did take the vows were referred to as the "religious." "Two ways of life were thus given by the law of Christ to His Church," writes Eusebius in the fourth century. "The one is above nature, and beyond common human living; it admits not marriage, child-bearing, property nor the possession of wealth, but wholly and permanently separate from the customary life of mankind, it devotes itself to to the service of God alone in its wealth of heavenly love!" On the other hand,

> the other more humble, more human [way of life], permits men to join in pure nuptials and to produce children, to undertake government, to give orders to soldiers fighting for right; it allows them to have a mind for farming, for trade, and the other more secular interests as well as for religion: and it is for them that times of retreat and instruction, and days for hearing sacred things are set apart. And a kind of secondary piety is attributed to them, giving just such help as such lives require, so that all men, whether Greeks or barbarians, have their part in the coming of salvation, and profit by the teaching of the Gospel.[50]

So again we have a ranking of human activities. The productive work of the common people lies at the bottom, providing for the necessities of the temporal life of the body, while the contemplative life of the monks resides at the top. There the human being is to find fulfillment through union with the divine. "Christianity," writes Hannah Arendt, "with its belief in a hereafter whose joys announce themselves in the delights of contemplation, conferred a religious sanction upon the abase-

50. Eusebius, *Demonstrata Evangelica,* bk. I, chap. 8.

ment of the *vita activa* [active life] to its derivative, secondary position."[51]

This ranking of human activities is reflected, as we have seen, in the general social structure of medieval society, which was similar to the one suggested by Aristotle, with a few alterations. The two domains of practical life were the political and the ecclesiastical; and the place of the philosophers was now occupied by the monks, who bided their time in the exercise of the spiritual disciplines in an attempt to draw nearer to God in contemplation. The entire edifice was supported not by slaves, but by tenant farmers, lay brothers, craftsmen, and serfs. They worked that others might pursue the religious life. By the earthly character of their occupations they could not directly participate in the religious life, but would have to remain content to have their life, such as it was, sanctified from without by the church. They themselves would receive grace through the church by means of the sacraments.[52]

The Renaissance Reversal

The low view of work generally prevailed in the West until the fifteenth century. At that time the dominant attitude toward work

51. Arendt, *Human Condition*, p. 16.

52. Herbert Lüthy characterized the medieval social hierarchy in the following way: "The unity of medieval hierarchical society, with the king, nobility, and clergy at its summit, maintained by the labour of common men, had simultaneously torn apart the unity of man. His faculties and aspirations were separated and distributed between different orders of society: for those of the first order the office of prayer, for those of the second that of warfare and command, and for the remainder the burden of toiling for their masters." Herbert Lüthy, "Variations on a Theme by Max Weber," in *International Calvinism: 1541-1715*, ed. Menna Prestwich (Oxford: Oxford University Press, 1985), p. 381. According to W. R. Forrester, "Every rank of life [in medieval times] was supposed to have its religious sanction and justification, but the whole ecclesiastical feudal structure of the medieval synthesis exhibits many of the features of the Greek aristocratic ideal." W. R. Forrester, *Christian Vocation* (New York: Scribner's Sons, 1953), p. 142.

and thought underwent a complete reversal at the hands of several leading philosophers of the Renaissance. As we noted earlier, the Greek philosophers largely thought of the gods as perfect minds—solitary, self-sufficient, uninvolved in the stuff of the world or the hubbub of human affairs. Human beings, then, were to become like the gods by withdrawing from the active life and devoting themselves to contemplation. In the Renaissance a new attitude toward work emerged from its regard of God as the all-powerful creator of the universe. No longer the passive and distant pure mind, God was conceived of as a cosmic craftsman, who, in an impressive display of wisdom and power, brought the entire universe into existence. In the writings of many Renaissance philosophers, God is typically referred to as the "Divine Artificer," the "Supreme Maker," or the "Mightiest Architect."[53]

According to these Renaissance thinkers, human beings were not to become like God through mere thinking, but through productive activity. To be created in the image of God meant not only possessing an intellect, but hands as well, so that what was envisaged by the mind could be ushered into reality by the formative powers of the body. God created nature out of nothing. Humankind would now create a world out of nature and thus become a demigod. For this reason Gordiano Bruno thought it was a good thing that human beings are subject to the necessity of work. For that necessity spurs human industry and the development of creative capacities whereby humankind will eventually exercise complete control over nature. "Whence, always removing themselves more and more from their bestial being by means of their solicitous and urgent occupations, they more closely approach divine being." Through work humanity maintains itself as a "god of the earth."[54] And just as nature glorifies God in his wisdom and power, so the world of culture glorifies humankind in its wisdom and power. The ideal human being is not the thinker who merely contemplates the idea of

53. For example, see Giovanni Pico Della Mirandola, *Oration on the Dignity of Man* (Chicago: Henry Regnery, 1956), pp. 5, 6.

54. Gordiano Bruno, *The Expulsion of the Triumphant Beast,* trans. by Arthur D. Imerti (New Brunswick: Rutgers University Press, 1964), Dialogue III, First Part.

beauty, but the artist, who both contemplates that idea and shapes the world accordingly.

Work as free productive activity is not only that which likens us to the divine; it also distinguishes us from the animals. In the productive activity by which they maintain their existence, the animals are bound to rigid patterns of instinctual behavior according to their species. Birds build nests out of twigs, beavers build dams out of branches, and spiders spin their webs. The same material is used to produce the same artifacts generation after generation. Animals display no discernible innovation or development, no creativity or imagination. But humankind, Marsilio Ficino contends, is bound by no law in its productive activity. Humankind does not merely carry out the instructions of nature, but "completes, corrects and amends the work of lower [material] nature."[55] In our productive activity, we range over the entire spectrum of material resources, using them for a freely invented variety of purposes. Especially in the production of artworks "we may notice how man handles all materials of the world and in all manners, as if they were all subjected to him. I say, he handles elements, stones, metals, plants and animals, and transforms them into many forms and figures, an achievement of which the animals are incapable." Accordingly, it is in this activity that we demonstrate our divinity, that we "imitate God the artisan of nature," achieving a god-like rule over the animals, the elements, even matter itself.[56]

Thus work, in the light of the Renaissance understanding, was no longer something that binds us to the necessity of nature and reduces us to the level of animal existence; rather, by it we can express our essence as free, creative, and sovereign beings, thereby achieving divine status. As Agnes Heller points out in her study of Renaissance man, work is now considered to be man's "essential activity" where typically hu-

55. Marsilio Ficino, *Platonica Theologica,* 3 vols. Raymond Marcel, ed. (Paris: n.p., 1964-70), XIII, 3.

56. Ibid.

man capacities are not thwarted but developed.[57] What the Ancients took to be beneath the dignity of a free person, the Renaissance thinkers took to be the very way in which we express our freedom. And what the Medievals took to be a hindrance imposed upon us by the necessity of nature, the Renaissance thinkers took to be an opportunity to exert our control over nature. Through work humanity can establish itself as a sovereign lord over a world of its own making.

Marx: Self-Realization Through Work

Karl Marx, the philosopher of labor *par excellence* and perhaps the most influential philosopher of the modern period, stands squarely within this Renaissance tradition.[58] What distinguishes human beings from the animals, according to Marx, is not the ability to think, but rather the ability to engage in free productive activity.[59] Unlike the animals, who are unreflectively immersed in their own patterns of behavior, human beings are conscious of what they are doing. They can step back from it. Through the use of their imaginations they can project a wide range of possibilities into the future. By the exercise of their will they can choose to realize one of those possibilities as opposed to others. Humans alone, Marx contends, are capable of genuinely free productive activity.[60]

In its freedom and lack of external determination, human productive activity is marked by a certain "universality." While

57. Agnes Heller, *Renaissance Man* (London: Routledge, Kegan and Paul, 1978), pp. 373, 400.

58. In her study of the Renaissance Agnes Heller notes that the Renaissance conception of work is "a good deal closer to the Marxian conception worked out centuries later than to the bourgeois work ethic of work." Ibid., p. 400.

59. Karl Marx, *The German Ideology* (New York: International Publishers, 1970), p. 42; Karl Marx, "Alienated Labor," in *Karl Marx: The Essential Writings*, ed. Frederic L. Bender (Boulder: Westview Press, 1972), p. 76.

60. Marx, "Alienated Labor," p. 76.

the animals produce the same thing with the same materials from one generation to the next, humanity ranges over the entirety of the earth's resources producing a seemingly limitless variety of things. The animals, Marx notes, "produce only in a single direction, while man produces universally."[61] The animals produce only out of necessity, but human production goes way beyond the bounds of necessity. The human house certainly provides shelter, but it provides much more than that. Consider the history of architecture. We produce not only what is needed, but what is beautiful as well.

Free productive activity is not only the activity by which we distinguish ourselves from the animals; according to Marx, by it we can find true fulfillment as human beings. Ultimate satisfaction is found in surveying the freely created works of our own hands. For the products of our activity contain within them something of ourselves. They are ourselves "objectified." When we stand back and gaze upon them, we "see our own reflection in a world which we have constructed."[62] In his comments on John Stuart Mill's *Treatise on Political Economy,* Marx states that in truly human productive activity "our productions would be so many mirrors of our nature."[63] Instead of contemplating God, we are to find our fulfillment in contemplating ourselves in the works of our own hands. There our nature, our essence as human beings, has been realized, set out before us in objectified form. As an artist would take profound satisfaction in his own artwork as a free expression of his own personality, so humanity would take satisfaction in the product of its free productive activity. Granted, in the primitive stages human productive activity had not worked itself out from under the necessity of nature. But with the steady development of technology humankind is on the road to self-realization through the free production and control of its own world.

This is at least the promise that labor holds for human-

61. Ibid.
62. Ibid., p. 77, (translation modified).
63. Marx, *Essential Writings,* p. 125.

kind. In the social reality of his day, however, Marx was confronted with the gross degradation and exploitation of human labor during the heyday of industrial capitalism: thousands of workers crowded into industrial centers, occupying substandard rental property, working fourteen hours a day at physically debilitating and mentally stultifying factory jobs; no education, no medical services, no municipal services; cities rife with crime and corruption, despair and disease, ignorance and alcoholism. At its best, work was a grim form of self-denial for the sake of mere physical survival. How could work, which contains within itself the glorious promise of human self-realization, have become the cruel scourge of modern life?

The problem, according to Marx's analysis, is that whenever the means of production are privately owned, human productive activity becomes distorted to the point where people can no longer realize themselves within it. The owners of the means of production achieve social dominance by virtue of their ownership. They will use the means of production to their own material advantage and increased profit. Those who do not own the means of production are powerless, and must work on the terms specified by the dominant social class if they are to survive. Work is then no longer a matter of free self-expression, but of necessity. Where the means of production are privately owned, we work in order to subsist—to maintain our existence, not to realize our essence.

Thus the worker is converted into a commodity of sorts, and sells his labor power in exchange for a wage determined by the market forces of supply and demand. He enters the factory and is assigned his place in the production process where he is then constrained to remain if he wants to keep his job and his livelihood. Work is not a freely chosen activity; rather a particular place within the division of labor is forced upon the worker on pain of dire poverty or even starvation. Nor is work an activity by which workers exercise a control over the world of their own making; rather that world controls them. Marx refers to this phenomenon as "alienated labor," and he took it to be especially prevalent in modern capitalist societies—where ample technology has been developed for the possibility of truly free production, but has been used only to augment profit and create a generation of "wage-slaves."

What Marx found particularly irksome about alienated labor is that it effectively eliminates the possibility of human self-realization through free productive activity. Assigning people to a specific slot within the division of labor, according to the objective requirements of the economy, capitalist society condemns them to doing the same thing with the same materials over and over.

In *Working,* a book of interviews with workers conducted and compiled by Studs Terkel, the job described by a Chicago steelworker is a case in point. This steelworker, Mike LeFevre, was to tend the "bonderizer"—evidently a machine consisting of a rack suspended over a vat of paint. Steel parts were put onto the rack and lowered into the vat where the paint was bonded to them. Then they were raised back out of the vat. His job was to load the parts on the rack, and then take the parts off the rack. "Put it on, take it off, put it on, take it off," he reports. "In between I don't even try to think. If I were to put you in front of a dock and I pulled up a skid in front of you with fifty hundred-pound sacks of potatoes and there are fifty more skids just like it, and this is what you're gonna do all day, what would you think about—potatoes?"[64] His job, consisting of nothing more than the mindless repetition of mechanical movements, is typical of manufacturing work or even office work which has been subdivided and simplified for the sake of efficiency and higher productivity.

Economists, Marx points out in his early manuscripts, tend to concentrate on the positive relation between the division of labor and productivity. They rarely ask what effect the division of labor has upon the producer.[65] But the tragedy of modern production processes is precisely its effect upon the producer. For the division of labor effectively converts the laborer into an animal, condemning him to a life of animal productiv-

64. Studs Terkel, *Working* (New York: Pantheon Books, 1972), p. xxxiv.
65. Marx, *Essential Writings*, p. 73.

ity. As the animals produce the same things with the same material, time after time for the sake of survival, so the modern worker produces the same thing with the same material for the sake of survival. As the spider spins its web out of the same solution and into the same design season after season to catch its food, so the auto worker cranks five nuts onto the wheel lugs every twenty seconds, day in and day out, in exchange for a weekly paycheck. Reflecting on his life on the job, the steelworker in Terkel's book exclaimed, "A mule, an old mule, that's the way I feel."[66] Precisely so, Marx would say. For in his work he has been reduced to a beast of burden. His productive activity is not free, as befits a human, but rigidly determined from the outside. Moreover his work is performed for the sake of self-preservation, not self-expression.

Since modern workers have been denied fulfillment in the potentially human activity of production, they will seek fulfillment in the typically animal activities of "eating, drinking and procreating, or at most also in his dwelling and in personal adornment." Under the aegis of capitalism work has been made so disagreeable it is "avoided like the plague."[67] We work only because we must. Human fulfillment is now sought outside the job—in acts of conspicuous consumption, in video entertainment, or erotic adventurism. We work in order to make a living. But no life is to be found in work.[68]

The solution to the problem of genuine human self-fulfillment will come, Marx predicted, when the working class's lot in life becomes so intolerable that it rises up in revolution and makes the means of production public property. The production process will then be used in the interests of the public good, rather than the private interests of a few. No one will be able to use the system of production as a means to exploit the labor of others. Instead, everyone will be able to realize himself in and through the system. The "free development of each" will be the

66. Terkel, *Working*, p. xxxii.
67. Marx, *Essential Writings*, p. 74.
68. Ibid., p. 125.

"condition for the free development of all."[69] Whereas under the private ownership of the means of production,

> each man has a particular, exclusive sphere of activity, which is forced upon him and from which he cannot escape . . . in communist society, where nobody has one exclusive sphere of activity but each can become accomplished in any branch he wishes, society regulates the general production and thus makes it possible for me to do one thing today and another tomorrow, to hunt in the morning, fish in the afternoon, rear cattle in the evening, and criticize after dinner, just as I have a mind, without ever becoming a hunter, fisherman, shepherd or critic.[70]

Here labor would become a "free manifestation of life and an enjoyment of life," rather than the alienation of human life for the sake of mere animal existence.[71] A communist society would, for the first time in human history, establish the conditions for the genuine fulfillment of human life through productive activity. After the revolution, humanity will come into its own—free, autonomous, and in total control of the world which it has created. Somewhat like God. In fact, Adriano Tilgher suggests that in the modern glorification of work as the activity by which humanity transforms and controls nature, "the ideal goal is to make mankind the master of the world, the supreme power—God."[72] If this is true, then for Marx humanity's self-realization through work is at the same time its self-divinization.

The coming of communist society is not just the idle wish of the alienated worker, according to Marx. For the demise of capitalism is inevitable. In the *Communist Manifesto,* Marx claims that capitalism, by virtue of pursuing its own goals, will bring about it own destruction. He gives two interconnected reasons for this. One is the "crisis of overproduction." The capitalist seeks increased profits in his business. To improve the profitability of

69. Marx, "The Communist Manifesto," in *Essential Writings*, p. 263.
70. Marx, *German Ideology,* p. 53.
71. Marx, *Essential Writings,* p. 125.
72. Tilgher, *Work,* pp. 135-36.

a business, he will try to make the production process efficient and keep overhead down, including wages. The efficiency of production can be enhanced through introducing machines, and so replacing human labor with capital assets. The company becomes more productive and at the same time requires fewer employees. If we assume all businesses are pursuing this policy, unemployment will rise, forcing wages down—a result of the law of supply and demand. At the same time productivity and profits will go up. But then, assuming that this process is taking place in a closed economic system, the market will be flooded with commodities that few people will be able to buy. For the vast majority of potential consumers are either unemployed, or making only subsistence wages. Eventually the economy will back up on itself and go into recession. Under the auspices of capitalism, the means of production have become so powerful, so productive, that the capitalists are no longer qualified to own and direct them. When they do, the economy stagnates.[73]

The second reason follows from the first and induces the event which will effectively push capitalism over the brink of self-destruction. It is the progressive impoverishment of the working class, the "pauperization of the proletariat." This process is actually just the social correlate of the inverse relation between profit and wages Marx cited in his economic theory of overproduction. As profits go up due to mechanized efficiency, more people are put out of work, and more are seeking the few remaining jobs. Thus wages go down. The downward trend of wages will mean that even the remaining core of jobholders will not reap any benefits from the increase in productivity and profits. The more the worker produces, the less he is worth.[74] This cruel inverse proportionality of capitalism will inevitably lead the workers to the revolutionary conviction that they have no stakes in the established economic system. As wages hit bottom and the remaining jobs become even more insecure, they will realize that they have nothing to lose by overthrowing the whole

73. Marx, *Essential Writings,* pp. 246-47.
74. Ibid., p. 69.

state of affairs in a violent political revolution and placing the means of production under public control. And this, Marx contends, is precisely what they will do.

Although the communist revolution begins with a political event—the violent seizure of political power—that event is only the beginning. The actual revolution entails a long process of social and economic transformation. Political power acquired through the revolution is used to centralize the system of production and place it under public direction and control. This is what Marx has in mind when he speaks of the abolition of private property as the key element in the program of the communist party. He does not mean that people will no longer have disposal over their personal property. He means rather that the means of production will no longer be privately owned. In every society to date the means of production have been, in one way or another, privately owned. Private ownership of the means of production in turn serves as the basis for class divisions and antagonisms in society. The owners of the means of production—be they the freemen of the Greek polis, the patricians of the Roman Empire, the nobility of the Middle Ages, or the modern bourgeosie—will constitute the dominant social class. They will use the material abundance, social standing, and political power to subjugate those who do not own the means of production. But once everyone owns the means of production, there will no longer be any basis for class divisions in society. Society will become "classless" and therefore free of social dominance and political repression. Thanks to the previous development of technology under capitalism, humanity will no longer be a slave to natural necessity; thanks to the social organization of communism, humanity will no longer be enslaved by the ruling class. For the first time in human history, the conditions will have been established for the possibility of true human freedom.

In making claims such as these, Marx thought he had discovered the laws of human history. He understood himself to be therefore in a position to predict the future course of history. In the modern industrialized countries of western Europe and

Great Britain, the rich would get richer and the poor would get poorer until the poor would finally rise up in revolt and establish a communist society. Evidently Marx was mistaken. Instead of the process of social polarization, we have seen the development of a sizable middle class. The union movement of the late nineteenth and early twentieth century, together with enlightened labor laws and government intervention, have turned the decline in wages around, improved working conditions, and created and enhanced fringe benefits. The workers of the advanced industrialized countries may be unhappy. But they are not revolutionary. They now have too much at stake in the system. Most of the communist countries today have not achieved their current political status through the kind of industrial worker revolutions Marx had envisioned. Rather, they have come about either as a result of peasant revolutions or national conquest.

By all appearances, the workers' lot in life has been substantially improved by recent developments in industrial and post-industrial society. At least those in union shops make good money. But to Marx this short-term gain, however salutory, is a historical disaster of major proportions. For it has effectively arrested the progress of history whereby a qualitatively new kind of human society is to come about—a society of genuine and total human freedom. An "increase in wages," Marx writes in his manuscript on alienated labor, "would be nothing more than a better remuneration of slaves, and would not restore, either to the worker or the work, their human significance and worth."[75] The workers must be allowed to bottom out and thereby become willing to overthrow the entire established system of class society and enforced division of labor. Anything short of that represents a sellout.

75. Ibid., p. 79.

Freud: Work as a Form of Self-Denial

Marx's glorified vision of the potentials of productive work will no doubt strike many as both romantic and utopian. The ideal of the all-sided development of the human personality through free productive activity ignores the finitude and limitations of the human individual. Likewise, society as a non-coercive association, where people are free to express themselves in productive activity—"just as they have a mind"—would most likely result in chaos. Furthermore, it seems unlikely that technology, no matter how advanced, will completely eliminate the element of necessity in work. Nor does it appear that the public ownership of the means of production will, by itself, eliminate relations of social dominance. For the actual management of the economy will inevitably fall into the hands of party-approved administrators and bureaucrats. And we have no guarantee that these managers themselves will not form a new social class, using their political power and authority to advance the interests of the party at the expense of the rest of society. In fact this is precisely what has happened in most communist countries.

It is likely that the Marxist exaltation of labor will leave the jaded worker thoroughly uninspired for more concrete reasons as well. "Why is it," asks Terkel's steelworker, Mike LeFevre, "that the communists always say they're for the workingman, and as soon as they set up a country, you got guys singing to tractors? They're singing about how they love the factory. That's where I couldn't buy communism. It's the intellectuals' utopia, not mine. I cannot picture myself singing to a tractor, I just can't. Or singing to steel. Oh whoop-dee-doo, I'm at the bonderizer, oh how I love this heavy steel. No thanks."[76] When LeFevre turns to his own vision of utopia, he thinks of college. Not that he wants to engage in learned discourse on the arts and sciences in the hallowed halls of academe. What he wants is to "live like a college kid. Just for one year. I'd love to. Wow! Wow!

76. Terkel, *Working*, p. xxxv.

Sports car! Marijuana! Wild sexy broads. I'd love that, hell yes, I would."[77]

Here LeFevre gives voice to a typical and pervasive attitude toward work, an attitude diametrically opposed to the historical optimism of the Marxist: dress work up as you will, it will never be more than a necessary evil, a disagreeable means to a more desirable end. True human fulfillment is not found in work, but somewhere outside of work—not in the making of money, but in the spending of it; not in productive activity, but in reproductive activity. Work is "good" not in itself, but only insofar as it makes certain preferred leisure activities possible. For at the end of the week comes the paycheck, and with the paycheck the pleasure of the things money can buy. The ends of human life are to be located in the life of consumption, not production; in leisure, not work.

If this is a faithful expression of the pervasive contemporary attitude toward work, then the account of work's place in human life given by another influential thinker of the West, Sigmund Freud, might sound more plausible and realistic than that of Karl Marx. For like many of us, according to David Reisman, Freud "viewed work as an inescapable and tragic necessity."[78]

However much we might want to deny it, Freud took it to be clear from our actual behavior that we are primarily pleasure-seeking organisms—the purest and most original form of pleasure being that which "convulses our physical being."[79] The problem, as Freud saw it, is that our physical constitution and our natural environment are not at all conducive to our original project. The pleasure program "is at loggerheads with the whole world."[80] A life of spontaneous and indiscriminant sexual activity would surely kill us through one social dis-

77. Ibid.

78. David Reisman, "The Themes of Work and Play in the Structure of Freud's Thought," *Psychiatry* 13 (1950): 2.

79. Sigmund Freud, *Civilization and Its Discontents* (New York: W. W. Norton, 1961), p. 28.

80. Ibid., p. 24.

ease or another. Continuous sexual activity would surely lead to death by starvation, if we didn't die of boredom first.

Moreover, if life itself is a necessary condition for the experience of bodily pleasure, then we must first take all sorts of precautions in order to ensure our basic viability within a hostile and unsympathetic natural environment: we must guard our bodies from disease, protect them from overexposure, and ward off starvation, among other things. Unfortunately, this means that we will have to postpone the immediate gratification of our desires and get down to work—work in order to create a civilization which affords us a measure of security in this threatening and inhospitable world; and work to make enough money to take advantage of the benefits of this civilization.

Prior to civilized life as we now know it, Freud held, humanity fashioned in its imagination an ideal image of itself in the form of the gods. Both wise and powerful, these gods presided over the manifold forces of nature. At the mercy of these forces, primitive people often appealed through ritual and sacrifice to the gods for protection. But with the development of science and technology, humanity has begun to claim for itself the omniscience and omnipotence it had formerly reserved for divine beings. Each piece of technical equipment, developed through human productive activity and in turn enhancing that activity, augments the native powers of the human body. The telescope extends the power of vision to the very distant; the microscope extends the power of vision to the very small. The telephone extends the range of the voice and the power of hearing; television extends the range of the eye and the ear. With the aid of modern forms of technology, humanity has achieved an undreamt mastery over nature and thus converted itself, as Freud puts it, into a "prosthetic God."[81] Yet, he admits, in acquiring the powers traditionally assigned to God "man does not feel happy in his God-like character."[82]

Although work, however technically enhanced, does not

81. Ibid., p. 43.
82. Ibid.

yield happiness in the form of pleasure, it is still required in order to avoid pain at the hands of nature. A vast cultural environment must be erected to protect us from nature's caprice. To accomplish this sizable task, we will have to cooperate with other people in a society where the tasks necessary for the maintenance of human life are parcelled out and fitted together. But this leads to another problem. The prevalence of violence and hostility in so-called "civilized life" convinced Freud in his later years that human beings are by nature hostile and aggressive. They evidently derive a solid sense of satisfaction from inflicting pain upon others. Among their "instinctual endowments," Freud contends, "is to be reckoned a powerful share of aggressiveness. As a result, their neighbor is for them not only a potential helper and sexual object, but also someone who tempts them to satisfy their aggressiveness on him, to exploit his capacity for work without compensation, to use him sexually without his consent, to seize his possessions, to humiliate him, to cause him pain, to torture and to kill him."[83]

This deep-seated lack of charity toward one's neighbor finds a humorous expression in a quaint piece by the German poet Heinrich Heine. In one of his notebooks, Heine made a list of his modest requests: "Mine is a most peaceable disposition. My wishes are: a humble cottage with a thatched roof, but a good bed, good food, the freshest milk and butter, flowers before my window, and a few fine trees before my door; and if God wants to make my happiness complete, he will grant me the joy of seeing some six or seven of my enemies hanging from those trees."[84] But what Heine expresses as a kind of joke is, according to Freud, a deep psychological truth: along with the innate human drive for pleasure there is also an equally innate drive to inflict pain upon others. This impulse estranges people from one another and renders them decidedly antisocial.

How then will it be possible to get human beings to live

83. Ibid., p. 65.

84. Heinrich Heine, *Gedanken und Einfälle,* Section I, as quoted in Freud, *Civilization*, p. 64n.

together in a harmonious and well-ordered society so that the work necessary for the preservation of human life can be carried out cooperatively? How can people be expected to work together if they are constantly at each other's throats? Freud's answer to this question is based upon his understanding of the peculiar mechanics of the human psyche. Left to itself, the pleasure drive will draw couples—or at most small groups—into erotic, loving relationships. If the pleasure drive is allowed to expend itself entirely in its original aim, the aggressive drive will hold sway over all social contacts outside the erotic relationship. It is only by severely restricting the opportunities for sexual activity and converting the unused, pent-up erotic energy into a lukewarm love for humanity that the aggressive drive will find its constructive counterpart in human social life. To maintain this artificially- induced sociability, society will find it necessary to install an internal monitor, the "super-ego," within each person, to detect any untoward erotic or aggressive urges and immediately bury them with guilt feelings or otherwise dispose of them.[85]

In this way people are accommodated to the requirements of civilization, which provides protection from the hostile forces of nature. But the price of such security is very high indeed. For the condition of membership in human society is the abstention from the two things that make people happy—sex and violence. "Civilized man has exchanged a portion of his possibilities of happiness for a portion of security."[86] Contained in this bargain, a bargain each of us strikes up with society, is the dilemma of civilized life: we all want to be happy; to be happy is to experience pleasure; but to experience pleasure we must, of course, be alive; to stay alive we must work together with a society; but to work together in society we must renounce practically all instinctual satisfaction, and the renunciation of instinctual satisfaction makes us unhappy. Stepping outside the protective confines of human society we might attain new and

85. Ibid., p. 79.
86. Ibid., p. 69.

hitherto unknown levels of happiness through the sudden satisfaction of untamed instincts. But such a life would be, for most, unacceptably brief.

Civilized life, Freud concludes, is a tragedy. Aspiring to be like God through the extension of our powers over nature in technologically enhanced work, we have become of all animal species the most miserable and neurotic. We work for the sake of self-preservation; but work itself is a form of self-denial. Civilization, originally designed to protect us from pain at the hands of nature, has now itself become a major source of suffering. And there is little hope for improvement in this situation. The problem is built into our biology.

Summary and Transition: The Promise of the Concept of Vocation

In our review of the history of work attitudes we have seen our own ambivalence about work divided up and taken to extremes. Our Western cultural tradition has swung back and forth over the issue of work and its meaning in human life, sometimes seeing work as a form of self-denial, sometimes as a form of self-fulfillment. We are the inheritors of both of these conceptions of work, and they war together within us with little hope of reconciliation. There is, however, another strand in our cultural tradition which has attempted to incorporate both the negative and the positive experience of work within a larger concept. That tradition is the Protestant tradition; that larger concept is the concept of work as vocation. And it is to both that we turn in the next chapter.

CHAPTER TWO

* * *

Our Work, God's Providence: The Christian Concept of Vocation

OUR SURVEY of the history of the philosophy of work in chapter 1 was far from complete. But it was enough to reveal a striking divergence in Western attitudes towards work: on the one hand, work seemed to debase human life to the level of mere animal existence, scratching out a living on the grim surface of the earth; on the other hand, work seemed to be the agent by which humanity elevates itself to the position of a god, proudly ruling over a cultural world of its own making. We might well wonder if there is a mean between these extremes, perhaps a way of thinking about work as a typically human activity, neither brutish nor divine. I am convinced that the Reformed Christian concept of work offers such an alternative. To appreciate the conceptual force of this alternative and its social implications we must start with the Reformer Martin Luther and his concept of "vocation." At the end of this chapter I shall argue that this alternative is not just the Reformed view, but is compatible with contemporary Roman Catholic social teaching as well.

Luther: God's Providential Presence in the Work of our Hands

Luther's concept of vocation was formulated largely in reaction to the medieval monastic ideal and its religious devaluation of all earthly occupations. As we have seen, during the Middle Ages work was not an activity that either directly promoted or contributed to the fulfillment of human life. It was seen instead as a disagreeable necessity, rooted in the temporary arrangements of this earthly life: we must work in order to eat; we must eat in order to sustain the body. But the body will soon pass away, returning to the dust from which it came. The soul, however, will pass into the next life and, if properly prepared, enjoy a state of perfect blessedness in the contemplation of God.

In itself then, work is of little spiritual significance. At best it might serve as an ascetic discipline, insofar as it forestalls the temptations of idleness, quells the passions, and promotes humility. The religious life can be lived fully only by abandoning one's earthly occupation, renouncing all attachments to this world, and withdrawing to the monastery. There the discipline of the body and the pursuit of devotional contemplation was practiced on a daily basis in the hope of achieving a mystical union with God as a foretaste of the eternal life to come.

In Luther's day, it was generally held that the monks, by taking the monastic vows and submitting to the rigors of the cloistered life, could actually merit special divine favor and thereby make their eternal salvation secure. Luther himself was a monk, a conscientious member of the Augustinian Order. For many years he was tortured by the idea that even after scrupulous observance of the prescribed religious practices, his sins still might not be forgiven. He regularly exasperated his confessor, subjecting him to hours of minute moral self-examination. How could he be sure he had remembered all of his sins, or felt sufficiently contrite about them, or performed enough penance for them? Of course there were always acts of supererogation. They could serve as a kind of backup. But how could he be sure that the merit acquired through such acts would surpass, or at least equal, the debit mounted up by his sin? Perhaps a heavenly audit would reveal a serious mistake in his calculations. Concerned not only with his own but with the salvation of others, Luther made a pilgrimage to Rome and dragged himself up the Scala Sancta, reciting the Lord's Prayer at each step, even kissing each step for good measure, so that the soul of his grandfather Heine might be released from purgatory. But how could he be sure that the means the church had established for the transfer of merit were effective?

It was Luther's discovery that we are saved by God's grace and not by our own works that eventually released him from his religious anxieties. That discovery also initiated a series of momentous events which sparked the Protestant Reformation of the sixteenth century. For our purposes it is important to note that Luther's discovery of grace also provided him with the leverage he needed to develop a new concept of the meaning of work in human life and at the same time wage a vigorous critique of the elitist social hierarchy of his time.

In order to place Luther's concept of vocation within the compass of his thought, it is important to recall a basic theological distinction he drew between the kingdom of heaven and the kingdom of earth. To the kingdom of heaven belongs our relationship to God, which is to be based upon faith; to the kingdom of earth belongs our relationship to our neighbor, which is to be based upon love. Vocations are located within the kingdom of earth. More precisely, a vocation is the specific call to love one's neighbor which comes to us through the duties which attach to our social place or "station" within the earthly kingdom. A station in this life need not be a matter of paid employment, although it may be. As conceived by Luther, our stations include all the typical ways in which we are related to other people. Being a husband or a wife is a station in life, as well as being a parent or a child, a magistrate or a subject, a master or a servant, as well as a baker, a cobbler, or a farmer.

Thus the call to love one's neighbor goes out to all, but what this call requires of me in particular is discovered in those stations which I presently occupy: as a parent I am called to care for my children; as a teacher, to provide an education for my students; as a member of a Christian congregation, to exercise my spiritual gifts in order to build up the community of faith; as a citizen of a democratic society, at least to vote intelligently. All of these callings represent concrete and specific ways of serving my neighbor, as I am commanded to do by God himself. God calls us to serve others; we serve others in our work.

Work itself, then, is a divine vocation. For that reason, when his parishioners wondered what God wanted them to do, Luther did not suggest that they abandon their worldly occupations and retreat to a monastery, but rather that they conscientiously serve their neighbor within the stations that God had placed them. In his lectures on Galatians, Luther insists that "all the duties of Christians, such as loving one's wife, rearing one's children, governing one's family, obeying the magistrate, etc., which they [the Papists] regard as secular and fleshly—are fruits of the Spirit. These blind men do not distinguish between vices and the things that are good creatures of God."[1]

Our vocation, according to Luther, comes to us through our station. What God would have us do with our time and talents is discerned from the duties which pertain to our stations in life together with the concrete opportunities he has placed before us. But what do we accomplish when we discharge the duties of a station in life, when we heed the call of God to serve our neighbor in and through our daily tasks? Luther's answer to this question is as astounding as it is humbling: the order of stations in the earthly kingdom has been instituted by God himself as his way of seeing that the needs of humanity are met on a day-to-day basis. Through the human pursuit of vocations across the array of earthly stations the hungry are fed, the naked are clothed, the sick are healed, the ignorant are enlightened, and the weak are protected. That is, by working we actually participate in God's ongoing providence for the human race.

1. Martin Luther, *Luther's Works,* vol. 26 (St. Louis: Concordia, 1958), p. 217. This English edition of Luther's works will be referred to as *LW* hereafter.

According to Luther then, the religious significance of human work is first apprehended in the light of the doctrine of creation. Having fashioned a world filled with resources and potentials, God chose to continue his creative activity in this world through the work of human hands. In his commentary on Genesis, Luther claims that God even milks the cows through those called to that work.[2] Through our work, humble though it may be, people are being brought under God's providential care. For God established the various stations of earthly life as channels for his love and providence for the human race; when people respond to the duties of those stations in the activity of work, God is present as the one who provides us with all that we need.[3] "With persons as his 'hands' or 'coworkers,'" writes Gustaf Wingren in his study of Luther's concept of vocation, "God gives his gifts through the earthly vocations, towards man's life on earth (food through farmers, fishermen and hunters; external peace through princes, judges, and orderly powers; knowledge and education through teachers and parents . . .)."[4] As we pray each morning for our daily bread, people are already busy at work in the bakeries.

Far from being of little or no spiritual account, then, human work is charged with religious significance—a significance which has been either wholly ignored or perverted by non-biblical attitudes toward work. In our work we neither lower ourselves to the level of the brutes, nor make ourselves into self-glorifying gods. Rather, by working we affirm our uniquely human position as God's representatives on this earth, as cultivators and stewards of the good gifts of his creation, which are destined for the benefit of all.

Now we can see what was wrong, in Luther's estimation, with those who pursued the monastic way of life. In the kingdom

2. Martin Luther, *Werke Kritische Gesamtausgabe,* vol. 44 (Weimar: Hermann Böhlaus, 1883), p. 6. This German edition of Luther's works—the "Weimarer Ausgabe"—will be referred to as *WA* hereafter.

3. See Gustaf Wingren, *Luther on Vocation.* Carl C. Rasmussen, trans. (St. Louis: Concordia, 1957), p. 9.

4. Ibid., p. 27.

of heaven they replaced faith in God with their own works in an attempt to make themselves worthy of God's acceptance. Rather than receiving eternal life as a gift of grace, they wanted, as Luther put it, to "do business and haggle with God."[5] Thus they were depending upon themselves, not God, for their salvation. "But God has commanded us," Luther insists in his major statement on monasticism in 1521, "to put our whole trust in his mercy and with utter certainty and without any doubt to have faith that we ourselves and all our works are pleasing to him not because of our worthiness or merit but because of his goodness."[6]

Of course good works have a place in the Christian's life—not as part of an attempt to justify one's self before a holy God, but rather as a response to having already been justified by God through the work of Christ. "Good works . . . do not really pertain to the remission of sins and a serene conscience, but are the fruits of a forgiveness already granted and still present, as well as of a good conscience."[7] The attempt to earn one's salvation by meeting the requirements of God's law, according to Luther's diagnosis, is the direct result of a lack of faith. For, as Wingren points out, "if a man cannot believe that the sin with which he struggles is forgiven, the law has risen up in his conscience . . . and faith gives way to works before God. Then eternal life does not depend on God's promise but on man's progress in the battle against sin."[8] To Luther, this led to the tragic spectacle of the monks, who "serve in the temples with noise and murmering, promising themselves halos in heaven for a faith that is dead."[9] In the kingdom of heaven they rely on their own works rather than God's grace.

Moreover, in the kingdom of earth, Luther contended, the monks withdrew from their neighbors into the isolated life of the cloister out of a self-centered concern for their own salvation. "Thus they corrupt both of them, faith and love. . . . They

5. *WA* 31I, p. 252.
6. *LW* 44, p. 277.
7. Ibid., p. 279.
8. Wingren, *Luther,* p. 52.
9. *LW* 44, p. 265.

deny their works to their neighbor and direct them to themselves."[10] In fact, Luther saw monastic vows as nothing but a thinly disguised form of religious egotism. "Our self-imposed good works," wrote Luther, "lead us to and into ourselves, so that we just seek our own benefit and salvation. But God's commandments drive us to our neighbor's need, that by means of these commandments we may be of benefit only to others and to their salvation."[11] The true motivation for our actions in the world ought to be our neighbor's good, not our own holiness.[12] But the monastic institutions actually promoted a callous disregard for one's neighbor, "for they say that a monk is dead to the world, dedicated to God, and must do so much in the monastery that parents, neighbors, indeed, the whole world, can suffer distress, collapse and perish."[13]

True, in the original monastic communities that followed the Benedictine Rule the monks worked as well as prayed. But they worked only to maintain their own communities. By the latter part of the Middle Ages, the liturgical practices within the major orders had grown to the point that the monks no longer had time to work to support themselves at all. Instead they lived off the gifts and endowments given by the aristocracy in exchange for a share of the spiritual benefits of the monastery.[14] The wandering monks of the mendicant orders—known as friars—did not work for a living either, but depended wholly upon the charity of those with whom they came in contact. In the monasteries of his time, Luther claimed he could find neither genuine faith in God's grace nor love of one's neighbor.

By maintaining that one's relation to God is established

10. *WA* 8, p. 363.

11. *WA* 6, p. 242; *LW* 44, 71. See also *WA* 8, p. 363.

12. Wingren, *Luther,* p. 54.

13. *LW* 44, p. 327. In the words of the Protestant theologian Emil Brunner, "To forsake the world absolutely is the absolute denial of love." *The Divine Imperative* (New York: Macmillan, 1937), p. 202.

14. See Luther's *De votis monasticis* in *WA* 8, pp. 564-669; Calvin's *Institutes of the Christian Religion* (Philadelphia: Westminster, 1960), Prefatory Address to King Frances I, pp. 19-20; and Wingren, *Luther,* p. 32.

through faith alone and relocating works of religious significance in the earthly realm, Luther showed it possible to respond to God's call even in the lowly and mundane occupations of this life. To follow Christ it is not necessary to abandon one's earthly station, for Christ commands us to do such works "as concern people here below who are in need, not those that concern God or angels. Therefore the Christian life does not consist of that which such men as monks invent; it does not drive people into the wilderness or cloister. . . . On the contrary, the Christian life sends you to people, to those that need your works."[15] According to Luther, virtually all occupations are modes of "full-time Christian service"—except those of the usurer, the prostitute, and the monk.[16] The point of the Christian religion is not to leave the world behind to live the life of faith, but to live the life of faith in the midst of the world. The religious life is not the prerogative of a small group of spiritual specialists. Rather, it must be lived by all; and it can be lived in the context of everyday work.

Thus it was through his concept of work as a divine vocation that Luther cut through the two-tiered spirituality of the medieval world. No longer will the common laborer be shuffled off to the second class section of the Kingdom of God, while first class seats are reserved for those who ostensibly go beyond the call of duty and elect to take monastic vows as a form of special dedication to God. As Paul Althaus points out in his book on Luther's ethical thought, "since the Christian has received the meaning and value of his life through God's gracious act of justification, all tasks and works of life are equally important and holy because they have been assigned to him by God's direction of his life. There are no particularly holy works. Everything that we do is secular. However, it all becomes holy when it is done in obedience to God's command and in the certainty that he will be pleased, that is, when it is done in faith."[17] It is not as if only

15. *WA* 29, p. 403.
16. *WA* 10I, 1, p. 317.
17. Paul Althaus, *The Ethics of Martin Luther* (Philadelphia: Fortress, 1972), p. 10.

a few super-spiritual people are able and expected to obey the full counsel of the gospel, while the rest of us get by on the minimum requirements. Rather, all Christians are called to wholehearted response to the gospel in its entirety.[18] That response, however, does not constitute a separate and distinctly religious vocation, but can be lived out through all the legitimate vocations of this earthly life.

Neither is there a need, as many monks thought, to withdraw from the world in order to experience religious suffering as a disciple of Christ. The monastic tradition in the West received its initial impulse from just such a search for religious suffering. When the Roman Emperor Constantine legalized Christianity in A.D. 312, Christians in the West were no longer persecuted by the state for their religious convictions. Life was suddenly comfortable for the confessing church. In fact, Constantine's public policy actually favored the Christian religion, granting to Christians benefits which were denied their pagan competitors. Many believers, however, began to wonder what it meant to follow Christ in the Constantinian era. Jesus had told his disciples to expect to be despised, reviled, and rejected for his name's sake. But now it seemed that no such tribulations were forthcoming. Monasticism made up for the lack of religious suffering in the world by inventing various forms of self-denial as means to identify with Christ's passion. The monastic vows of poverty, chastity, and obedience were themselves voluntary acts of self-denial, by which a monk foregoes the usual comforts of property, the pleasure of sex, and the freedom of choice. Many monks went far beyond the requirements of the vows in their denial of self for the sake of Christ. St. Simon the Stylite is said to have spent some forty years atop a pillar under constant exposure to the elements; other monks have recited the psalms in their entirety while standing on a frozen lake in their bare feet.

18. Against the "double Christianity" created by the distinction between the precepts and the counsels of the gospel, Luther's fellow reformer John Calvin claimed that "men must of necessity obey every little word uttered by Christ." Calvin, *Institutes,* IV.xiii.12.

Against the monastic practice of self-imposed suffering, whether bizarre or routine, Luther said that genuine religious suffering is still to be found in everyday life. For every earthly occupation has its cross to bear. "I ask you where our suffering is to be found. I shall tell you: Run through all the stations of life, from the lowest to the highest, and you will find what you are looking for . . . therefore do not worry where you can find suffering. That is not necessary. Simply live as an earnest Christian preacher, pastor, burgher, farmer, noble, lord, and fulfill your office faithfully and loyally."[19] To follow Christ in his suffering we need not abandon our stations. Rather, when we faithfully discharge the duties of our stations we will find ourselves suffering for the sake of others, and thus in some small way imitating Christ, who suffered greatly for our sake. Our works "should be done freely and for no reward, to the benefit and advantage of our neighbor, just as the work of Christ was done freely for us and for no reward."[20]

Neither does our love for God demand that we withdraw from our neighbor. We saw in the last chapter how the medievals often posited a conflict between the command to love God and the command to love one's neighbor: the command to love God, it seemed to them, directs us to the contemplative life, which is best lived in social isolation; the command to love one's neighbor pulls us back into the bustle of the active life, making it exceedingly difficult to find time for prayer and meditation. While not denying that time spent apart with God in prayer is important, Lutheran spirituality also finds God to be present in the form of one's neighbor. As we noted earlier, Luther held that God is providentially present in the sustaining work of other persons. When I receive what I need from the hand of my neighbor, it is as if I have received it from God himself. But Luther also thought that God encounters us in our neighbor's needs. For Christ identifies himself with the poor and the needy of this world (see Matt. 25:31-46). So to turn away from a neighbor in

19. *WA* 51, p. 404.
20. *LW* 44, p. 301.

need is to turn away from God himself; to serve a neighbor in need is to serve God himself. While on this earth, we are to spend our powers in the service of our neighbor; "but in heaven," Wingren points out, "it is made evident that the poor neighbor whom we served was Christ, the King."[21] Thus, "for Luther," Althaus writes, "our love of God and our love of our neighbor cannot be separated."[22]

The Calvinist Elaboration: Work and the Organic Structure of Social Life

In his concept of vocation Luther rejected the medieval devaluation of work. At the same time he initiated a long and rich line of Protestant reflection upon the place of work in human life. Incorporated into the theology of the Genevan Reformer John Calvin, the Protestant concept of calling made its way into the countries of northern Europe and the British Isles. There it was elaborated in new social circumstances and, as we shall see, modified in certain important respects.

Calvin's solidarity with Luther on the issue of the religious dignity of work is perhaps most strikingly apparent in his commentary on Luke 10:38-42. In this passage Luke relates an incident which occurred when Jesus paid a visit to the home of two sisters, Mary and Martha. As Jesus held forth in the living room, Mary sat at his feet and listened to all he said, while her sister Martha was frantically busy in the kitchen, making elaborate preparations for the guest of honor. Exasperated, Martha came to Jesus and said, "Lord, don't you care that my sister has left me to do the work by myself? Tell her to help me!" But Jesus answered, "Martha, Martha, you are worried and upset about many things, but only one thing is needed. Mary has chosen what is better, and it will not be taken away from her."

21. Wingren, *Luther*, p. 143.
22. Althaus, *Ethics*, p. 14.

According to the dominant medieval allegorical interpretation of this passage, Jesus, in commending Mary over Martha, is at the same time commending the life of contemplation over the life of action. In this interpretation, Mary represents the contemplative life. She does nothing but sit at the Master's feet and listen, pondering what he says. Martha, on the other hand, stands for the active life. She is busy at work in the kitchen, making provisions for the common bodily needs and comforts of the Lord. When Martha complains that her sister Mary is not working, Jesus says that Mary chose "what is better." Given that "Mary figures the contemplative life," the scholastic theologian Thomas Aquinas concluded that what Jesus intends to teach us here is that "the contemplative life is more excellent than the active."[23]

When we turn to Calvin's comments on this passage, what we find stands in stark contrast to the traditional interpretation. Refusing to assign an allegorical meaning to the persons of Mary and Martha, Calvin claims that Jesus was simply commending Mary's response to his presence over Martha's. Since Jesus was easily satisfied with modest accommodation, it was more important for Martha at that time to listen to what Jesus had to say than to make a big fuss about the food. But she was working too much, and had no time to hear his instruction. "It was as if one were to give a magnificent reception to a prophet, and yet not to care about hearing him, but, on the contrary, to make so great and unnecessary preparations, as to bury all the instruction."[24] In commending Mary over Martha Jesus was not commending a whole way of life over another—for certainly at times Mary also worked just as Martha also listened. Rather, he was addressing himself to the relative merits of their responses to his presence and message at that particular time. When he paid them a visit, one listened; the other did not. There is a time to work, and a time to listen.

23. Thomas Aquinas, *Summa Theologica* II, 2nd, Q. 182, art. 1.

24. John Calvin, *A Commentary on the Harmony of the Evangelists,* vol. 2, trans. by William Pringle (Grand Rapids: Eerdmans, 1949), p. 144.

Jesus faulted Martha not for working in general, but for working at the wrong time.

When Calvin makes explicit reference to the traditional interpretation of this passage, however, we find that his criticism of it is not limited to the forced allegorization of the persons of Mary and Martha. Rather, he rejects the whole vision of the proper ends of human life which stands at its source, a vision he believes drawn from the pagan Greek philosophers. The difference between Calvin's interpretation of the Mary and Martha passage and the traditional interpretation is not just the result of different methods of interpretation. What is at issue are fundamentally different understandings of the purpose of human life.

> As this passage has been basely distorted into the commendation of what is called a Contemplative life, we must inquire into its true meaning, from which it will appear that nothing was farther from the design of Christ, than to encourage his disciples to indulge in indolence, or in useless speculation. It is, no doubt, an old error, that those who withdraw from business, and devote themselves entirely to a contemplative [life], lead an Angelical life. For the absurdities which the Sorbonnists [the scholastic theologians in Paris] utter on this subject they appear to have been indebted to Aristotle, who places the highest good, and ultimate end, of human life in contemplation, which, according to him, is the enjoyment of virtue. When some men were driven by ambition to withdraw from the ordinary intercourse of life, or when peevish men gave themselves up to solitude and indolence, the resolution to adopt that course was followed by such pride, that they imagined themselves to be like the angels, because they did nothing; for they entertained as great a contempt for active life, as if it had kept them back from heaven. On the contrary, we know that men were created for the express purpose of being employed in labour of various kinds, and that no sacrifice is more pleasing to God than when every man applies diligently to his own calling, and endeavors to live in such a manner as to contribute to the general advantage.[25]

25. Ibid., pp. 142-43.

Aristotle placed the highest end of human life in contemplation. That way of life was, to him, the most divine. He conceived of the gods as distant minds wrapped up in their own thoughts, in a state of perfect rest, essentially unconcerned with human affairs. To become like them, and to participate in a measure of their supreme beatitude, we must turn from the demands of work and politics and pursue the contemplative life. To the degree that mere mortals can, we should imitate the gods in their solitary mental self-sufficiency and calm distance from practical matters.

Calvin vigorously rejected this pagan philosophical conception of the divine, along with any Christian adaptations of it. The God of Abraham, Isaac and Jacob, Calvin insists, is "not the empty, idle, and almost unconscious sort that the Sophists [the Sorbonnists] imagine, but a watchful, effective, active sort, engaged in ceaseless activity."[26] It follows, on Calvin's view, that we express the image of God within us, that we become most Godlike not when we turn away from action, but when we engage in it. For God is not the cold, pure intellect of the pagan philosophers, but a full-fledged person, actively engaged in the governance and redemption of this world. He is the creator and sustainer of the universe. He is the redeemer of the human race. Thus when we shape and administer his creation in service to others and pursue his righteousness in the context of human society we express something of his nature in our lives. Ulrich Zwingli, Calvin's fellow Swiss reformer, claimed that it is not those who "are concerned to find a quiet life" but rather those who exercise themselves in righteousness that they may "serve the Christian community, the common good, the state and individuals" that are "the most like to God."[27]

Referring to the early monastic communities envisioned by St. Augustine, Calvin admits that "it was a beautiful thing to forsake all their possessions and be without earthly care." But

26. Calvin, *Institutes,* I.xvi.3.

27. Ulrich Zwingli, "Of the Education of the Youth," in *Zwingli and Bullinger: Selected Translations,* trans. by Geoffrey W. Bromiley (Philadelphia: Westminster, 1953), p. 113.

he insists that God is not better served in this mode of life. For "God prefers devoted care in ruling a household, where the devout householder, clear and free of all greed, ambition, and other lusts of the flesh, keeps before him the purpose of serving God in a definite calling." Indeed, "It is a beautiful thing to philosophize in retirement, far from intercourse with men. But it is not the part of Christian meekness, as if in hatred of the human race, to flee to the desert and the wilderness and at the same time to forsake those duties which the Lord has especially commanded."[28]

Of course the knowledge of God and the exercise of the intellect have a place in the Calvinist scheme of things. But the knowledge of God in itself does not represent the final end and ultimate purpose of human life for Calvin. He frequently dismisses knowledge of God for its own sake, together with subtle inquiries into God's nature as the Scholastics were wont to make, as "merely toying with idle speculations."[29] The kind of knowledge of God that Calvin holds to be important is the knowledge that bears fruit in a person's life, knowledge that is taken up within the question of how we ought to live and act in this world. Apprehending God as he gives himself to be known in creation, in Scripture, and in Christ, the pious mind responds with fear and reverence, worship and gratitude, commitment and obedience. It is, of course, always possible to pry into the nature and essence of God in order to satisfy our intellectual curiosity. But if such knowledge does not serve to edify the life of faith, it is to be thrust aside as "unprofitable."[30] In Calvin, the contemplative life is subordinated to the ends of the active life.

Thus all work, provided it contributes to the common good, possesses an inherent religious dignity, no matter how mean or low it may be in outward appearance. For the divine intent for human life is that we be employed in mutual service. This is one of the abiding convictions of the Reformed Christian

28. Calvin, *Institutes,* IV.xiii.16.
29. Ibid., I.ii.2.
30. Ibid., I.xiv.4.

conception of work. Luther wrote that "it looks like a great thing when a monk renounces everything and goes into a cloister, carries on a life of asceticism, fasts, watches, prays, etc. . . . On the other hand, it looks like a small thing when a maid cooks and cleans and does other housework. But because God's command is there, even such a small work must be praised as a service of God far surpassing the holiness and asceticism of all monks and nuns."[31] So too with Calvin. In his *Institutes* he claims, "no task will be so sordid and base, provided you obey your calling in it, that it will not shine and be reckoned very precious in God's sight."[32] "A man therefore that serves Christ in serving of men," maintains the Puritan divine John Cotton, "doth his work sincerely as in God's presence, and as one that hath an heavenly business in hand, and therefore comfortably as knowing God approves of his way and work."[33] Because of the intrinsic spiritual significance of work, the Puritan preacher Thomas Gataker proclaims that "A man must not imagine . . . , when he is called to be a Christian, that he must presently cast off all worldly employments . . . and apply himself wholly . . . to prayer and contemplation, but he must retain the calling still as well as the other, following the one still with the other."[34]

31. Luther, *Werke,* vol. 5, Erlanger edition, p. 100.

32. Calvin, *Institutes,* III.x.6. In fact, Calvin took the notion that work is a purely secular matter to be a satanic deception. In his sermon on 1 Corinthians 10:31–11:1 he claims that "The devil has so blinded men that he has persuaded them to believe that in little things they do not have to worry whether God is honored or served: and this he accomplished on the pretext that such things are of the world. When a man works in his labor to earn his living, when a woman does her housework, and when a servant does his duty, one thinks that God does not pay attention to such things, and one says that they are secular affairs. Yes, it is true that such work is proper to this present and fleeting life; however, that does not mean that we must separate it from the service of God." As quoted (in French) in Ronald S. Wallace, *Calvin's Doctrine of the Christian Life* (Edinburgh: Oliver and Boyd, 1959), p. 155. (My thanks to Ellen Monsma for her assistance in the translation of this passage.)

33. John Cotton, "The Christian Calling," in *The Puritans,* ed. Perry Miller and Theodore Johnson, vol. 1 (New York: Harper & Row, 1963), p. 322.

34. Thomas Gataker, "Sermon," in *Capitalism and the Reformation,* ed. M. J. Kitch (London: Longman & Green, 1967), p. 155.

The Calvinists not only retained the Lutheran insistence on the dignity of labor, but they also elaborated the Reformed theology of work into a general understanding of the divinely intended order for human society. This understanding begins from the fact that God did not create us as individuals sufficient unto ourselves. We cannot by ourselves meet all of our needs, even our basic bodily needs, through our own efforts. Rather we depend upon others, as they depend upon us. This indicates God's intent that human beings should live in a society bound together by common needs and mutual service. Our lack of self-sufficiency necessarily draws us together into an interdependent society of persons. Furthermore, although we were created with the same basic needs, we were not created with the same talents and abilities. Each one of us cannot do all things equally well. Not all of us would make good neurosurgeons. That requires, among other things, a rare degree of manual dexterity. Not all of us would make good theoretical physicists. That requires a formidable amount of mathematical ability. Not all of us would make good finish carpenters. Some of us couldn't connect hammer to nail if our lives depended upon it. Possessing different gifts, each person is to occupy that particular station in life where those gifts can be exercised for the common good.

On the Reformed understanding then, human life is to be lived out in a society of mutual service and support, each member contributing according to his specific talents and receiving according to his need. The emphasis on the connection between work and social justice was clearly sounded by Calvin, and continued to reverberate in the subsequent works of English and American theologians in the Calvinist tradition. Commenting on 2 Corinthians 8:13, Calvin claims that "the Lord recommends to us a proportion [of material goods], that we may, in so far as every one's resources admit, afford help to the needy, so that there may not be some in affluence and others in need."[35] But not only are

35. John Calvin, *Commentary on the Epistles of Paul the Apostle to the Corinthians*, vol. 22 of *Calvin's Commentaries* (Grand Rapids: Baker Book House, 1979), p. 295.

we to share what we have, but also share in what we do. "As there is a distinction of several creatures," writes the Puritan theologian Stephan Charnock, "so among men there are several inclinations and several abilities, as donations from God, for the common advantage of human society . . . one man is qualified for one employment, another marked out by God for a different work . . . all men . . . mutually return an advantage to one another . . . so the variety of inclinations and employments in the world is a fruit of the wisdom of God, for the preservation and subsistence of the world by mutual commerce."[36] "God hath made man a social creature," writes the English Puritan John Robinson, "and hath not only ordained several societies, on which persons are to unite themselves for their mutual welfare, but withal so dispensed his blessings, as that no man is so barren, but hath something wherewith to profit others: nor any so furnished, but that he stands in need of others to supply his wants."[37] This voice finds its echo in the writings of the prolific American Puritan preacher Cotton Mather: "God hath made man a societal creature. We expect benefits from human society. It is but equal that human society should receive benefits from us. We are beneficial to human society by the works of that special occupation in which we are to be employed, according to the order of God."[38]

This understanding of human society serves in turn as a basis for apprehending our social obligations. Our talents and abilities were not given to us as tools to heap up fame and fortune for ourselves; rather they are to be exercised for the common good. In his *Institutes,* Calvin asserts that "all the gifts we possess have been bestowed by God and entrusted to us on condition that they be distributed for our neighbors' benefit."[39]

36. Stephen Charnock, *Discourses upon the Existence and Attributes of God,* 1680 Reprint (New York: Robert Carter and Bros., 1873), p. 531.

37. John Robinson, *Works I* (Boston: Doctrinal Tract and Book Society, 1851), p. 157.

38. Cotton Mather, "A Christian at His Calling," in *Puritanism and the American Experience,* ed. Michael McGiffert (Reading, MA: Addison-Wesley, 1969), p. 122.

39. Calvin, *Institutes,* III.vii.5.

"For as God bestows any ability or gift upon any of us," Calvin points out in his sermon on Galatians 6:9-11, "he binds us to such as have need of us and as we are able to help."[40] God has "knit us together" and "let us in the world on the condition that every one of us should consider wherein he may be able to help such as have need of him."[41] For "we are the stewards of everything God has conferred on us by which we are able to help our neighbor, and are required to render account of our stewardship."[42] "So every man by doing of his duty," writes the English Puritan Thomas Lever, "must dispose unto others that commodity and benefit, which is committed of God unto them (to be disposed unto the other) . . . by the faithful and diligent doing of their duties."[43]

As such, the Calvinist concept of the proper order for human society has its parallel in the New Testament picture of the principle of church organization. In the epistles the church is represented as an organic whole: differently gifted members of the church make their various contributions to the community of faith just as different organs have their distinct role to play in the overall functioning of the body. In 1 Corinthians 12 St. Paul makes an explicit comparison between the members of the church and the parts of a body. The role of each bodily part is different, and yet important. For the eye cannot say to the hand, "I don't need you" (1 Cor. 12:21). Likewise, God has appointed different works to different members of the church—some he gave to be apostles, some prophets, some teachers, some workers of miracles, some administrators, and so forth (1 Cor. 12:28). Each depends upon the other, and together they build up the community of faith. Furthermore, just as parts of the body are governed by the head, so the members of the church, their individual differences notwithstanding, find their

40. *Sermons of M. John Calvin upon the Epistle of Saint Paul to the Galatians* (London: Lucas Harison and George Bishop, 1574), p. 307 (translation modified).

41. Ibid., p. 308.

42. Calvin, *Institutes,* III.vii.5.

43. Thomas Lever, *Sermons* (London, 1870), p. 106.

unity in Christ. For Christ himself is the head of that body, and "from him the whole body, joined and held together by every supporting ligament, grows and builds itself up in love, as each part does its work" (Eph. 4:16).

The reformers taught that the members of human society are to exercise their natural gifts for the benefit of their neighbors, just as St. Peter taught the members of the church to exercise their spiritual gifts for the edification of fellow parishioners (1 Pet. 4:10). Although the New Testament passages about gifts and their exercise are restricted to the discussion of the church, it stands to reason that God, being the originator of both the church and society, should make use of similar organizational principles. "We must recognize," Calvin points out in his sermon on 1 Timothy 6,

> that God has wanted to make us like members of a body. When we regard each other in this way, each will then conclude: 'I see my neighbor who has need of me and if I were in such extremity, I would wish to be helped; I must therefore do just that.' In short this communication of St. Paul speaks here of the fraternal affection which proceeds from the regard that we have when God has joined us together and united us in one body, because he wants each to employ himself for his neighbors, so that no one is addicted to his own person, but that we serve all in common.[44]

The Calvinist Modification: The Call to Reform Fallen Structures

However much Luther's concept of vocation enriched the Christian understanding of work, it subsequently required modification in the light of the effects sin can have on the order of stations

44. Calvin, Sermon 53 on 1 Timothy 6:17-19, *Opera* 53, p. 634. See also Pope Pius XI, *Quadragessimo Anno,* II, 5, for an explicit comparison between the right order of society and the structure of the church.

in the earthly kingdom. Luther lived at a time when labor was divided up along fairly natural lines in a relatively modest economy. It appeared to him that this division of labor was part and parcel of the creation order itself. Had he lived in the industrialized world and witnessed the often dehumanizing division of labor in modern production processes, or the proliferation of jobs in today's consumer society no longer connected with legitimate human needs, he may have had second thoughts about maintaining that the existing order of stations directly reflects the will of God.

It was largely the Calvinists who realized that the institutional shape of our earthly occupations is also a product of human culture. During Luther's time and for many centuries preceding him, the given structure of human society was seen as something as stable and incapable of change as the order of nature itself. The social hierarchy and the order of stations in human life were taken to be just as independent of the human will as the biological foundations of the family. This view quite naturally led to a social conservatism: one was to accept the order of society as one would acquiesce to the order of nature. Everyone was to fit into the divinely ordained stations of life—these stations being ascribed, for the most part, rather than chosen.

To flit from one station to the next—out of ambition, avarice, or simple lack of discipline—was seen as an act of insubordination, an attack upon the order of human society. "Every man is to remain in his class and condition, carrying on from father to son the family profession," writes Adriano Tilgher of this period's conception of the social order. "He must not use work to pass from one class of society to another, for that would mean the ruin of the social order. Labor must fit into a world firmly and permanently organized not by man but by God, who has set limits beyond which no one must step. Social classes and professions are divine and immutable forms of society; they existed before labor, which does not create them but must adapt itself to the already existing forms which they offer."[45]

45. Adriano Tilgher, *Work: What It Has Meant to Men Through the Ages* (New York: Arno, 1977), pp. 40-41.

For Luther the given order of stations, as God's design, is unquestionably good. Human sin and the work of the devil, as Wingren points out, make their appearance only in the "misuse of a good and divine office."[46] There were scoundrels, of course, who operated apart from the divinely-ordained system of stations—prostitutes and highwaymen—but the evil here was always seen as personal deviation from the order of society, not a defect in the order of society itself.

Shortly after Luther's time, however, European civilization underwent a dramatic transformation under the combined influence of a rapidly expanding market economy, accelerated urbanization, technological innovation, and vast political reorganization. In the face of these astounding changes on all fronts of social life, it became increasingly apparent that the structure of human society is in part a product of human activity. In turn, to the degree this activity is motivated by sinful desires and worldly ambitions the society thus formed is likely to be structurally unsound and in need of drastic reform. An economy based on greed and a government given over to the arbitrary use of power stand in just as much need of change as the individuals who are a part of them. For this reason Calvinists have typically insisted that not only people's personal lives but also human society be reformed according to the Word of God. The social order must not be merely accepted without complaint, but surveyed with the critical eye of an Old Testament prophet.

An anticipation of this subtle but significant shift in the Reformed understanding of the status of stations can be found in Calvin's sermon on Ephesians 6:5-9. In that passage St. Paul addresses himself to masters and slaves. He does not condemn the institution of slavery outright, but rather reminds both masters and slaves of their duties to each other: slaves are to obey their masters, and masters are to treat their slaves with fairness. But in his exposition and application of this passage Calvin does not confine himself to criticizing cruel masters or in-

46. Wingren, *Luther*, p. 87.

dolent slaves. He procedes to attack the whole institution of the bondservant as "totally against the order of nature," i.e. against the order of creation. It is not just that individuals can act contrary to God's will. Social institutions can in their structure reflect the fallenness of humankind as well.[47]

This shift in attitude toward the existing societal structures is also signalled in the language Calvinists use to express their theology of vocation. Instead of claiming that God has a place for each person in the order of stations in this life, Calvinists often put it this way: God has given each person certain talents and abilities which they should exercise for their neighbor's good. Whereas for Luther our vocation is discerned in the duties of our station in life, for the Calvinists it is derived from our gifts. We have a duty to use our talents and abilities for our neighbor's sake. Therefore we are obliged to find a station in life where our gifts can indeed be employed for the sake of our neighbor's good. The station is no longer itself normative, but must be judged by its suitability as an instrument of social service. If it is found to be faulty or ill-adapted to its end, it must be either altered or discarded altogether. We must not only serve God in our calling; our calling itself must be brought into alignment with God's Word.

By the seventeenth century the Calvinist impulse toward social reform became fully manifest. The address of the Puritan minister Thomas Case to the English House of Commons in 1641 is a case in point: "Reformation must be universal. Reform all places, all persons, and callings; reform the benches of judgement, the inferior magistrates. . . . Reform the universities, reform the cities, reform the countries, reform the inferior schools of learning, reform the sabbath, reform the ordinances, the wor-

47. John Calvin, *Sermons on the Epistle to the Ephesians* (Edinburgh: Banner of Truth Trust, 1973), p. 634. It must be noted that although Calvin took the institution of the bondservant to be contrary to the order of nature, he did not recommend that it be abolished. It may be a fallen structure, but Calvin thought that it may be God's will that fallen people be subject to fallen structures. The emphasis on active social reform comes in later Calvinism, especially that of the Puritans.

ship of God . . . you have more work to do than I can speak. . . . Every plant which my heavenly Father hath not planted shall be rooted up."[48]

For Calvinists, then, it is not so much serving God within the station one finds oneself as it is serving God by one's station. The station is no longer conceived as a form of life imposed upon one from the outside, but as an instrument of life. "Thus," writes Ernst Troeltsch of the Calvinists, "the ideal was now no longer one of surrender to a static vocational system, directed by Providence, but the free use of vocational work as the method of realizing the purpose of the Holy Community. The varied secular callings do not simply constitute the existing framework within which brotherly love is exercised and faith is preserved, but they are means to be handled with freedom, through whose thoughtful and wise use love alone becomes possible and faith a real thing."[49]

Ecumenical Convergence: The Contemporary Catholic Position

In tracing the development of the Protestant concept of vocation from Luther's reaction to the medieval monastic ideal, it is easy to give the impression that the official Catholic position on work crystallized at some point in the high Middle Ages and has been dutifully collecting dust ever since. But that is not the case. In the course of modern Catholic social teaching, beginning with Pope Leo XIII's encyclical *Rerum Novarum* of 1891, we can detect a distinct "reformed shift" in the Catholic estimation of the meaning and place of work in human life. In their recent pastoral letter on the U.S. economy, the U.S. Catholic bishops state

48. Thomas Case, *Two Sermons Lately Preached* (London, 1642), II, pp. 13, 16.

49. Ernst Troeltsch, *The Social Teaching of the Christian Churches*, vol. 2 (London: George Allen and Unwin, 1931), pp. 610-11.

that Catholics "have much to learn from the strong emphasis in Protestant tradition on the vocation of lay people in the world."[50] But the "reformed shift" involves more than just an openness on the part of the Catholic church to the Protestant tradition. With the publication of Pope John Paul II's *Laborum Exercens* in 1981, the official Catholic theology of work virtually coincides with the traditional Protestant position at every major point.

The modern tradition of Catholic social teaching began in the nineteenth century as a pastoral response to the social reality that occupied the center of Karl Marx's concerns: the great inequities and class antagonisms brought about by unrestrained industrial capitalism. At that time, the captains of industry and trade were enormously rich, and getting richer, while the great mass of workers labored long and hard for bare subsistence wages with virtually no prospect of improvement. Commenting on the society of his day, Pope Leo XIII, in *Rerum Novarum,* notes with regret that "a small number of very rich men have been able to lay upon the masses of the poor a yoke little better than slavery itself."[51] This lamentable state of affairs constituted what was often referred to at that time as the "Social Question." In this question, the church was confronted not only by certain theoretically interesting social and economic developments, but by a great moral problem of the modern age, where "Working Men have been given over, isolated and defenseless, to the callousness of employers and the greed of unrestrained competition."[52] Although not in a position to devise or criticize economic theories or hand out fiscal advice, the church was bound to address a morally unacceptable situation. In the words of Pope Pius XI in *Quadragissimo Anno,* a very small minority "enjoyed practically all the comforts so plentifully supplied by modern invention," while the rest, made up

50. National Council of Catholic Bishops, *Economic Justice for All* (United States Catholic Conference, 1986), sec. 59.

51. Pope Leo XIII, *Rerum Novarum,* sec. 2.

52. Ibid.

of workers, were "oppressed by dire poverty," and "struggled in vain to escape from the straits which encompassed them."[53]

The moral problem encompassed not only the material deprivation of the workers, but also the dehabilitating spiritual effect of modern methods of production upon the human soul. Labor, which was originally given for man's good, Pope Pius XI noted with sad irony, "has everywhere been changed into an instrument of strange perversion: for dead matter leaves the factory ennobled and transformed, where men are corrupted and degraded."[54]

In the face of this social reality, the Catholic church unabashedly took up the cause of the working class.[55] Its aims were to defend the rights of the workers, reduce the level of class conflict, and reverse the process of social polarization. As means to those ends, however, it did not jump onto the socialist bandwagon and advocate the abolition of private property. In fact, it maintained that the abolition of private property would lead to a state of affairs much worse than the one it was designed to improve. Rather, while maintaining that private property is an inalienable natural right, Catholics called attention to the social obligations correlative to that right. For the right to private property is not "absolute," but relative to the right of "common use," that is, the right that all people have to the goods of creation which are required to meet their basic human needs. What private property comes my way, then, imposes upon me the obligation to use that property to meet my own needs *and* the needs of others. The right to private property does not justify me in doing anything I please with what is mine. In *Populorum Progressio* (1967), Pope Paul VI writes ". . . private property does not constitute for anyone an absolute and unconditioned right. No one is justified in keeping for his exclusive use what he does not need, when others lack necessities."[56] Thus, as Pope John XXIII

53. Pope Pius XI, *Quadragessimo Anno,* Occasion.

54. Ibid., III.3.

55. Ibid., II.3; Pope Paul VI, *Populorum Progressio,* sec. 1; and Pope John XXIII, *Mater et Magistra,* sec. 8.

56. Pope Paul VI, *Populorum Progressio,* sec. 23.

points out in *Mater et Magistra* (1961), he who uses his private property "must take into account not only his own welfare but that of others as well."[57] "In the right of private property there is rooted a social responsibility."[58]

The private owners of the means of production have such a responsibility as well. Because they own the means of production, they are under the social obligation to use those means to promote the common good, not to enhance their private advantage at the expense of their employees and society. This constitutes the duties of the rich. But the poor also have rights—the right to sustenance, to work, to a just wage and decent working conditions, and to assembly for the purposes of collective bargaining. Furthermore, the state has the duty to protect the rights of workers.

The answer to the Social Question, according to the Catholic Church, was not to be found in social revolution as promoted by the Marxists, but in the faithful discharge of the duties by all parties involved: the workers, the employers, and the government. The workers have the duty to provide a fair day's work; the employer has the duty to provide a fair day's wage and decent working conditions; and the state has the duty to protect the rights of both—the right to private property as well as the right to sustenance.

Although the initial encyclicals in the modern tradition of Catholic social teaching express a positive estimate of work, they are primarily directed toward the resolution of certain social problems. As such they do not contain or elaborate a theology of work. Pope John Paul II in his encyclical entitled *Laborum Excercens,* published in 1981, carried out the official rethinking of the Catholic theology of work. Drawing upon the implicit theological reorientation of the previous encyclicals and the new directions in Catholic theology established in the Vatican II documents, especially *Gaudium et Spes* (1965), John Paul II

57. Pope John XXIII, *Mater et Magistra,* sec. 19.
58. Ibid., sec. 119.

laid down a position on human work which is remarkably Reformed in both substance and spirit.

The medievals had by and large assigned the activity of work to the periphery of human life. Work was indeed necessary, but it pertains to the temporal goods of this life, not the eternal goods of the next, to the lower, not the higher elements of the human person. The reformers, on the contrary, held that work stands at the center of the divine intent for human life. Using the biblical account of creation, the contemporary Catholic theology has come to the same conclusion. In the first chapter of Genesis we read that humankind, created in God's image, was placed on this earth with the mandate to "fill the earth and subdue it" (Gen. 1:28). Commenting on this portion of Scripture, Pope Paul VI writes that "the Bible, from the first page on, teaches us that the whole creation is for man, that it is his responsibility to develop it by intelligent effort and by means of his labour to perfect it, so to speak, for his use."[59]

Through work we fulfill our God-given mandate to develop, give shape to, and care for the earth. It is not a burdensome necessity which draws us away from true fulfillment; rather, work represents, in the words of John Paul II, a "fundamental aspect of man's existence."[60] It represents the divine intent for human life. "By the work of his hands and with the aide of technical means," we read in *Gaudium et Spes,* "man tills the earth to bring forth fruit and to make it a dwelling place for all mankind . . . in so doing he is revealing the design, which God revealed at the beginning of time, to subdue the earth and perfect the work of creation."[61]

The reformers held that work is not only an activity by which we respond to God's original command, but by it we also express God's image within us. With wisdom and power God created the world. But the activity of creation did not stop there.

59. Pope Paul VI, *Populorum Progressio,* sec. 22.

60. Pope John Paul II, *On Human Work: Laborum Exercens,* sec. 4.

61. Pope John Paul II, *Gaudium et Spes,* sec. 34.

In the Genesis account we read that God created human beings in his own image and entrusted them with the task of carrying on the activity of creation, giving further form to the raw material of nature, actualizing the potentials tucked away in the world in a way which serves human society and at the same time glorifies God and his lavish benevolence. When we carry out this project in our own work we do something godlike. We image God. The contemporary Catholic theology of work solidly agrees with this point. In *Laborem Exercens* John Paul II states that "man is the image of God partly through the mandate received from his creator to subdue, to dominate, the earth. In carrying out this mandate, man, every human being, reflects the very action of the Creator of the universe."[62]

The reformers also said that in our work we participate in God's providence. God works in this world with human hands. Through our work, God provides. The contemporary Catholic theology of work concurs. The Vatican II document, *Gaudium et Spes,* claims that

> Man was created in God's image and was commanded to conquer the earth with all it contains and to rule the world in justice and holiness: he was to acknowledge God as maker of all things and relate himself and the totality of creation to him, so that through the dominion of all things by man the name of God would be majestic in all the earth. This holds good also for our daily work. When men and women provide for themselves and their families in such a way as to be of service to the community as well, they can rightly look upon their work as a prolongation of the work of the Creator, a service to their fellow man, and their personal contribution to the fulfillment in history of the divine plan."[63]

Expanding on this passage from *Gaudium et Spes,* Pope John Paul II writes that "the word of God's revelation is profoundly marked by the fundamental truth that man, created in the image of God, shares by his work in the activity of the Crea-

62. Pope John Paul II, *Laborum Exercens,* sec. 4.
63. Pope John Paul II, *Gaudium et Spes,* sec. 34.

tor and that, within the limits of his own human capabilities, man in a sense continues to develop that activity, and perfects it as he advances further and further in the discovery of the resources and values contained in the whole of creation."[64] The U.S. Catholic bishops repeat the theme when they maintain that men and women, as faithful stewards in caring for the earth "can justly consider that by their labor they are unfolding the Creator's work." In work, they "share in the creative activity of God."[65]

The reformers couched their theology of work in a comprehensive vision of the divine economy at work in human society. Human society, like the church, was to be organized as an organic unity, with interdependent members each contributing to the whole according to their specific gifts. So with contemporary Catholic theology: in *Rerum Novarum,* Pope Leo XII noted that "there naturally exists among mankind innumerable differences of the most important kind; people differ in capability, in diligence, in health, and in strength; and unequal fortune is a necessary result of inequality of condition. Such inequality is far from being disadvantageous either to individuals or to the community; social and public life can only go on by the help of various kinds of capacity and the playing of many parts, and each man, as a rule, chooses the part which peculiarly suits his case."[66] Pope Pius XI remarked that this organic image of the proper order and structure of human society at large bears a strong formal resemblance to the New Testament understanding of church organization.

> If then the members of the social body be thus reformed [in a spirit of mutual service], and if the true directive principle of social and economic activity be thus re-established, it will be possible to say, in a sense, of that body, what the Apostle said of the Mystical Body of Christ: 'The whole body, being compacted and fitly joined together, by what every joint supplieth,

64. Pope John Paul II, *Laborum Exercens,* sec. 25.
65. National Council of Catholic Bishops, *Economic Justice,* sec. 32.
66. Pope Leo XIII, *Rerum Novarum,* sec. 14.

according to the operation in the measure of every part, maketh increase of the body, onto the edifying of itself in charity.'[67]

The reformers insisted that religious suffering ought not to be sought through the artificial means invented by the monks. For possibly, indeed inevitably, one will suffer for Christ's sake in the occupations of this world. Work, then, is not only a matter of participating in the creative activity of God, but also a matter of following Christ in his example of redemptive suffering. This point has not been lost on the contemporary Catholic theology of work. In *Laborem Exercens* Pope John Paul II points out that

> Sweat and toil, which work necessarily involves in the present condition of the human race, present the Christian and everyone who is called to follow Christ with the possibility of sharing lovingly in the work that Christ came to do. This work of salvation came about through suffering and death on a cross. By enduring the toil of work in union with Christ crucified for us, man in a way collaborates with the Son of God for the redemption of humanity. He shows himself a true disciple of Christ by carrying the cross in his turn every day in the activity that he is called upon to perform.[68]

Thus, "the Christian finds in human work a small part of the cross of Christ and accepts it in the same spirit of redemption in which Christ accepted his cross for us."[69] By faith, as *Gaudium et Spes* puts is, we believe "that through the homage of work offered to God man is associated with the redemptive work of Christ."[70] When faithful Christians "apply themselves to temporal affairs," maintains Pope John XXIII, "their work in a way is a continuation of the labor of Jesus Christ Himself."[71]

The reformers also taught that no conflict exists between

67. Pope Pius XI, *Quadragessimo Anno,* II, 5.
68. Pope John Paul II, *Laborum Exercens,* sec. 27.
69. Ibid.
70. Pope John Paul II, *Gaudium et Spes,* sec. 67.
71. Pope John XXIII, *Mater et Magistra,* sec. 259.

the love of God and the love of one's neighbor. For God identifies himself with our neighbor in need. To serve that neighbor, then, is to serve God. This contention is also strongly represented in the contemporary Catholic theology of work. The U.S. Catholic bishops, for instance, make the same point in their letter on the U.S. economy. "Jesus," they maintain, "is hidden in those most in need; to reject them is to reject God made manifest in history."[72] For this reason we are warned in *Gaudium et Spes* that "the Christian who shirks his temporal duties, shirks his duties towards his neighbor, neglects God himself, and endangers his eternal salvation."[73] Pope John XXIII also warns against playing the religious life off against the active life: "Let no one imagine that there is any opposition between these two things so that they cannot be properly reconciled: namely, the perfection of one's own soul and the business of this life, as if one had no chance but to abandon to activities of the world in order to strive for Christian perfection, as if one could not attend to these pursuits without endangering his own dignity as a man and as a Christian."[74] For "it is in full accord with the designs of God's providence that men develop and perfect themselves by exercise of their daily tasks."[75] Distancing itself from the traditional interpretation of the Mary and Martha passage in Luke 10, *Gaudium et Spes* holds that Christ does not recommend the contemplative life over the active, but rather commands the Christian "to devote himself to the service of his fellow man."[76]

The reformers came to see that not only the human heart, but also the given order of human society is corrupted by the presence of sin. Therefore the demand that society too be reformed in accordance with the Word of God. The social order was not to be simply accepted as a direct reflection of God's will, but must be made to comply with God's will. The call for reforming society is also issued in the social teachings of the

72. National Council of Catholic Bishops, *Economic Justice*, sec. 44.
73. Pope John Paul II, *Gaudium et Spes*, sec. 43.
74. Pope John XXIII, *Mater et Magistra*, sec. 255.
75. Ibid., sec. 250
76. Pope John Paul II, *Gaudium et Spes*, sec. 57.

Catholic church. This is especially true when it addressed the Social Question. In *Populorum Progressio,* Pope Paul VI insisted that "the present [social] situation must be faced with courage and the injustices linked with it must be fought against and overcome. Development demands bold transformations, innovations that go deep."[77] He called upon the Christian layperson "to take the initiative freely and to infuse a Christian spirit into the mentality, customs, laws and structures of the community in which they live. Changes are necessary; basic reforms are indispensible: the layman should strive resolutely to permeate them with the spirit of the Gospel."[78]

In sum, we are witnessing a remarkable ecumenical convergence in the practical theology of work. That theology, both Protestant and Catholic, gives to human work a central role in the understanding of human life in its relation both to God and the world. Through work we respond to God's mandate to humanity to continue the work of creation by subduing the earth; through work we realize ourselves as image-bearers of God; through work we participate in God's ongoing creative activity; through work we follow Christ in his example of redemptive suffering for the sake of others; through work we serve God himself as we serve those with whom he identifies. As opposed to the ancient pagan and modern secular views of work, the Christian conception claims that working does not elevate us to the position formerly occupied by God, lord and master of the universe. Neither do we, in working, debase ourselves to the level of animal existence. Although in working we become like God, giving further shape and form to the earth for the good of humanity, we remain subordinate and responsible to God as stewards of his creation. Although through work we meet many of the basic bodily needs that we share with the animals, our work goes far beyond such needs in the development of culture, and it goes far beyond the instinctual behavior of animals when it is carried out with intelligence, foresight, imagination, and responsible choice.

77. Pope Paul VI, *Populorum Progressio,* sec. 32.
78. Ibid., sec. 81.

PART TWO

*　*　*

Applications

CHAPTER THREE

* * *

Work, Life, and Vocational Choice: Investing Yourself in the Divine Economy

HAVING REVIEWED what the Christian tradition has made of work on the basis of God's self-revelation in the Holy Scriptures, we might very well ask what all this has to do with us today. How does this newly acquired information help us with the practical and often difficult problem of choosing a vocation? What about those of us who are presently stuck in a job in which we experience no sense of vocation? What about those of us who feel that the accepted practices and standard operating procedures of our profession have seriously eroded our moral integrity? What about those of us who are coming to the unsettling realization that the demands of our career have taken over our entire life and given us little in return but an empty promise of happiness through worldly success and material abundance?

These are difficult questions indeed. And the answers to them will necessarily vary from one case to the other. Yet by considering these questions in the light of the preceeding discussion of the Christian understanding of work as vocation, we may be able to discover some basic guidelines for specific answers.

Making the Match: Career Choice

How exactly does the Christian concept of work as a divine calling bear upon the problem of choosing a vocation? Before we answer this question, we would do well to make two preliminary observations. First, to those of us who are familiar with the language of the Bible, there is something odd about the phrase "choosing a vocation." For in the New Testament the primary, if not exclusive, meaning of the term "vocation"—or calling *(klesis)*—pertains to the call of the gospel, pure and simple. We are called to repentance and to faith (Acts 2:38); we are called into fellowship with Jesus Christ (1 Cor. 1:9); we are called out of the darkness and into the light (1 Pet. 2:9); we are called to be holy (1 Pet. 1:15, 1 Cor. 1:2); indeed, we are called to be saints (Rom. 1:7). Here we are not being asked to choose from a variety of callings, to decide which one is "right" for us. Rather, one call goes out to all—the call of discipleship. For it is incumbent upon all Christians to follow Christ, and, in so doing, to become the kind of people God wants us to be. The call of the gospel is not to a particular occupation, but to sainthood.

Yet we are also as Christians commanded, and therefore called, to love and serve our neighbors with the gifts that God has given to us. Each one of us, writes St. Peter, "should use whatever gift he has received to serve others, faithfully administering God's grace in its various forms" (1 Pet. 4:10). For each of us has certain gifts, certain talents and abilities. Those gifts were not given that we might heap up fame and fortune for ourselves. Rather, the possession of those gifts places an obligation upon us to use them for the building up of the community of faith and the human community at large (Rom. 12:4-21). We are called, then, not only to be certain kinds of persons, but also to do certain kinds of things.

Because of this twofold character of God's call, the Puritans used to distinguish between the "general" and the "particular" calling. The general calling is the call to be a Christian, that is, to take on the virtues appropriate to followers of Christ, whatever one's station in life. St. Paul refers to these virtues as the "fruit" of the Spirit: love, joy, peace, patience, kindness, goodness, faithfulness, gentleness, and self-control (Gal. 5:22-23). It is not for us to pick and choose among these virtues. When it comes to being a Christian, the virtues come in one package. They are the fruition of the work of the Spirit in our lives.

The particular calling, on the other hand, is the call to a specific occupation—an occupation to which not all Christians are called. With respect to occupations within the church, St. Paul refers to such particular callings as the "gifts" of the Spirit: to be an apostle, a prophet, a teacher, a worker of miracles, an administrator, and the like (1 Cor. 12:28-31). Not all are called to be apostles, prophets, or teachers. For here the Spirit fits each member of the body of Christ differently for a specific work: we are not expected or able to do all things, but only the things which God has enabled and called us to do. In the discharge of our various particular callings we together build up the interdependent society of the saints, which finds its unity in Christ, the head of the church.

With the distinction between the general and the particular calling in mind, talk about "vocational choice"—in the sense of choosing a particular occupation in which we will exercise our gifts—is both biblically appropriate and religiously important.[1] At certain junctures in our lives we are confronted with the need to identify our gifts and choose an occupation; and an occupation can provide us with the concrete opportunity to employ our gifts in the service of our neighbor, as God commanded us to do. This holds not only for the occupations within the church, but in society as well. For although the Bible concentrates on the spiritual gifts and their employment in the commu-

1. A technical note: earlier vocation had been defined by the duties and obligations a person has in occupying certain stations or possessing certain gifts. As such, a vocation is still not something a person can choose. Strictly speaking, what we choose are occupations, where our vocations can be fulfilled. The locution "choosing a vocation" in this book, then, must be understood as shorthand for "choosing an occupation where one can pursue one's vocation." Although the shorthand version has the virtue of brevity, it fails to challenge the modern identification of vocation with occupation. It is important to keep the distinction in mind.

nity of faith, the Christian tradition has generally extended the Biblical principle, confessing that our "natural" gifts also come from God and are to be employed for the benefit of the wider human community.[2]

As a second preliminary observation, lest we move too quickly from the question of vocation to that of paid occupation, we ought to remind ourselves that vocation is the wider concept. One need not have a paid occupation in order to have a vocation. Indeed all of us have, at any one time, a number of vocations—and only one of them might be pursued as a paid occupation. To put it in Luther's language, at any given time we occupy a number of stations: parent, child, citizen, parishioner, and so on. Each one of these stations entails a specific vocation. As a parent it is my vocation to love, discipline, and care for my children; as a child it is my vocation to honor and obey my parents; as a citizen it is my vocation to participate in the political process and abide by the decisions and rulings of the government; as a parishioner it is my vocation to exercise my spiritual gifts for the edification of the body of Christ. I may not have a paid occupation. But that doesn't mean I have no calling in life.

Furthermore, it follows from the broad concept of vocation that we will always have a number of vocations as a result of certain social relations and historical circumstances which we ourselves have not chosen. I, for instance, was born in a modern nation state known as the United States of America in the mid-twentieth century of white Anglo-Saxon Protestant parentage. I did not ask or choose to be so born. I just was. From the purely human perspective it seems almost accidental that I should be who I am. Could I not just as well have been a Chinese woman born during the Ming dynasty, or a Nicaraguan campesino born during the glory days of William Walker? Why was I born of this

2. Miroslav Volf contends that the traditional concept of vocation, being based on the given order of stations, is neither socially nor biblically tenable. He procedes to give a programmatic sketch of a theological concept of work based on the idea of gifts as if it were a fresh proposal. One can already find, however, the language of gifts and duties in the Calvinist doctrine of vocation. See his "Arbeit und Charisma," *Zeitschrift für Evangelische Ethik* 31: 4 (1987): 411-433.

particular race and nationality, with this particular body and temperament? It's hard to say.

Existential philosophers of atheist persuasion have dwelt upon the apparently accidental nature of our identities, and refer to such as the brute "facticity" or "thrownness" of human existence. We find ourselves thrown into a particular situation with no apparent rhyme or reason, and our task as human beings is to appropriate our absurd circumstances into a meaningful life project which we ourselves freely choose.

But from a theistic point of view things look quite different. That I am who I am is not a result of chance, a mere cosmic accident. Rather it is the result of God's intention. There is a reason why I am who I am, although that reason may not be immediately apparent to me. I was placed here for a purpose, and that purpose is one which I am, in part, to discover, not invent. The facts about me are indicators of the divine intent for my life, indicators which are to be interpreted in the light of God's revealed Word. Perhaps, through no choice of my own, I inherit a vast family fortune and suddenly find myself wealthy to the point of embarrassment. An absurd event? No. A providential one in which I am to discern God's will for the shape and direction of my life. For the rich have at least one divine vocation just by virtue of being rich, namely to use their money to benefit others. Many things about me I did not choose. But that does not mean that they are not meaningful, or that they have to be made meaningful through other choices that I make.

Even a vocation as a paid occupation may not be a matter of choice. In fact, for most people it never has been. Down through the ages and in many parts of the world today people did and do not have much choice in the kind of work they do. Their work was and is simply imposed upon them by circumstances beyond their control: the economic niche of the family into which they were born, or a combination of financial necessity and the existing job market. One is born a rice farmer or becomes a factory worker because that is the only line of work open at the time. "Today we consider it an imperfection of society for people to be fixed in their opportunities and jobs by class and birth," management theorist Peter Drucker observes, "where only yesterday this was the natural and apparently inescapable condition of mankind."[3] Freedom of choice regarding occupation is a relatively novel social phenomenon. Those of us who are faced with such a choice are, historically speaking, a very small minority indeed.

It shouldn't come as a surprise, then, that guidelines for the responsible choice of an occupation have not been thoroughly worked out by the Christian community at large. The fact that in many parts of Christendom today work is still considered a secular matter, with little or no connection to religion, has not helped either.

But an initial attempt to formulate the principles of vocational choice was made by the Protestant reformers of the sixteenth and seventeenth centuries. They were, on the one hand, firmly convinced that all of life, even the life of everyday work, ought to be lived to the glory of God. On the other hand, they were aware that in their time people were being granted a greater measure of freedom in the choice of occupations. The rigid structures of medieval society were crumbling around them and social life was opening up, differentiating, and becoming more flexible. Higher education was no longer the prerogative of the aristocracy alone. As a direct result, an increasing number of people had access to an increasingly wider range of occupational options. Thus it was given to them to work out the principles of vocational choice in the light of the Word of God.

How did they go about this? Taking their initial bearings from the biblical witness together with a reflection upon the human condition, they began with a definition of work that went something like this: work is the social place where people can exercise the gifts that God has given them in the service of others.[4] For God did not create us as self-sufficient individu-

3. Peter F. Drucker, *Management: Tasks, Responsibilities, Practices* (New York: Harper & Row, 1974), p. 9.

4. This summary of the Reformed theology of work is based on such comments of Puritan preachers as the following. William Perkins: "The main

als.[5] We all have needs which we alone cannot meet. By necessity we live in communities of interdependent individuals. And we are to make use of what talents we do have to serve others as they, in turn, serve us. Together we build up society as a mutual support system.

With this concept of work, two practical items immediately arise: the gifts God has given me, and the exercise of those gifts for the sake of others. The first step then, in making a responsible choice of vocation, is ascertaining precisely which gifts God has bestowed upon me.

This in itself can be a difficult, painful, and protracted process. We were not born with job descriptions taped to our backs. Our vocational aptitudes have to be discovered in that process by which we come to know ourselves. But the road to self-knowledge can be a long one, and often we don't possess a clear idea of exactly what our talents are at the time we must make vocational decisions. If we are not sure what we are good at, it often pays to reflect upon our past experience with precisely that question in mind. What have I done, and done well? What kind of skills did I make use of? Planning, investigating, implementing, building, repairing, creating, writing, teaching, supervising? What kind of knowledge did I acquire? Knowledge about cars, computers, finance, administration, food, flowers, music, mathematics? What kind of objects did I work with? Numbers, words, people, mechanical things, living things, programs, institutions? In what capacity was I relating to others? As

---

end of our lives . . . is to serve God in the serving of men in the works of our callings," from his "Treatise of the Vocations or Callings of Men." To Richard Baxter, the main purpose of labor is a matter of "obeying God and doing good to others," in his *A Christian Directory.* Again, William Perkins: a person's vocation is "a certain kind of life, ordained and imposed on men by God, for the common good."

5. In his sermons on the book of Galatians, Calvin claimed that God could have created each one of us as self-sufficient individuals, each inhabiting his or her own solitary universe. The fact that God did not so create us indicates that He intended us to live in a community of mutual love and service. See *Sermons of M. John Calvin upon the Epistle of Saint Paul to the Galatians* (London: Lucas Harison and George Bishop, 1574), p. 308.

a team member, team leader, lone ranger, coach, manager, expert? Was I in a position with a lot of freedom and responsibility, or was I working in a highly structured situation, where my activity was thoroughly specified?[6] With an autobiographical grasp of my talents I can begin, perhaps with some additional guidance, to see what kind of work I could do well.

Beside reflecting on past experience, remaining open to future experience is equally important. For self-knowledge is an open-ended process, a fact twentieth-century theologian Karl Barth underscored in his *Church Dogmatics:*

> In relation to the personal presuppositions which he himself brings, the action of man must be one which always and in all directions is open, eager to learn, capable of modification, perpetually ready, in obedience to the exclusively sovereign command of God, to allow itself to be orientated afresh and in very different ways from those which might have seemed possible and necessary on the basis of man's own ideas of his ability and capacity. In the last analysis man has no more knowledge of himself than mastery over himself. Again and again he must let himself be shown who he is. His faithfulness to himself, then, [consists] only in constant attention and openness to that which, as God claims him, will be continually disclosed to him as his true self, as the real aptitude which he has been given together with its limits, and then in the corresponding decision for perhaps a much more daring or possibly a much more humble action than that to which he has hitherto considered himself called.[7]

6. For further guidance on this point, try SIMA (System for Identifying Motivated Abilities) as explained in Ralph Mattson's and Arthur Miller's fine book, *Finding a Job You Can Love* (Nashville: Thomas Nelson, 1982). Much assistance in identifying skills can also be found in Richard Bolles, *The New Quick Job-Hunting Map* (Berkeley: Ten Speed Press, 1985). The Strong-Campbell Interest Inventory test is a standard instrument for identifying interests and their typical locations in the world of paid employment. Another tool of self-evaluation is "Performax." To find out where this self-evaluation is locally administered write to Performax Systems International, Inc.; 12805 State Highway 55; Minneapolis, MN 55441.

7. *Church Dogmatics,* III, 4, 52.2 (Edinburgh: T. & T. Clark, 1961). Barth's emphasis on "openness" to future experience comes from his conviction that there

Some experimentation, then, may be required in the process of career choice. If several occupational options lie before me, and they all look equally valid and interesting, rather than allowing myself to be paralyzed by the lack of a deciding factor, it would be better simply to choose one and pursue it. In the course of pursuing that occupation I will inevitably learn something I couldn't have known prior to its pursuit. I may become convinced that I had in fact made the right choice. On the other hand, I might find out in no uncertain terms that I made the "wrong" choice. Not to worry. I can still benefit from that. I have learned something about myself. And I can cross one occupational option off my list.

Besides, career decisions are rarely irrevocable. Most people nowadays go through four or five career changes in the course of a lifetime. When I was in high school I wanted to go into cinematography. I loved movies, and I wanted to make some. Instead I became an advertising artist. But later, while working in an art studio in the San Francisco Bay area, I found myself drawn into the discipline of philosophy. I needed to clarify certain issues in life. Today I am a professor of philosophy at a liberal arts college. And I suspect most people past their twenties have similarly crooked accounts of how they came to their present occupations. Career paths are rarely straight. Typically they are afflicted by detours, unmarked intersections, forced exits, blind alleys, and cul-de-sacs. When the philosophy majors I advise at Calvin College hesitate to go to graduate school because they are not sure if philosophy is their calling, I usually tell them that going to graduate school is the best way to find out if philosophy is their calling. We can't know everything before we act. An element of trial and error is unavoidable in the carving out of a niche for oneself in the world of work. Barth was entirely correct when he said that "a man can really

---

is very little that we can discern about God's will for our lives in general from the order of creation. Although this conviction differs from the one promoted in this book, it remains the case that openness is essential for the acquisition of certain forms of self-knowledge which are crucial for vocational decision-making.

learn to know his sphere of operation only as he sets to work in it."[8]

Vocational counseling and testing can also help here. Not that the results of a vocational test are to count as the last word. The validity of the results depends upon how well the test was designed, how accurately and honestly you were able to answer the questions, and how carefully the results are interpreted. But a vocational test can at least do this: it can comfort you by confirming what you already thought you knew about yourself, but weren't sure; or it can challenge you by suggesting occupational possibilities you had never considered before.

An honest lack of self-knowledge is not the only problem in making a career choice. The sins of greed, pride, envy, and fear can enter into the picture too, clouding our vision of who we are and what we were cut out to do. We might have our eye on a certain career because of the salary. We approach our career as a means to untold riches and material delights. Or perhaps we find ourselves attracted to a certain career because of its social prestige. We want to prove to others—and perhaps to ourselves—that we are much more talented and capable than either thought. We treat our prospective career as a wand to wave before the crowds to command their respect, awe, and admiration. Or perhaps we are unhappy with the way God has made us, and we are envious of another person's gifts and accomplishments. In the course of our prospective career, we resolve to become just like her and excel where she has excelled. Our career becomes the tool of our covetousness. Or we begin by being aimed at certain careers due to family expectations about what we are going to do with our lives, and we are afraid to disappoint our parents. We live in fear of what others would think of us were we to strike out on our own. Our career becomes a place where we hide from others, and especially ourselves. On the basis of these and similarly errant motives, we can convince ourselves that we are qualified for certain careers, while what led

8. Ibid.

us to choose those careers had very little to do with our particular gifts or the human needs around us.

Perhaps I have been raised in a community where intellectual prowess is held in high esteem. Perhaps other features of my upbringing led to an overwhelming psychological need to be highly esteemed by others. Or, I may have been raised in a community with a substantial anti-intellectual bias and, due to other features of my upbringing, I have an overwhelming psychological need to distinguish myself over against that community, thereby establishing my social independence. At any rate, on the basis of some subterranean motive of which I am not fully aware, I find myself quite naturally drawn in the direction of intellectual pursuits. When I get to college I might even boldly stage a direct assault on the very pinnacle of mental achievement, surrounded by the chill, thin air of theoretical abstraction—I declare a philosophy major.

Thus I become convinced that in philosophy I have found my true calling. But have I? Has God really given me the appropriate intellectual gifts and a genuine zeal for the truth? Or am I just fooling myself? These are difficult questions to answer on the basis of private self-examination. The opportunites for self-deception along these lines are almost limitless. Even if I received lousy grades in all my philosophy courses—enough to thoroughly discourage the average mortal—I could still convince myself that this failure was wholly due to the clumsy pedagogy of my professors, or their inability to detect the secret genius of my work. Resolute in purpose, I go on to graduate school against the advice of my mentors. No one will deny me the glory associated with my chosen field—and I proceed to make a total fool of myself trying to prove to everyone else that I am not a complete idiot.

Because of the innate human talent for self-deception, it is a good idea to seek the advice of others known for mature and balanced judgment. I may be convinced that God has especially called me to a particular occupation. But do others recognize in me the gifts I think I possess? Can my friends detect in the pattern of my life the passions, the interests, and the concerns I claim to have? Do my teachers take me to be mentally competent and personally well-suited for the career of my own choosing? Their counsel may be encouraging. Or devastating. But it must be sought. Often I must seek the help of others if I am to be honest with myself before God.

It seems, then, that perceived social status combined with certain psychological needs can push people into occupations for which they are not at all qualified. But it can work the other way too. Low social status plus similar psychological needs can drive people away from an occupation for which they are eminently qualified. I may have formidable mechanical abilities and a genuine love for the automobile as an engineered system of intake and exhaust manifolds, regulators and alternators, camshafts and crankshafts. In the world of car repair, infested as it is by rip-off artists, I may be able to perform a genuine service to the community as a mechanic. But I chafe at the suggestion. After all, who wants to be a "grease monkey"? What would my parents think? My friends?

Finding our niche in life may not only require that we be honest with ourselves. It may also require a stiff dose of humility. Yet, as John Calvin said, "No task will be so sordid and base . . . that it will not shine and be reckoned very precious in God's sight."[9] An occupation held to be of no account in the eyes of the world can nonetheless be important to God. The ranking of occupations in our society and in the kingdom of God are often two very different things. And it's important to keep the difference in mind. The garbage collector performs an infinitely more valuable social service than the advertising executive about to launch a campaign to convince the American homemaker that Pink Froth dish detergent is indispensible to gracious living. But the latter, for reasons difficult to fathom, enjoys more social status.

The first step, then, in responsible vocational choice is to identify the abilities and talents God has given us. Those talents

9. Calvin, *The Institutes of the Christian Religion,* III.x.6.

and abilities, however, will probably not be unique. For that reason they will not, by themselves, lead a person to a unique job. That is especially true if we consider such things as the ability to grasp objects between the thumb and fingers. That ability is regularly exercised by the dentist, the electrician, and the surgeon—as well as the paperboy. Even rarer gifts, like a lightning-quick analytical mind, do not suggest only one profession. One could use such a mind in law, philosophy, or the CIA.

Although the absence of a unique gift may leave us in the lurch when it comes to choosing a specific career, we can take positive comfort in the fact that as generic human beings we already possess a wide range of abilities. And we can meaningfully put these ordinary abilities to use in a number of perfectly acceptable occupations. What is lost by way of unambiguous guidance is made up by flexibility. And we are thereby relieved of the frustrating and ultimately self-defeating quest for "the right job," as if there were only one per person. As a simple matter of fact, we are qualified to do a number of things. And a number of the things we are qualified to do would be good things to do.

Nonetheless, God can give us two other things that will narrow down the field considerably. First, he can give us a concern. Of course, we are all concerned about ourselves and how we will fare in this life. No special work of God is required for that. But if we can detect within a growing concern for others, then we can be sure God is at work within us. But not all of us will be concerned for others in the same way. Some may be concerned for their health. Others may be concerned for their emotional well-being, their spiritual condition, or the integrity of their natural or cultural environment. Once we become aware of the specific concern God has given us, we can go about cultivating the skills required to follow through on that concern effectively.

Furthermore, God may have endowed us with certain lively interests apart from any other-directed concerns—interests in mathematics, music, or microbiology. Those interests lead us to cultivate skills which we can in turn use in the service of others. For example, based on an innate love of literature I might acquire the skills of appreciation and criticism that would later qualify me, as an English teacher, to introduce others to the wonders of the written word. Or I might become a writer myself, and proceed to open up God's world to others through the medium of language.

The assumption behind these recommendations is that discovering God's will for one's life is not so much a matter of seeking out miraculous signs and wonders as it is being attentive to who and where we are. It is not as if our abilities, concerns, and interests are just there, as an accident of nature, and then God has to intervene in some special way in order to make his will known to us in a completely unrelated manner. Rather, in making a career choice, we ought to take seriously the doctrine of divine providence: God himself gives us whatever legitimate abilities, concerns, and interests we in fact possess. These are his gifts, and for that very reason they can serve as indicators of his will for our lives. In coming to know ourselves and our situation, we come to know God's will. The Protestant theologian Emil Brunner claims, in fact, that "the idea of the Calling and of the Call is unintelligible apart from that of Divine Providence. The God who says to me here and now: 'Act where you are, as you are,' is not One who comes on the scene after all that has been done previously has been done without His knowledge. Nothing can happen apart from Him. . . . To Him it is no accident that you are what you are here and now, an accident with which He must come to terms. He Himself places you where you are."[10] Too often our search for God's will in our lives has been skewed by a highly secularized view of the world. We don't really believe that God is present and at work in the concrete events and circumstances of this world. Rather we think of Him as distant, removed, putting in only occasional appearances here on earth. If God speaks to us at all, he must speak to us in the freakish and miraculous, but not in the normal, everyday course of affairs.

At this point, however, we might step back and wonder

10. Emil Brunner, *The Divine Imperative* (New York: Macmillan, 1937), p. 200.

if doing what God is calling us to do is always a matter of doing that for which we are best qualified. Certainly the Bible records numerous instances in which this was emphatically not the case. Are we developing a truly biblical approach to career choice? After all, a stuttering Moses was called by God to speak before Pharaoh; Jonah was instructed to call the city of Nineveh to repentance, a city he himself would have liked to see burn under God's judgment; and the personally unimpressive Paul was prevailed upon to present the gospel to the entire Gentile world. It seems unlikely that a modern vocational counseling agency would have directed these biblical characters to their respective tasks on the basis of their native interests and talents.

True. And the point is well taken. God does sometimes call people to do that for which they are outstandingly unqualified; and sometimes he calls people to do what they are entirely disinclined to do. But when he does that, it is because he is about to give a special demonstration of his power. That is, he is about to perform a miracle—which is, by definition, a departure from the normal course of affairs. As a rule people are to do that for which they are qualified. Of course, there are exceptions to the rule. And we must remain open to the possibility of an exception in our own case through prayer and awareness of God's leading hand.

Finding the Fit: Job Placement

The second step in vocational decision-making is locating the place where our native abilities and acquired skills can be put at the disposal of those who need them. Deciding on a career is not the only issue in vocational choice; we must also decide on where and how we are going to pursue our career. Choosing a "sphere of operation" is one thing, but, as Barth points out, we must also ask ourselves what constitutes "obedient existence in the chosen sphere."[11]

11. Barth, *Church Dogmatics,* III, 4, 52.2.

This too can be difficult. Selfish motives often stand in the way of making the best decision. For example, I may enter the job search process with an undue fondness for the earthly treasures that moth and rust corrupt. When it comes right down to it, what I really want out of a job is enough money to buy that five-bedroom Tudor with a private pool, a couple of Swedish cars replete with fifty-watt compact-disc stereo systems, a cottage on the lake, and an annual winter trek to the Bahamas—all required equipment for the good life as it is so vividly set forth in TV commercials and magazine advertisements. I then set out with grim determination to acquire those skills which, given the current job market, will give me a good shot at the six-figure salary bracket.

But can we assume that those careers promising the highest pay are at the same time those careers that best serve our neighbor? Because of the presence of sin in this world, I'm afraid we are not entitled to this assumption. Pope John XXIII was entirely correct when he noted that "in the economically developed countries, it frequently happens that great, or sometimes very great, remuneration is had for the performance of some task of lesser or doubtful utility."[12] There are such things as "illusory services" and to deny that, writes the French Catholic philosopher Yves Simon, is "to assert that any and every desire is an expression of genuine need, which is something no one really believes, despite all profession to the contrary."[13] Take the pornography industry today, for example. No one can deny that a substantial demand exists today for slick pictures of naked bodies. And much money—perfectly legal money—can be made in meeting this demand. But those who adhere to the Christian understanding of persons refuse to help meet such demands, for they judge them to be improper, perverse, or in some way morally errant. And rightly so. Existing demand is not necessarily a reliable guide to legitimate need.

12. Pope John XXIII, *Mater et Magistra,* sec. 70.

13. Yves R. Simon, *Work, Society, and Culture* (New York: Fordham University Press, 1971), p. 124.

Even when we move into the realm of the morally unobjectionable, however, clearly some jobs—given the priorities of the kingdom of God—are to be preferred over others. Here all things may be permissible, but not all are equally expedient. In some jobs my neighbor is less well served than others. My neighbor is less well served by the production of diamond-studded eyebrow pencils than in the production of prescription eyeglasses; my neighbor is less well served by the production of another TV game show than a drama which locates and explores significant issues in human life; my neighbor is less well served by the publication of the lurid confessions of a rock and roll groupie than a sensitive guide to the choral works of Heinrich Schütz.

Unfortunately, many of the available jobs in our economy are geared to the production and sale of that which is cheap, frivilous, environmentally hazardous, and socially unsound. Our highly commercialized culture is filled with goods and services of dubious value. And the techniques of modern advertising have proven lamentably effective in generating a demand for them. Simply having the right attitude, the "Christian attitude," towards one's work is not enough. One must also take into consideration the social content of one's work: am I, in my job, making a positive contribution to the human community; am I helping to meet legitimate human needs; am I somehow enhancing or promoting what is true, what is noble, and what is worthy in human life?

Attitudes and motivations certainly will play key roles in the moral evaluation of a person engaged in work. One must do the right thing for the right reason. Here, I daresay, none of us will come out looking very good. Our motives are rarely pure. Nevertheless, "good works" can be performed even out of bad motives. Such works do not redound to the moral credit of the person who performs them, but in and of themselves they can carry a social, or even a spiritual utility. For this reason St. Paul could thank God that the gospel of Jesus Christ was being preached, even though he was well aware of the often errant motives behind the preaching of it. And St. Augustine could say that although the glory-seeking of the Romans was a private vice, it was still a public virtue insofar as it led them to establish a well-ordered government of law that they might be highly regarded by their citizens. Likewise, a business person might treat his or her customers well solely for the sake of future sales and profit—a happy, but accidental, coincidence of self-interest and social good.

Conversely, people can engage in "bad works" with the best of intentions. A politician motivated by a strong desire to bring about social justice may proceed to develop a social welfare program which will only serve to entrap and stifle the poor rather than help them. A parent anxious to bring up a child in the fear of the Lord may succeed only in alienating that child from every form of divine presence. More to the point, a person may enter a job with all the right attitudes and motives, and yet find himself or herself involved in a project with socially disastrous results. One might wind up making a substantial contribution to the amount of human suffering in this world by doing a marvelous job as copywriter for an advertising firm whose principal client just happens to be a tobacco company.

In the light of such possibilities, it would seem that the process of career choice should involve not only a personal inventory of talents and interests together with a moral self-examination of motives and attitudes, but also a serious evaluation of various types of work according to their social value. Let's say I've decided on a career in medicine. God has given me a compassion for the sick; he has given me the necessary intellectual abilities; and I am currently acquiring the relevant diagnostic skills and knowledge of therapeutic strategies. Now at some point in medical school I must begin to think about where I want to fit into the medical profession. A highly paid plastic surgeon with regular hours in an urban area with a high doctor-to-patient ratio and all the amenities of high culture? Or a family practitioner in an economically depressed rural area where the doctor-to-patient ratio is low—that is, where basic medical services are most needed?

Or let's say I'm going through law school. God has given

me, in the idealism of my youth, a genuine concern for justice; he has given the requisite intellectual abilities, and I am currently acquiring the relevant knowledge of the law and forensic skills. Will I allow myself to be enlisted in the growing ranks of corporate lawyers, developing tax strategies, engineering takeovers, and fighting seemingly endless battles in the suit and counter-suit of vested interests? Or will I seek to find a place where my skills can serve the disadvantaged who traditionally have been denied adequate legal representation?

Of course, vocational choices are rarely set out in such stark contrasts. There are usually more options. And there are always additional considerations in any concrete situation. Moreover, I am not casting a blanket of disapproval over plastic surgery or the practice of corporate law. Both definitely are needed. They are by no means inherently wrong or unchristian. In fact—in the light of their talents, skills, personal history, and family obligations—Christians may be justified in pursuing precisely these occupations. The point I want to make is this: since there are plenty of people willing to take up such appealing positions, those convicted by the Christian conception of the nature and purpose of work will undoubtedly feel an uncomfortable tug in the direction of the greatest human needs, where their presence will make a difference. "Personal decisions, policies of private and public bodies, and power relationships must all be evaluated by their effects on those who lack the minimum necessities of nutrition, housing, education, and health care," insist the U.S. Catholic Bishops in their pastoral letter on the U.S. economy. "Meeting fundamental human needs must come before the fulfillment of desires for luxury consumer goods, for profits not conducive to the common good and for unnecessary military hardware."[14]

As I mentioned earlier, the constant temptation is to evaluate a job solely on the basis of salary, security, status, and satisfaction—all, oddly enough, benefits which accrue directly to ourselves. Certainly adequate pay, financial stability, a measure

14. National Council of Catholic Bishops, *Economic Justice for All,* (United States Catholic Conference, 1986).

of social dignity, and a sense of vocational fulfillment are significant considerations in applying for jobs. But the most important consideration for the Christian is service. Those who belong to the household of faith, Calvin counsels, should "choose those employments which yield the greatest advantage to their neighbors."[15] As Christians we are obliged to evaluate a job by its actual social content—the way in which it benefits, or harms, others. For God "let us in this world," Calvin adds, "on the condition that every one of us should consider wherein he may be able to help such as have need of him."[16] Because of the effects of sin upon the institutional shape and social direction of work, we cannot automatically assume that all existing occupations are equally legitimate, nor can we assume that the highest paying ones are the ones that fill the greatest and most important needs.

Nor can "job satisfaction" serve as an infallible guide to the right occupation. Much is made these days of self-fulfillment. We must to our own selves be true. When it comes to work, we are inclined to think that jobs exist primarily for our sake, to assist us in the realization of our selves. That is what we expect from a good job. If it happens that others are served or edified in the process, then so be it—we will count it as a happy by-product. If, however, we find our work unsatisfying, then even if we are serving others in it, we take ourselves to be entirely justifed in quitting.

The Christian understanding of work does not deny that job satisfaction is a good and valuable thing. But job satisfaction cannot, for the Christian, serve as the sole or even primary criterion by which a job is evaluated. For an occupation must be first considered in terms of how it provides a fitting place for the exercise of one's gifts in the service of others. If job satisfaction comes along with the work, then one must count that as a blessing and be thankful. But it cannot be a goal. "The greatest reward of faithfulness to vocation," writes Barth,

15. Calvin, *Opera,* XLI, p. 300.
16. Ibid., p. 308.

> is to be able to devote ourselves to our concern not only with interest but with desire and love, with gladness that we are what we are. But this is a reward which we cannot expect nor demand, and at which we are not to aim. Our task is to do justice to what is demanded at the place which we have occupied, whether gladly or otherwise. Yet these may not be absolute alternatives. There will always be exceptional cases of men who can gladly fulfill their sphere of operation from first to last and in all its dimensions; just as there will always be those who do so with the greatest reluctance. For most of us the reality will lie somewhere between. We shall have much cause for sighing, yet also for joy, and *vice versa.* There will be much to make us glad but also much to depress us.[17]

These are hard words of advice. They suggest that making the best decision about what to do with one's life may involve a degree of personal sacrifice, even self-denial. But behind these hard words lies the exquisite paradox of the gospel message: those who seek to gain the world will lose themselves in the process, while those who deny themselves for the sake of Christ will gain themselves back again a hundredfold. This ground rule of the kingdom of heaven, plus Christ's identification with the poor and the needy of the world, should make the overall vocational direction of our lives disturbingly clear.

A poignant example of how Christian convictions may bear upon career choice or career change can be found in an interview conducted with Debbie Price by John Bernbaum and Simon Steer, authors of *Why Work?* Debbie had received a bachelor of science degree in interior design and had worked for five years for an interior design company based in Aspen, Colorado. She was both highly successful and well-paid. Then, quite suddenly, she left her job and became an administrative assistant and education director for a Baptist church; later, she became the scheduling secretary for Senator William Armstrong of Colorado. Why the career change from interior design? "It was a hard decision," Debbie admits.

17. Barth, *Church Dogmatics,* III, 4, 52.2.

> I finally made it when I realized I wasn't being valuable to anyone. Nor was I able to be enthusiastic about any aspect of my work. I also realized that it wasn't right for me to be doing what the job required. Not that there was anything dishonest or illegal involved, but I was being paid on a commission basis—30 percent of the gross profit. One client spent twenty thousand dollars on furnishings for a 10 × 12 room. I began to question my motivation for encouraging people to buy—I really couldn't believe that it was good stewardship of my talents to be persuading customers to spend huge sums of money on furniture. So, although it was a lucrative position, I decided to leave.[18]

As Debbie considered her job options, it became clear to her that "you should consider what the job is asking you to do. The product of your work is most important. Is the result of your labor truly worthwhile, serving the community and honoring God?"[19]

The above examples of vocational choice might easily lead us to think that choosing a vocation is basically a matter of choosing a paid occupation. Indeed, that's the way we usually think about vocational choice. But it can be, and often is, something other than that. Earlier we noted that any one person has a number of vocations, each pertaining to different dimensions of his or her life. The examples of vocational choice I gave—becoming a doctor, becoming a lawyer, or an administrative assistant—were examples of paid occupations. But once we realize that the concept of vocation extends to domains of life far beyond occupation, we can see that there is no reason to think that the vocational focus of one's life will necessarily coincide with one's job. The most important things we do in life may not be those for which we are paid.

God may have given me a concern for the condition of the poor, those whose material needs are not being met by the pres-

18. John A. Bernbaum and Simon M. Steer, *Why Work? Careers and Employment in Biblical Perspective* (Grand Rapids: Baker Book House, 1986), p. 70.

19. Ibid., p. 69.

ent economy. If my present job does not relate to those needs, and I cannot find such a job, I may become active in the diaconal ministry of the church, or become a volunteer worker for a charitable organization, or join a political organization which serves as an advocate for the interests of the poor. That activity may then become the axis around which the rest of my life revolves. My job then becomes the means to a higher end: it enables me to support myself as I help people in my chief vocation.

An aquaintance of mine, Vince Scotti, was a self-employed light hauler in Pittsburgh. With his trusty step van he moved refrigerators and pianos, stoves and mattresses, firewood and trash to various points in western Pennsylvania. That was his job. But it was not the focus of his vocation, as he understood it. For the bulk of his energies were spent on prophetic social witness—pouring blood over files in the offices of defense contractors, staging "die-ins" in front of the company manufacturing trigger devices for the neutron bomb, and scaling the fences of nuclear defense sites. Light hauling was simply what he did in order to support himself between such dramatic activities. While many of us might disagree with his political convictions and his method of making those convictions known, nonetheless his conduct of life points to the fact that one's mission in life need not be identical with one's employment.

Similarly, the paid employment of one's professional skills might make it possible to volunteer one's professional skills where there is much need but no monetary recompense to be had. Work as a medical specialist in an urban center may serve as a base for volunteer work in the field. In May of 1988, two Grand Rapids plastic surgeons, Dr. Robert Mann and Dr. Matthew Shambaugh, spent two weeks in Guatemala with a medical team of twelve doctors, nurses, and support staff. They performed twenty-eight operations on children from the rural areas in the surgical room of an indigenous hospital, repairing severe burn scars and correcting cleft palates. Their visit was coordinated by the Michigan chapter of Heal the Children, a volunteer medical organization committed to the delivery of medical services to children in the Third World.

The donation of professional time and skills can also be arranged on a more local and regular basis. Dr. Robert Bulten is a highly respected pediatrician in the Grand Rapids area. His office is located in the suburban neighborhood of Alger Heights. But every Tuesday afternoon Dr. Bulten is down at the Baxter Community Center, making his services available free of charge to the economically disadvantaged inhabitants of the inner city. Following his example, his associates, Dr. Ron Hofman and Dr. Douglas Daining, spend Monday and Friday afternoons at the community center as well. Bulten's expertise and credentials have made it possible for him to support himself and to deliver medical services both to those who can and those who cannot pay for them. He could be making more money by staying at his office on Tuesday afternoons. But ever since his exposure to the plight of the poor during a vacation to the South a number of years ago, he has had a desire to serve the needy professionally. His vocation and employment overlap. But they are not identical. His vocation to heal the sick is partly realized in his paid occupation, and partly in his volunteer work.

As the focus and emphasis of our economy becomes further removed from primary and legitimate human needs, it becomes increasingly difficult within the vast expanse of subdivided labor to make the connection between one's work and genuine service to one's neighbor. Many of us may be led to shift the vocational focus of our lives outside the domain of paid employment. St. Paul was a tentmaker, after all, and no doubt he served many in that capacity. But tentmaking was never more than a means by which he supported himself in his chief vocation: the preaching of the gospel to the Gentile world (Acts 20:34-35). Likewise we may find the center of our vocation located outside the domain of paid employment. Perhaps we will find our vocational focus in a specific area of church life, or in volunteer work for a neighborhood association, or in providing a foster home for neglected children, or in volunteering professional services or trade skills, or in a combination of such activities.

On the other hand, those of us with paid occupations

must not give up on the attempt to find meaningful employment and some sense of vocation within the domain of work. No doubt this often will be difficult. Both wage labor and the division of labor have conspired to "de-vocationalize" human work. The system of wage labor encourages us to look at work as simply a way of making money, and nothing more. The division of labor has made it difficult for us to discern the social purpose of our work. "Where the individual worker is simply a minute wheel (which at any moment may be exchanged for another) in a vast piece of machinery," Brunner writes,

> when he does not know for what purpose or persons his work will serve, when all he knows is that others will be enriched by his labor, while he himself remains poor, humanly speaking, he can no longer regard his calling as a Divine vocation. In it he does not experience his superiority over nature, nor his connection with others in mutual service. At the present time the life of labor has reached such a state of moral disorganization that the 'order' of labor has become a dis-order; it is scarcely possible to speak of serving the community in the midst of anarchy.[20]

Hence the social organization of work today often invites cynicism. Talk about serving one's neighbor on the job sounds like just so much pious self-deception. Let's be honest. Why make such a big theological deal about work? We work, like everyone else does, in order to make a living. We are in it for the money. And because we need money to survive—and to enjoy ourselves in the meantime—we are willing to play by the rules of the game, even if those rules run contrary to our personal values and ideals.

One powerful voice in the contemporary Christian intellectual scene, French social theorist Jacques Ellul, has not only given up on any attempt to make a straightforward connection between work and divine vocation; he denies that there ever was one. Beginning with the fallenness of human social structures within which work is carried out, he has concluded that work

20. Brunner, *Divine Imperative,* p. 393.

"is the human condition resulting from the rupture with God."[21] After the Fall, work has become "painful and compulsory in the attempt to survive . . . it does not represent a service to God."[22] Belonging, then, to the "order of necessity," work is quite naturally "alienating, overwhelming and insignificant."[23] It has "no ultimate value, no transcendental meaning."[24] Furthermore, "nothing in the Bible allows us to identify *work* with *calling*."[25] The reformers' attempt to dignify work theologically simply reflects in the ideological realm the growing importance of work in the capitalist economy during the sixteenth and seventeenth centuries.[26]

It is impossible, Ellul maintains, to realize one's calling, one's vocation, in the world of work. And it would be a misguided piece of cultural optimism to try to change the world of work in order to allow for the genuine pursuit of vocations within it. We are, after all, dealing with the order of necessity. But if one does not want to capitulate to the fallenness of the world and become a wholly irrelevant "Sunday Christian," where can one discover that form of activity in which a vocation can be incarnated? Ellul suggests, by way of an example from his own life, volunteer work—not just any volunteer work, but volunteer work which draws upon the skills and insights gained in the domain of paid employment and proceeds to apply them to genuine human needs in a redemptive way. In his own case, Ellul worked with a "Prevention Club"—a club geared to the needs of teenage "social misfits." Here he was free to relate in a personal way to human needs and brokenness without the constraint and irrelevancies imposed upon him in his professional life as a university professor. Many of his abilities and concerns as a university professor, however, carried over into his work in

21. Jacques Ellul, "Work and Calling," *Katallagete* 4, 2-3 (Fall/Winter 1972): 13.

22. Ibid., p. 8.

23. Ibid., p. 13.

24. Ibid., p. 14.

25. Ibid., p. 8.

26. Ibid., pp. 9-10.

the Prevention Club. In this way his employment as a university professor, which he must consider insignificant and of no ultimate value, receives a measure of meaning by virtue of being related to what he does outside of work on a volunteer basis.

What we have in Ellul's statement on work is in many ways the mirror opposite of the Lutheran view—but with the same practical result: an acquiescence to the status quo. While Luther took the given social order of stations to be the direct result of the creative work of God, Ellul takes it to express only the fallenness of humankind. While Luther maintains that to obey the duties of one's station is at the same time to heed the call of God, Ellul asserts that the discharge of one's professional role at best has nothing to do with what God is calling one to do, and may often go contrary to the values of God's kingdom.

We seem then to be caught in a dilemma: we must either say yes or no to the existing social structure. In either case, however, we will not endeavor to change it. We will not endeavor to change it either because it is a part of the fixed and unalterable order of God's creation, and therefore neither can nor should be changed. Or we will not endeavor to change it because it belongs to the order of necessity brought about by the Fall, an order we must endure until God brings in his kingdom.

The dilemma, however, is a false one. In this life there will always be a mixture of what bespeaks the continuing goodness of God's creation and what announces the terrible effects of sin. For that reason we cannot resort to either a wholesale rejection or acceptance of existing economic, political, social, sexual, or cultural practices. We must discern what, in each, we must endorse and develop and what we must oppose and reject.

Furthermore, although much of human life remains in the grip of sin and its consequences, the renewing power of God's Spirit is already at work through Christ and his body, the church. Miracles have happened. Dramatic turnabouts for the good have occurred. The future of God's kingdom is already breaking into our present reality. This is of utmost practical significance because redemption in Christ means nothing less than the renewal of the whole of God's creation—not just the transportation of human souls to the heavenly realms while the rest of creation drops off like a spent booster rocket (see Rom. 8:18-25). To participate in the redemptive life of Christ means to oppose and, where possible, to eradicate evil, sin, and the perversion of God's good order for human life. Of course we cannot change the world overnight, or even in our lifetime. To think so is sheer triumphalist fantasy. But just as surely the world is not bound by the iron laws of fallen necessity. Each one of us has domains of responsibility, however restricted. Each one of us is called upon, in various ways and at various times, to make significant choices. And the cumulative effects of such choices can, by God's grace, make for significant change.

What is called for, then, in the face of fallen human society is not fatalistic acquiescence, nor revolutionary activism, but unrelenting reform. In the existing situation we must be able to discern what is good and worthy of preservation, and what is bad and in need of change. "Thus God's Command requires from us," counsels Brunner,

> both adaptation and protest, acceptance of the existing order and resistance to it, because our service of our neighbor requires it. In the actual working out of the obedience the believer will be found now in the camp of those who maintain and justify the existing order, now in that of those who protest and demand a new order. In itself obedience is neither conservative, as the world is conservative, nor radical, or revolutionary as the world is revolutionary . . . it is based upon the one, unchangeable will of the Creator and Redeemer, who, on that account, because He makes his will effective in a world which is always changing, demands us for Himself, and is always bidding us to serve Him in varying ways."[27]

This more balanced "case by case" approach to the problem of the fallenness of the social institution of work is aptly summarized in Nicholas Wolterstorff's response to Ellul's position on work and vocation: "Is what we do in our occupations

27. Brunner, *Divine Imperative,* p. 218.

through and through what God would have us do? Of course not. Is it not at all what God would have us do? Usually not that either. A Yes and a No is what must be spoken. Can we *entirely* alter what we do, so that here and now we practice the occupations of heaven? Of course not. Can we *somewhat* alter what we do, so that our occupations come closer to becoming our God-issued vocation? Usually, yes."[28] While harboring no illusions of establishing a Christian society by our own efforts prior to the complete realization of God's reign on earth, we must nonetheless labor to heal and restore a broken world where we can, in anticipation of what God will accomplish in the future.

Changing the System: Conflict and Strategy

When we consider what the lone individual can do to change established social practices in the world of work, Ellul's pessimism seems quite plausible. The way things are done in a particular trade or profession has been determined by forces which go far beyond any individual's sphere of influence. Consequently, when a conflict arises between the way things are done at work and our ethical intuitions about how things ought to be done, we are put in a difficult position. Either we conform to the offensive practice and assuage the residual pangs of conscience with a thousand excuses, or we quit—or at least risk getting fired as a direct result of our noncompliance. At any rate, the system will remain the same because it has the power to accommodate or reject any potentially troublesome individuals. If a company demands eighty hours a week from its salespeople, and if I am to be a salesperson for that company, then I must be willing to put in eighty hours a week—even if that means I cannot possibly fulfill my obligations to my family, church, or community. If I am not willing to put in eighty hours a week, then I must look for another job.

28. Nicholas Wolterstorff, "More on Vocation," *The Reformed Journal* 29 (May 1979): 20-23.

Other options open up, however, when we consider what groups of individuals can do—especially those groups of individuals which are in some way responsible for shaping the work of others. The contours that a particular line of work has in the present, after all, were formed by the decisions of such groups in the past; it follows that the present contours can be altered to some degree by the subsequent decisions of such groups. Examples of positive change brought about by like-minded groups within a particular trade or profession are not hard to find. In what follows I shall cite two examples from the legal profession. One represents change brought about within the established profession; one represents change brought about alongside the established profession.

Law firms are notorious for the demands they typically make on an attorney's time. But that is the way they make money. Law firms are owned by partners. Partners share the profits between themselves. The associates of a law firm are mere employees: they are paid a straight salary, with bonuses thrown in from time to time. The more hours of work the partners can get out of their associates, the more profits they will have to share between themselves. The associates must accept the assigned work loads if they want to remain with the firm and eventually achieve partnerhood themselves.

The ratio of associates to partners in a law firm is known in the profession as "leverage." The more associates per partner, the more profit for the partners. When potential associates interview with a firm, they are not only informed about their salary level, but also the number of "billable hours" they will be expected to put in for the firm per year. Although the average number of billable hours runs around 2,000, the number can range as high as 2,400, 2,600, even 2,800. That translates into roughly sixty, seventy, even eighty hours of work per week, given that not all of the hours the associate puts in are billable. Obviously, to work for law firms with these kinds of requirements is to sacrifice the rest of one's life on the altar of professional success—family life, civic life, church life, and spiritual life will inevitably get insufficient attention. In the face of such demands there is little an individual can do. He or she must either bite the bullet and make an idol of work, or look for employment elsewhere. If any change is to happen, it must be initiated by the partners.

On the southeast corner of Pearl and Ottawa streets in downtown Grand Rapids stands the sturdy edifice of the Trust Building—the first "skyscraper" built between Detroit and Chicago. The eleventh floor houses the offices of one of the oldest law firms in the city: Wheeler, Upham, Bryant, and Uhl, P.C. Although this traditional law firm is well-established and well-respected in the Grand Rapids legal community, it differs from many other law firms in several significant respects. Shaped by a succession of partners who were also active churchmen—Jacob Kleinhans, Marshall Uhl, and Harold Bryant—it maintains a strong tradition of respect for the validity of those dimensions of life which lie outside the confines of its walls. And it has limited its claims upon its employee's lives accordingly. Associates are generally held accountable for fewer billable hours than the average law firm. As a consequence, the salaries are also slightly lower than firms which require more hours. But many of the attorneys who now work for Wheeler, Upham, Bryant, and Uhl have come from other firms, gladly accepting a salary cut in order to work for a firm which, according to its corporate statement of purpose, strives "to recognize the importance of our employee's personal development, and their family, community, religious, and other like commitments unrelated to the practice of law."

Hourly workers receive similar considerations. Secretaries are rarely asked to work overtime—a shocking abnormality in the legal profession. They are expected to make only six Saturday mornings a year available to the firm. Secretaries are also allowed three weeks of vacation per year, while attorneys are encouraged to take four.

Although the way this firm limits its demands on employees might seem to dull its competitive edge, John Roels, attorney at the firm, says the opposite. Rested, attuned, focused, and personally integrated employees are sharper, fresher, and less likely to make errors than those who are tired, burned-out, overworked, and whose personal lives are falling apart due to neglect. In his experience, the quality of legal services rendered is positively enhanced when the quantity is carefully controlled.

Concerted efforts by those in control can make for significant changes, even within the confines of an established profession. But the shortcomings of a profession can also be addressed by establishing para-institutions.

It is well known that the courts of our country are not only overburdened with criminal cases but besieged by disputants seeking favorable settlements. Tenants against landlords, customers against merchants, consumers against manufacturers, patients against doctors, children against parents, spouse against spouse, neighbor against neighbor — all seek their day in court. And there is no shortage of lawyers ready to jump into the fray of the adversarial system and help their clients get the most favorable settlement possible. But the verdict of the jury or the decision of the judge often does not resolve the deep alienation between persons. Anger may have been vented, the spirit of revenge satisfied, and in many cases even justice may have been done. But there was no reconciliation. We have become a litigious society, and the process of litigation in the adversarial system often serves only to exacerbate the divisions between persons rather than overcome them, to rend the fabric of society even further rather than repair it.

On the northwest side of Grand Rapids, in the protective shade of the Basilica of St. Adalberts church, stands a two-story brick building housing the offices of the Grand/Kent Community Reconciliation Center. Marty Weirick, director of the Center, says she is there because, as a Christian, she is called to be a peacemaker. The Reconciliation Center is designed to bring people with disagreements together rather than fortifying them in their opposition, to "defuse" personal disputes through the process of mediation before they explode into acrimonious legal battles. Typically the disputants are brought together with a trained mediator. After having told their story to the mediator, and some private consultation, the parties work together toward a resolution of the conflict. The role of the mediator is not that of judge, deciding who is right and who is wrong, but rather to serve as one who reconciles the disputants by helping them overcome their difference through understanding, compromise, and agreement.

The Reconciliation Center handles about 200 cases a year. Not all of them are successfully resolved. But many of the attempts at mediation have produced dramatic results. One recent case involved a patient's claim against his dentist. The patient wanted $2500 for alleged damages; the dentist claimed no responsibility and refused to pay. After two mediation sessions and a two-week cooling-off period, the dentist and his patient came to a remarkable impasse: the dentist was willing to pay the entire sum requested, and the patient was willing to drop the request altogether. A happy compromise was worked out and they parted in a good spirit.

Founded in 1986 as a response to the shortcomings of the existing adversarial legal system, the Reconciliation Center exists through the financial support of local churches, foundations, and individuals. Over thirty people from different professions volunteer their time as mediators, including six attorneys. St. Adalberts provides rent-free office space. The Center ekes out a meager existence on the margins of the legal community. But by a recently enacted law in Michigan, the Center will soon be eligible for state funds derived from an increase in court fees; and it has already begun to receive referrals from state and local government agencies which recognize the practical and social value of resolving disputes before they reach an already overloaded court system.

Balancing Commitments: Work and Vocation

Work and vocation are not the same thing. Work may be a part of my vocation, but it is not the whole of my vocation; work may be one thing that I am called to do, but it is not the only thing I am called to do. As a husband I am called to love, honor, and encourage my wife; as a parent, to care and provide for my children; as a citizen, to be an informed participant in the political process; as a parishioner, to identify and make use of my spiritual gifts, edifying the community of faith; as a teacher, to instruct and advise my students. My vocation has many facets. If I am gainfully employed, my employment will count as only one of those facets.

This broad, rich, and variegated sense of vocation, encompassing all of life, goes back, as we saw, to Martin Luther's initial formulation of the concept of vocation in the sixteenth century. In Gustaf Wingren's study of Luther we read that "one's occupation and place of work are, according to Luther, contained in vocation, but it is also a vocation to be a father, mother, son, daughter, husband, wife, etc. Everything that brings me into relation with other people, everything that makes my actions events in other people's lives is contained in 'vocation.'"[29]

In spite of its auspicious beginnings, however, the concept of vocation soon fell upon hard times. By the late seventeenth century the meaning of the word "vocation" had, in the vocabulary of the Puritans, been whittled down to the point where it meant little more than paid employment.[30] One's particular calling was simply one's "special business."[31] And one's special business was often thought a secular affair, along-

29. Gustaf Wingren, *Luther on Vocation.* Carl C. Rasmussen, trans. (St. Louis: Concordia, 1957), p. 94.

30. In his study of the secularization of the concept of vocation, Paul Marshall claims that "amongst the Puritans of the period between the turn of the [seventeenth] century and the civil war, callings came to be understood more in terms of employments. The words trade, employment, occupation, calling and vocation become interchangeable." "The Calling: Secularization and Economics in the Seventeenth Century," (Unpublished Manuscript, 1978), p. 14.

31. See Paul Bayne, *Exposition of Ephesians* (ca. 1600). Reprint. (Evansville: Sovereign Grace, 1953), pp. 475, 558; William Prynne, *Histrio-Mastix* (1633). Reprint. (New York: Johnson Reprint, 1972), pp. 325, 873, 985; Thomas Scott, "Vox Dei," in *Works* (Utrecht, 1624). Reprint. (New York: Da Capo, 1973), pp. 3, 4; and Charles H. and Katherine George, *The Protestant Mind of the English Reformation* (Princeton: Princeton University Press, 1961), p. 130.

side, or even in competition with, one's general calling to be a Christian.[32]

This is an unfortunate development. But it leads directly to our present-day notion that a vocation is nothing more than a job. "Vocational training" means "job training." If we are asked what our vocation is, we are expected to say what we do for a living. It follows that finding one's "calling in life" is a matter of finding an occupation; that a person without a job is also without a vocation; and that the aspects of a person's life outside work do not have the dignity of being vocations—they are merely the insignificant details of personal life.

To gain a full-orbed, properly nuanced and balanced view of the place of work in human life, it is imperative to recover the broad sense of vocation. For an occupation is only one element in the total configuration of my vocation. After I've done my job as an employee, I still have other things to do as a spouse, a parent, a parishioner, a neighbor, and a citizen—not to mention the fact that I am also called to rest in leisurely contentment with God's goodness on the Sabbath. If I pour myself into my work, with nothing left over to give to my spouse, my children, church, community, or country, I have neither heard not heeded the full scope of God's call in my life. For, as Barth points out, human life "is not exhausted in the process of labor."[33] Work, family, church, education, politics, and leisure must each of them find their place, shoulder to shoulder, under the concept of vocation.

The fact that our vocation has many dimensions brings with it the problem of "vocational integration." Luther once remarked that once we comprehend the full range of our duties to our neighbors we will quickly realize that we couldn't

32. William Gurnall, for instance, maintained that one of the signs of sanctification was that "the Christian's particular calling doth not encroach upon his general—[for]—The world is of an encroaching nature, hard it is to converse with it—so will our worldly employments jostle with our heavenly." *The Christian in Complete Armor* (1655). Reprint. (London: Banner of Truth Trust, 1969), pp. 435-37.

33. *Church Dogmatics*, III, 4, 52.2.

possibly fulfill them all, even if we each had four heads and ten hands. Over-responsible people tend to burn out quickly. The limitations of time and energy create dilemmas and call for trade-offs: do I go to my daughter's track meet or the church council meeting? Do I go out with my wife on Thursday night for coffee, or stay home and polish the Kant lecture for Friday? Do I take advantage of an opportunity to hear my congressional representative speak on aid to the Contras, or do I spend more time with the Gospel of Mark? We are constantly making choices as to how we will spend our time. The question is: do our claims reflect the right priorities and proper balance?

Few of us can claim that our lives are well-balanced. And in our own culture, work is often the part of our vocation which claims disproportionately large amounts of our time and energy. Especially for those in the professions, the constant temptation is to make an idol of one's work. Other human relationships, even the relationship to God, must often make way for the high-speed pursuit of a successful career.

We often associate the dominance of work with the materialism of our age. People tend to evaluate themselves by the things they own. Because they see little else to life than the ownership of things, they readily give themselves entirely to the vehicle for acquiring more things—their work. So many put in extra hours or moonlight because they want—or think they need—more money for the downpayment on their dream house, for the monthly payments on their third car, or to finance some other expansion of their worldly estate. Indeed, the god of gain is a demanding employer. But his rewards are strictly temporary, and rarely satisfying.

While the desire for more may motivate many to invest a disproportionate amount of time in their work, there is often something else at stake for the bona fide workaholic. In his portrayal of what life is really like in the high-profile professions, Glenn Kaplan notes that, for many of us, "Getting rich is not enough. We want to get rich in the most spectacular and comprehensive way. Our labors must bring us not just money but also power, prestige, and fulfillment."[34] Many of those passionately devoted to their careers are not just out to get rich. They have, it seems, an insatiable need for challenge, accomplishment, and public recognition. It is not so much the god of gain that they serve as the god of glory. And they are willing to render their lives a living sacrifice on the altar of their chosen profession so their god may grant what they so desperately desire.

Take management consulting, for instance. Typically consultants travel incessantly, work long hours, and have very little time outside their jobs. Consulting for the big firms is not just a way to make a living, remarks Kaplan; it is a way of life. What's the attraction? James Farley of Boos-Allen Corporation remarks in a candid moment that "when you've done a fine piece of work for a client, and he says so, it's absolutely a high. The psychic rewards are unbelievably good. You get instant gratification. This is such a turn-on business; you don't get that typically at a major corporation. I think that's why the profession gets addictive."[35] Career advancement to partnership in a consulting firm is important for similar reasons. "Ego is an important part of partnership. People look at you as an expert. They pay more than $1000 a day for your advice. That's ego. Partnership is your recognition. It's proof of your achievement."[36]

Turn to the big-name law firms. When a person is hired by a law firm, he or she typically has five to ten years to achieve partnership. The move from being a mere associate to a partner is the most important career achievement because it is, in effect, the move from being an employee to being an owner. Partnership means "a princely income, fascinating work, and abundant prestige, guaranteed for life."[37] Often to become partners, however, associates must prove that they have the capacity to work hard, and to work endlessly. They must take whatever assign-

34. Glenn Kaplan, *The Big Time: How Success Really Works in 14 Top Business Careers* (New York: Congdon and Weed, 1982), p. ix.

35. Ibid., p. 12.

36. Ibid., p. 22.

37. Ibid., p. 33.

ments are given them by the partners, work on them through the night, and through the weekends, if necessary. Nothing short of all-out dedication will do. The whole process, notes Kaplan, "is designed to sort out those people who want partnership more than anything else."[38] One associate, upon being informed that he had achieved partnership, reports that he couldn't even shake the hand of the partner who informed him. "This meant everything to me. It was my whole life, everything I'd worked for, everything I'd ever hoped for. I sat in front of him and began to cry."[39]

The same picture emerges from Wall Street. It is not so much the money, it seems, as the challenge and the thrill of victory, the prestige and the glory. A top partner in an established Wall Street firm admits "I have all the money I could possibly use. I own four beautiful homes. I own all my cars and boats and everything free and clear. I have at least a million and a half in my cash account that I don't even know what to do with. I don't come to work because I'm gonna get paid. I come for the challenge of winning. Money is important because it's the chip that says how well you're doing. But the money itself? No, that's not important . . . once you have enough."[40] An investment banker describes what attracts him to his job: "I like the excitement of it. When all the phones are ringing at once. All those deals are coming off. I'm telling this guy one thing and the other guy something else. You have a clear strategy for each of the players. It's great. When the company president calls you from the phone booth at the airport and at the same time you've got the guy on the other side of the deal on the other line—God, it's exciting. Some days, it'll take me a couple of hours to unwind—just from a long day of playing the telephone."[41] Another investment banker entered his field with a very clear idea of what he wanted from his job. "My objective

38. Ibid., p. 35.
39. Ibid., p. 36.
40. Ibid., p. 37.
41. Ibid., p. 89.

was—and still is—to be an important person. And I have been able to do just that in investment banking."[42]

All this is not to suggest that everyone who enters high-profile professions does so for fame and fortune. Nor that everyone who works hard is necessarily motivated by such concerns. But it is entirely likely that the attitudes expressed here are not unusual. What many find irresistible about their work is that it represents an arena of contest and recognition, of challenge and achievement, of stimulation and excitement. One small taste of success and public affirmation creates an appetite for more, until work becomes the reigning passion of a person's life—while everything else recedes into insignificance. And those firms and corporations which equate their employees' total dedication to work with market competitiveness will find no shortage of success addicts who are willing to sacrifice everything for the sake of career advancement.

But the personal cost of work idolatry is high indeed. In the wake of those in hot pursuit of professional advancement lie broken marriages, children filled with resentment, forgotten friends, and a God put on hold; those who race ahead often turn to alcohol to relieve the stress, or drugs to forestall burnout. Living in constant fear of failure, chained to the evaluations of others, their lives become filled with anxiety and caught up in a web of pretense. When an occupation is no longer freely taken as a way of responding to a call from God, it can be a cruel taskmaster indeed. Luring the unwary into the portals of its temple with heady promises of worldly success, it demands more and more of their lives and gives very little by way of lasting satisfaction in return. Those who initially devoted themselves to their careers as a means of self-fulfillment now find themselves entrapped and enslaved by a capricious and unforgiving god.

When the virtue of hard work becomes the vice of workaholism, it is likely that an underlying spiritual problem needs to be addressed. The addiction to work as a source of affirma-

42. Ibid., p. 90.

tion and self-esteem needs to be broken by an encounter with a God of grace who can provide all that we need apart from our own efforts, thereby freeing us for a life in pursuit of the righteousness of his kingdom.

Work is an important part of life, but it is not the whole of life. Moreover, the proper place of work in a person's life is an issue that must be posed anew from time to time, and may demand creative answers. Life is dynamic. It changes over time. The various facets of a person's vocation will interact with each other in different ways as that person enters into new relations with other persons and as those persons change. The old answers to the question of work will not always be adequate to new situations. When a single person marries, the question of work must be posed anew, for married persons must learn how to adjust the pursuit of their vocations to each other: shall only the husband seek paid employment, or only the wife; or shall both seek full-time employment; if both seek full-time employment, should they do so at the same time, or should they "take turns"; or should both seek part-time employment? If children enter the picture, new considerations arise concerning their care and feeding as they grow up from being wholly dependent kids to surly teenagers to relatively independent adults with their own vocations to fulfill. Should the mother care for the children while the father goes to work, or should a more equitable distribution of parental responsibilities be sought? Illness in the family, aging parents, unemployment, retirement, economic downturns, war, crucial moments in the life of the church or the nation that call for extraordinary involvement—all such eventualities can demand a reevaluation of the place of work in a person's life. There is nothing particularly sacred about being employed full time at the same job from age 21 to 65. A certain amount of flexibility is required in the organization of life; those who remain too rigid may miss their calling as it comes to them afresh.

Reformed Monasticism: The Work of Prayer

Our vocation is complex, not simple. It may have a focus, but it will also have many facets. Included in the many facets of our vocation is the general calling to be a Christian: to be the kind of person God wants us to be; to take on the virtues appropriate to a follower of Christ. The earnest pursuit of this vocation requires much prayer, meditation, and regular participation in the Eucharist. As these practices are a part of what is often referred to as the "contemplative life," we can say that all Christians are called to pursue the contemplative life along with the active life. That is, they are called to pursue what the medievals referred to as the "mixed life." The mixed life is not purely contemplative, nor purely active, but a combination of contemplation and action, a regular alternation between the two. Sometimes we are to be actively engaged in the pursuit of our particular callings; other times we are to withdraw in prayer and meditation. This pattern of engagement and withdrawal is exemplified in the ministry of our Lord. His work on behalf of the crowds was regularly preceded by time spent alone with the Father (see Mark 1:32-39, for instance). The Christian life too should be characterized by the rhythm of work and rest, the expenditure of energy and the recollection of the self, of action and prayer. "The careful balance," writes Henri Nouwen, "between silence and words, withdrawal and involvement, distance and closeness, solitude and community forms the basis of the Christian life and should therefore be the subject of our most personal attention."[43]

The contemplative life, then, will always be a facet of the Christian's vocation. But might it also be the focus of a Christian's vocation? Might the life of prayer and meditation not only be a way of fulfilling one's general calling, but one's particular calling as well? Might it be the "work" that God is calling one to do? In other words, might one still be called to the monastic life? Prayer and meditation within the cloister continue to be rec-

43. Henri J. M. Nouwen, *Out of Solitude* (Notre Dame: Ave Maria Press, 1974), pp. 14-15.

ognized as a legitimate vocation in Catholic circles. But given the torrent of criticism unleashed by the reformers on the institution of monasticism, we would expect the Protestant answer to these question to be a resounding "no." But such is not the case. Although both Luther and Calvin were highly critical of the monasticism of their day, both of them allowed for the legitimacy of the monastic calling—provided a number of conditions were met.

In his classic statement on the taking of monastic vows, Luther admits that the vows of poverty, chastity, and obedience could be taken as useful forms of self-discipline for the sake of growing in the virtues of faith. He enumerates three conditions, however, if this calling is to be legitimate. First, the vows are not to be taken as a way to righteousness or to make satisfaction for sin.[44] Second, the vows are to be taken up in a spirit of freedom, not as a higher law for the achievement of spiritual perfection in this life.[45] Third, the vows were to be taken up like any other vocation, like farming or trade.

The contrast between early and late monasticism played an important role in Calvin's estimation of the monastic vocation. The monasticism described by St. Augustine in *On the Morals of the Catholic Church*[46] Calvin deems to be a "holy and lawful monasticism," in contrast to the perversion of monasticism in his own day.[47] In the early monastic communities, Calvin contends, the rule of life was not construed as a rigid law for living a more holy life, but as an instrument for the promotion of piety. The rule was made flexible and adopted to the various conditions of the monks. Success or failure to live by the rule was not judged to be good or bad in itself, since the rule was an instrument rather than a standard of piety. Furthermore, the early monks were not allowed to "live upon others in idleness. . . . Our

44. *Luther's Works,* vol. 44 (St. Louis: Concordia, 1958), pp. 294-95.

45. Ibid., p. 303.

46. See sections XXXI.67 and XXXIII.70-73 of "On the Morals of the Catholic Church," in *The Nicene and Post-Nicene Fathers,* vol. 4 (Grand Rapids: Eerdmans, 1956).

47. Calvin, *Institutes,* IV.xiii.10.

present-day monks find in idleness the chief part of their sanctity. For if you take idleness away from them, where will that contemplative life be, in which they boast they excel all others and draw nigh to the angels?"[48]

Perhaps the most important consideration for Calvin is the question of how the monastic vocation can count as a form of service to one's neighbor. He could not condone the monastic life of complete withdrawal from human society as an end in itself, for he was convinced that God had created us for a life of service in the human community. The early monastic communities, in Calvin's understanding, served the Christian community in two ways. One was to provide a spiritual training ground for those who were ultimately headed for active service in the church as clergy.[49] The second was to serve as a model of a kind of piety incumbent upon all Christians. All Christians are called to a life of prayer and meditation. The monastic communities specialize in this. When the monasteries open their doors to guests, when they impart instruction in the spiritual life, when they serve as retreat centers, there is a genuine service being performed for the church, a help to one's neighbor in the way of piety.

It still troubled the reformers, however, that the monastic life was carried out in self-enclosed communities, separate from the rest of human society. It should be pointed out, however, that physically removing oneself from the press of human affairs does not necessarily represent a callous turn from the troubles and concerns of the world. For much of the work of prayer to which monks and nuns are called is intercessory in nature. They pray for others; they hold up the needs of the world before the throne of a gracious God. In such prayer, though physically distant, they are nonetheless spiritually present to the deepest needs of the world. Thus the monastic life still represents a legitimate vocation, even in the Reformed understanding of the Christian life with its emphasis on the compassionate service to one's neighbor.

48. Ibid.

49. Ibid., IV.xiii.8.

Summary and Transition: From Career Choice to Job Design

In this chapter we have made an attempt to draw out the implications of the Christian concept of work as vocation for the practical question of career choice. We saw that this question has essentially two components: namely, what are my gifts, and where shall I employ them?

Responsible career choice involves the discovery of my talents and abilities, and the location of a place where those talents and abilities can be exercised in the service of others. Furthermore, we saw that the question of vocation is more than just the question of paid employment. For the concept of vocation covers our whole life as we relate to God, to other persons, and to creation within the stations, or social roles, that God has placed us. Our work, then, is just one facet of our overall vocation, and it must be integrated with the other facets of our vocation if we are to hear and heed the full scope of God's call within our lives.

Most of the available literature on career choice focuses on questions pertaining to the discovery of one's talents, interests, and abilities. Careers where those gifts can be put to use are then suggested. As far as finding a place where those gifts can be exercised for the benefit of one's neighbor, most job-hunting advisors simply assume that people will go for those jobs within their chosen profession which they find most attractive in terms of salary, satisfaction, security, and the like. The job hunters need only know what they want; the job-hunting advisor will tell them how to get it. Rarely is the social responsibility we have to make ourselves of genuine service to others even mentioned; rarely is the social content of a prospective job brought up as a serious consideration. Yet work as a social service, as a way of making a contribution of the welfare of the human community, is just as much a part of the original concept of vocation as the use of one's talents and abilities.

When the issue of service, of making a contribution to the common good, is brought up, however, our attention must invariably turn to the social structure of work. For it is largely the social structure of work that determines the value of our work as a contribution to society and hence the degree to which our work can count as a vocation. Furthermore, it is the structure of our work which will determine whether a significant range of our talents and abilities are being employed in our jobs, and whether we are being made responsible in their employment. In the next chapter we will turn to the implications of the Christian concept of work as vocation for the structure of work in institutional contexts. For we may, as individuals, be wholly committed to the idea that our work should be a place where a significant range of our talents and abilities can be exercised in the service of our neighbor, but whether our work in fact has that characteristic will depend on the way it is organized.

CHAPTER FOUR

* * *

The Shaping of Human Work: Management Theory and Job Design

THUS FAR our consideration of the practical implications of the Christian concept of vocation has been limited to individual concerns. From the perspective of the previous chapter, if work is a social place where our gifts are to be employed in the service of our neighbor, then two obligations follow: to discover and cultivate our gifts, and to locate the place where those gifts can be exercised for the good of the human community. In this way the concept of calling serves as our guide as we wend our way in the world of work, as we make personal choices in a social context. But the concept of calling has practical implications for the social context of our personal choices as well. From the standpoint it provides, we can ask of any particular job or line of work this question: is this indeed a social place where I can respond to my calling? Is the work so structured that I can pursue my calling within it through the responsible use of a significant range of my talents and abilities in the service of others?

The answers to these questions will vary over time and place simply because the social organization of human work is neither uniform nor stable. We have represented work as a niche in society, a place where we carry out certain kinds of activities. Thus the contours of our work are shaped by a variety of social and historical forces: technological change, government policy, international trade, labor markets, patterns of investment, shifting gender roles, management practices, and the like. This is especially true in today's society, where most work is carried out in social institutions. A mere 100 years ago most working people in the United States were "self-employed." The farmer and his family worked on their own land; the craftsman worked in his own shop; the shopkeeper ran his own store; the doctor and the attorney had their own offices. They were their own bosses and they ran their businesses as they saw fit. In today's society, the manufacture of goods and the delivery of services are social tasks which have been taken over, for the most part, by institutions. Health care is delivered by hospitals and clinics; food is produced by agribusiness and retailed by supermarket chains; consumer goods are manufactured by large corporations; and legal services are provided by firms. The majority of working people are now employees. They work for someone else, and most of them work in some small corner of fairly large institutions. Their work is organized, directed, coordinated, and controlled by managers. But managers are also employees; they are responsible to the executive officers. The executive officers, in turn, are responsible to the board of trustees. The board is responsible to the owners. And the owners—typically—have disappeared into anonymous crowds of stockholders.

In these relatively new social contexts for work, many people have found it difficult, if not impossible, to think of their work as a calling. To speak of work as a divine vocation to a robust adult of sound mind whose workdays are spent inspecting Ping-Pong balls must sound like a cruel joke, or at best a disconnected piece of theological romanticism. Often people do not find that any significant talents or abilities are being employed on the job; nor do they believe that what they are doing is of any particular value to society. Their work is just a job, just a way of making money. Indeed, modern technology, notes the Protestant theologian Emil Brunner, "with its extreme specialization, has made it hard for good Christians to look on factory work as a divine vocation."[1] This is not only true of factory work, but of

1. Emil Brunner, *Christianity and Civilization*, pt. 2 (New York: Scribner's Sons, 1949), pp. 68-69.

office work as well. Talk to almost anyone who processes claims for a large insurance company. As a rule, human work in institutional contexts has been subdivided, simplified, routinized, and distanced from its end result.

For these reasons and more, it is often hard to see the meaning of work that has been traditionally ascribed to it by Christian theology. One of the most pessimistic statements of this fact comes from Jacques Ellul in his major study entitled *The Ethics of Freedom:*

> Our age is characterized by non-meaning. All psycho-sociologists agree ultimately that the work we do is marked by this fault. It makes no sense. It has no obvious value of its own. We have on the one side the dividing up of tasks, monotony, and the production of articles of no evident utility, while on the other side we find a break with matter, then with the machine, then a break between the function of thought and that of execution, the growth of an enormous labor organization and bureaucracy, a mass of paper work, often with no recognizable content, for every conceivable function, and finally the wastage of giving complex and highly advanced training to men who are then entrusted with jobs far below their competence. These things, and many others, contribute to the fact that work has no meaning in modern society.[2]

Ellul contends that there is little we can do about this state of affairs, aside from lamenting it. To be sure, there is very little the individual alone can do about the surrounding social structure. But the social structure is not a part of the unchanging order of nature. It is a social product. It can and does change, as examples in the previous chapter demonstrate. If there is something about the social structure which is contrary to the divine intent for human life it is often possible for individuals, acting in concert, to have some effect on the future direction of its evolution. In fact, it is their duty to do so. "The Christian community," writes Brunner, "has a specific task in just this field,

2. Jacques Ellul, *The Ethics of Freedom* (Grand Rapids: Eerdmans, 1976), p. 461.

namely, to work out a concrete doctrine of vocation through its lay members who know the jobs and their threat to working morale, and to demand and to create such technical and psychological conditions as are necessary to regain the lost sense of work as a divine calling."[3]

In this chapter we intend to take up Brunner's challenge by tracing the effects of management theory—for good and for ill—on the institutional shape of human work. The content of a job in an institutional context is not automatically determined by the task of that institution together with the current state of relevant technology. Rather, it is intentionally organized in a particular way, as opposed to a number of other ways in which it could be organized. Typically, it is organized according to certain managerial assumptions about what makes human beings work, and what makes their work productive. The examination, criticism and elaboration of those assumptions is the province of that sub-discipline in management theory known as "job design."

Thus we turn to the problem of the appropriate design of human work. We begin with the normative idea that work ought to be, as Dietrich Bonhoeffer put it, a "place of responsibility."[4] That is, work ought to be a social place so structured that it is possible for people to serve others through the free and responsible use of a significant range of their gifts, talents, and abilities. This normative idea of the proper organization of human work was well expressed by Pope John XXIII when he proclaimed that,

> Justice is to be observed not merely in the distribution of wealth, but also in regard to the conditions under which men engage in productive activity. There is, in fact, an innate need of human nature requiring that men engaged in productive activity have an opportunity to assume responsibility and to perfect themselves by their efforts. Consequently, if the organization and structure of economic life be such that that human dignity of workers is compromised, or their sense of responsibility is

3. Brunner, *Christianity and Civilization*, p. 69.
4. Dietrich Bonhoeffer, *Ethics* (New York: Macmillan, 1964), pp. 222ff.

> weakened, or their freedom of action is removed, then we judge such an economic order to be unjust, even though it produces a vast amount of goods, whose distribution conforms to the norms of justice and equity.[5]

One of the structural demands the Christian concept of work makes, then, is that jobs be designed to allow for—and even encourage—responsible action. "Work is intimately related to our being human, that is, our being created for responsibility in freedom," according to Harry Antonides, Director of Research and Education for the Christian Labour Association of Canada.[6] "Therefore, as much responsibility as possible should be handed to workers themselves."[7] One of the earliest and most influential forces in management practice, however, was characterized by the attempt to make human work productive by eliminating the employees' responsibility for their own work and concentrating it in the hands of a science-based managerial elite. To see why this happened, and what came of it, we must turn to the beginnings of management theory at the close of the last century.

Frederick W. Taylor: The Imposition of Science and the Brutalization of Work

The mid- to late-nineteenth century was a period of great change in the economy of the United States. The tremendous logistical demands of the Civil War had set the wheels of the Industrial Revolution in motion on American soil. The methods of mass production used for armaments, uniforms, and supplies spread to other sectors of the economy after the war. In the span of a few decades, the shift had been made from local manufacture in

5. Pope John XXIII, *Mater et Magistra,* sec. 82-83.

6. Harry Antonides, "A Christian Perspective on Work and Labour Relations (1)," *The Guide* 35 (July-August 1987): 4.

7. Harry Antonides, "A Christian Perspective on Work and Labour Relations (3)," *The Guide* 35 (September-October 1987): 10.

small shops to centralized industrial production. Machines replaced hand tools; factories replaced shops; factory workers replaced artisans; large cities replaced small villages; mass-produced goods replaced handicrafts.

Without a doubt, the industrial economy raised the general standard of American living to new levels of prosperity. The shift to industrial economy, however, was not without its problems. Among other things, it created a tension between the new demands of the industrial organization of work and the workers whose skills, methods, and expectations were rooted in the former age of artisan labor. This tension was compounded by demographics. In the 1870s and 1880s the American industrial labor force swelled with successive waves of immigrants from the European continent and British Isles. Leaving the small shops and rural settings of their homelands, scores of immigrants teemed into the huge industrial centers of the New World. Independent Old World artisans and peasants, bringing with them their own tools, skills, and often only a dim comprehension of the English language, suddenly found themselves in a strange work environment. Now placed under foremen in a factory setting, they received their daily assignments and were largely left to themselves and their machines to get the job done in the best way they knew how. Typically relegated to only a small part of the overall production process, they rarely understood how their work fit into the overall scheme of things. Yet there were few complaints. Many had been driven across the Atlantic by a desperate poverty. Their jobs now provided them with a social toehold in the New World. For such security most were thankful.

Into the rank and file of this largely immigrant labor force of the late-nineteenth century stepped the unlikely figure of Frederick Winslow Taylor. The privileged son of an established Quaker family in Philadelphia, Taylor had entered Phillips Exeter Academy in 1872 at the age of sixteen to prepare for Harvard and, eventually, a career in law. He was a hard, if not compulsive worker, and quickly rose to the top of his class, immersing himself in the study of the classical languages. But two years later, complaining of failing eyesight, he dropped out of Exeter and—

much to the surprise and bewilderment of his family—became an apprentice to a machinist at Enterprise Hydraulic Works. There he identified completely with the industrial workers in their dress, their manner, and their speech. It is reported that he not only adopted the habit of swearing, but raised it to the level of high art.

It was at the Hydraulic Works that Taylor also become aware of the woeful inefficiency of American industry at that time. A typical factory might have employed workers representing not only diverse ethnic groups, but over twenty separate trades. Moreover, each worker within a particular trade had his own way of going about things according to his apprentice tradition and private intuitions. Production planning was still at a fairly low level of development. Often materials were scattered at random locations in a factory with little, if any, inventory control. In addition, the overall process of production was poorly designed. Factory operations were, by contemporary standards, far from efficient.

This state of industrial affairs ran against the very grain of Taylor's being. Raised in a strict and orderly household under the iron rule of his mother, he had thoroughly internalized the domestic demands for order, regularity, rigor, efficiency, and precision. His behavior was at times compulsive, and his childhood playmates thought him something of a crank. Entire summer mornings were spent in the precise measurement and rigorous geometrical determination of a playing field before any game of which Taylor would be a part could begin. In the biographical portrait of Taylor drawn by Sudhir Kakar, we find that "in a game of croquet he would carefully work out the angles of the various strokes, the force of impact, and the advantages and disadvantages of the understroke, overstroke, and so on, before he started to play. In cross-country walks he constantly experimented with his legs in an endeavor to discover the step which would cover the greatest distance with the least expenditure of energy."[8]

8. Sudhir Kakar, *Frederick Taylor: A Study in Personality and Innovation* (Cambridge, MA: MIT Press, 1970), p. 18.

In 1878 Taylor finished his apprenticeship at the Hydraulic Works and went to work at Midvale Steel Works. A dedicated and hard-working machinist, he was soon appointed foreman of the lathe operators. He was now in a position that gave full reign to his penchant for finding the one best way to accomplish a task. With the permission of his supervisor, he conducted over 30,000 experiments on the lathe to determine the optimum rate of rotation, speed of feed, and depth of cut for diverse materials. He then analyzed the work routines of the lathe operators. The most efficient methods were determined. Tools were also evaluated and redesigned. Then the entire operation—machine setting, work routines, and tools—was standardized with an eye to maximum efficiency. Each lathe operator was in turn given a specialized slide rule for determining the proper machine settings for various kinds of materials and trained in the one right way of doing his job. Quotas were set on the basis of time studies, and the work was continuously monitored. Nothing was left to the worker's judgment. Everything had been planned, organized, and controlled "scientifically."

Although Taylor's attempts at the scientific reorganization of industrial work were met with something less than universal enthusiasm by the workers, his years at Midvale were marked by great personal achievement and innovation. There he developed the principles of what he would later call "scientific management." He had also, through home study after hours, received a Master's degree in mechanical engineering from the Steven's Institute of Technology. In 1890, however, he left Midvale for the Manufacturing Investment Company. His new job was organizing the production processes of several new paper mills being built in New England. But he failed miserably. The mill workers bitterly resented the imposition of scientific management, and the financiers resisted its expense. After a series of acrimonious disputes with both the employees and the owners, Taylor resigned and thereupon suffered a nervous breakdown.

In 1897, after several disasters in the consulting business and another nervous breakdown, Taylor was offered a job with Bethlehem Iron Works (later to become Bethlehem Steel). One of his most outstanding efforts at Bethlehem resulted in his well-known "Science of Shoveling."[9] At the Iron Works there was a lot to do, and many different kinds of material that had to be moved around. And most of it was moved around by gangs of men with shovels. Coal had to be shoveled into the blast furnaces; ashes had to be shoveled out; iron ore had to shoveled into carts, etc. When Taylor came to Bethlehem there were between 400 and 600 men on the shovel gangs. Each brought his own shovel to work; each had his own style of shoveling.

As we might expect, this haphazard approach to work was wholly unacceptable to Taylor. He immediately set out to determine, through scientific methods, the one best way to shovel. After much study and experimentation, Taylor established the optimal load and design of the shovel. He also proceeded to conduct motion studies of the best shovelers in the Iron Works in order to determine the most efficient method of shoveling (as it turned out: with the knees bent, thighs supporting elbows, sliding the shovel along the floor). He also conducted experiments to find out the optimal surface upon which to exercise the optimal method of shoveling. In addition, the daily work flow at the Iron Works was to be carefully planned in advance and constantly monitored, so that no one gang of shovelers had to be kept idle while waiting for another gang to finish its work.

As a direct result of the development and application of the science of shoveling, Taylor claimed to have reduced the number of workers on the shovel gangs from 600 to 140, and raised the average number of tons shoveled per day per man from sixteen to fifty-nine. This dramatic increase in productivity was accompanied by a raise from $1.15 to $1.88 in the daily earnings of the average worker. At the same time scientific management single-handedly lowered the cost of handling a ton of ore from $.072 to $.033.[10]

9. Frederick W. Taylor, *The Principles of Scientific Management* (New York: Harper & Bros., 1911), pp. 66ff.

10. Ibid., p. 71.

The wholesale replacement of the traditional know-how and individual style of the worker with scientific knowledge and standardized working methods is a good example of the systematic reorganization of human work Taylor both envisioned and demanded. Prior to scientific management, the manager or boss left both the planning and execution of the work to the workers themselves. The chief task of management was to provide effective incentives in order to get the workers to finish their work on time. Most of the thought that went into management prior to Taylor was devoted to the question of monetary incentive plans—the pros and cons of piece rates, hourly rates, bonus plans, etc. Under the new regime of scientific management however, management assumes "new burdens, new duties, and responsibilities never dreamed of in the past."[11] For one, the planning and method of work was no longer left up to the best judgment of the workers. Rather, management was, first of all, to determine scientifically the most efficient method for every operation. This method was to replace all traditonal "rule of thumb" methods.[12] Second, management was to select and train workers scientifically in the new methods of work. Third, management was to supervise the workers constantly to make sure that all work was being done in strict accordance with scientifically established methods.

Thus human work was to be made efficient and productive: management would provide the brains, while the workers supplied the brawn. No longer would those who do the work also plan the work. Their job was simply to follow instructions issued from above. Taylor called this functional division of labor "task management": each task assigned to the worker had to be scientifically analyzed for optimum productivity and specified down to the last detail by management. "The work of every workman," Taylor writes, "is fully planned out by the management at least one day in advance, and each man receives in most cases complete written instructions, describing

11. Ibid., p. 36
12. Ibid., p. 16.

in detail the task which he is to accomplish, as well as the means to be used in doing the work. The task specifies not only what is to be done but how it is to be done and the exact time allowed for doing it."[13]

Despite the glowing accounts Taylor gives of his accomplishments at Bethlehem Iron Works, he again met strong resistance from both above and below. The owners were unwilling to pay for the extensive studies, training, and administration demanded by scientific management, and the workers resented its authoritarian style. After another round of bitter disputes, Taylor again suffered a nervous breakdown and was summarily fired in 1901. Unwilling and perhaps unable at this point to reenter the world of industrial work, Taylor decided to seek no more paid employment. Instead, he assumed the role of a prophet, devoting his time to publication, correspondence, and consultation, preaching the gospel of higher productivity through scientific management.

Ironically, the man whose ideas fomented so much strife in industry couched his message of higher productivity through applied science within the larger concern for harmony in labor relations. Traditionally, the employer and employee have been at odds with one another: the employee seeks to get the most pay for the smallest quantity of work, while the employer tries to get the most work out of the employee for the least amount of pay. Taylor proposed to resolve this conflict of interests through scientifically achieved higher productivity. This would allow both parties to get what they wanted most: larger profits for the owners and higher wages for the workers.

Taylor was also convinced that the benefits of scientific management would not be contained to relations internal to industry alone. Rather, they would spill over the factory walls and make a substantial contribution to the flourishing of human life in general. Scientific management could effectively double the productivity of the average worker. "Think of what this means to the whole country," Taylor asks, "think of the in-

13. Ibid., p. 39.

crease, both of the necessities and in the luxuries of life, which becomes available for the whole country, of the possibility of shortening the hours of labor when this is desirable, and of the increased opportunities for education, culture, and recreation which this implies."[14]

Despite the often fierce resistance from the industrial workers, and the financial foot-dragging of the captains of industry, Taylor's ideas were taking hold in key sectors of American society in the first decade of the twentieth century. Scientific management had been appropriated by a number of prestigious business schools, including Dartmouth and Harvard. In 1911 Taylor published his classic work, *The Principles of Scientific Management.* By 1915 his book had been translated into nine languages, including Japanese. Taylor himself was inundated by requests for speeches, articles, and advice on scientific management—especially from businessmen who saw its potential for enhancing their company's profits.

Organized labor, however, perceived the upsurge of interest in scientific management as an unmitigated threat. Convinced that the new style of management would be used to get more work out of the workers for the same wages, the Executive Council of the American Federation of Labor passed a resolution opposed to what it called Taylor's "premium bonus plan." Not only did they fear exploitation, but also the dehumanizing effects of the "scientific approach" to management. The well-known labor leader of the day, Samuel Gompers, expressed these anxieties in a flight of sarcasm during an address to American laborers: "So there you are, wage-workers in general, mere machines—considered industrially, of course. Hence why should you not be standardized and your motion-power be brought up to the highest possible perfection in all respects, including speeds? Not only your length, breadth, and thickness as a machine, but your grade of hardness, malleability, tractability, and general serviceability can be ascertained, registered, and then employed as desirable. Science would thus get the most out

14. Ibid., p. 142.

of you before you are sent to the junkpile."[15] In 1911 the organized labor lobby was successful in getting Congress to appoint a special "Committee to Investigate the Taylor and Other Systems of Shop Management." Taylor himself was brought before the congressional hearings and relentlessly questioned—and ridiculed—by politicians and labor leaders.

Contrary to Taylor's predictions, the introduction of scientific management rarely eliminated the opposition between labor and capital, and often intensified it. For the owners—who were, after all, in charge—saw no reason why higher productivity should not be translated almost entirely into higher profits, allowing wages to remain roughly the same. And the labor unions, with some justification, perceived Taylor's method—what they called "speeding"—as an ingenious scheme to get workers to work harder without partaking in the economic rewards of their efforts.

If anything, scientific management actually made workers more vulnerable to abuse at employers' hands. For it stripped the workers of the one thing that gave them power and authority in the workplace—the opportunity to apply informed judgment to their own work and thereby acquire an expertise of their own. With the wholesale replacement of traditional skills with scientific knowledge, decision-making power became the exclusive prerogative of management. As a direct result, the workers were rendered wholly passive and dependent. They had no say in how they were to work. They had nothing special to contribute. The only thing they brought to the job was muscle power, and there were plenty of others standing on the industrial sidelines who could supply the same.

Another negative effect of scientific management might be called the "de-vocationalization" of human work. In the last chapter we stated that it is our vocation to follow Christ and to use our gifts and abilities in the service of our neighbor. But when work has been systematically emptied of responsibility, of

15. As quoted in Milton J. Nadworney, *Scientific Management and the Unions* (Cambridge, MA: Harvard University Press, 1955), p. 51.

the exercise of the intellect and the imagination, when it has been reduced to carrying out simplified routines that any robot or well-trained animal could do, then it is no longer a place where we can make use of our typically human gifts and abilities in the service of others. Such gifts and abilities lie fallow on the job, of no use to anybody.

Taylor envisioned no adverse reactions to the de-vocationalization of work by scientific management. After all, he thought that the only thing workers wanted out of work was a good wage.[16] And since scientific management would make it possible for them to be more productive and thus to earn more money, he could see no reason—apart from ignorance—why the workers would not embrace his program as an unalloyed blessing. He assumed, as management theorist Frederick Herzberg put it, that the workers would "be delighted with the fact that they did not have to make decisions."[17] Evidently it never occurred to Taylor—who himself derived much meaning from work without pay in his later life—that work, apart from any monetary compensation, might be meaningful in itself, that certain human needs might be met within work itself: e.g., accomplishment, social contact, personal development, and the like. As we shall see, it was left to later management theorists to discover the complexity of human needs and motivations on the job.

Taylor's assumptions about worker motivation, even worker intelligence, were perhaps plausible given the social circumstances of the day. As already noted, during the last half of the nineteenth century America was flooded with immigrants. By and large they were poor and in desperate need of employment. Their survival and the well-being of their families depended on it. In such circumstances, money does become an overriding consideration and the primary motive for work. "Man lives by bread alone," noted management theorist Douglas

16. Ibid., p. 53.

17. Frederick Herzberg, *Work and the Nature of Man* (New York: World, 1966), p. 37.

McGregor, "when there is no bread."[18] Furthermore, most immigrants had relatively little formal education; and that many of them had only a rudimentary grasp of the English language gave at least the appearance of stupidity.

Social circumstances in America have changed since then. Most students of today's labor force contend that scientific management is no longer adequate. A 1973 report to the Department of Health, Education, and Welfare, entitled *Work in America,* points out that workers today generally are native-born, well educated, and unlikely to tolerate the monotonous, servile jobs that provide them a paycheck, but no power.[19]

The sentiment of the *Work in America* report has been joined by a chorus of management theorists and work ideologues who have roundly rejected Taylor's system of scientific management as the source of most, if not all, the evils of the workplace today. To be sure, there is much to be criticized in Taylor's approach. But there is also an element that must be both appreciated and retained: the analysis of the work process. As contemporary management theorist Peter F. Drucker points out, Taylor was the first to subject the process of work to rigorous and systematic analysis. Such analysis has in fact contributed greatly to productivity. "The tremendous surge of affluence in the last seventy-five years which has lifted the working masses in the developed countries well above any level recorded before," rests, Drucker claims, on "scientific management."[20] While this may be an overstatement, it cannot be denied that there is something valuable in eliminating inefficiencies in the workplace through a careful analysis of work processes. In an industry which depends upon a lot of shoveling, determining the optimal load and design of a shovel makes good sense.

The problem with Taylorism is not the analysis of work,

18. Douglas McGregor, *The Human Side of Enterprise* (New York: McGraw Hill, 1960), p. 36.

19. *Work in America:* Report of a task force to the Secretary of Health, Education, and Welfare (Cambridge, MA: MIT Press, 1973), p. 18.

20. Peter F. Drucker, *Management: Tasks, Responsibilities, Practices* (New York: Harper & Row, 1973), p. 181.

but the synthesis of work. After having analyzed the process of work into its basic elements, identified the most efficient methods and eliminated the unnecessary elements, Taylor recombined those components as if machines, not human beings, were to perform the work. Taylor's scientific approach to work treated job design as if it were nothing more than a problem in mechanical engineering. The tasks were simplified and standardized. The work pace was made uniform. Such organization of effort is ideally suited to the work of machines. The problem is that human beings are not machines. In fact, they make lousy machines. "Machines," Drucker points out, "work best if they do only one task, if they do it repetitively, and if they do the simplest possible task. . . . Machines work best if run at the same speed, the same rhythm, and with a minimum of moving parts."[21] On the other hand, "the human being is engineered quite differently. For any one task and any one operation the human being is ill-suited. He lacks strength. He lacks stamina. He gets fatigued. Altogether he is a very poorly designed machine tool. The human being excels, however, in coordination. He excels in relating perception to action. He works best if the entire human being, muscles, senses, and mind is engaged by the work."[22] Furthermore, "there is no 'one right' speed and no 'one right' rhythm for human beings. Speed, rhythm, and attention spans vary greatly among individuals. . . . Nothing, we now know, creates as much fatigue, as much resistance, as much anger, and as much resentment, as the imposition of an alien speed, and an alien rhythm, and an alien attention span, and above all, the imposition of one unvarying and uniform pattern of speed, rhythm, and attention span."[23]

Well-designed jobs for human beings must incorporate an analysis of the process of the work to be done. Inefficiencies must be eliminated if work is to be made productive. At the same time, the design of the job must take into account the fact that

21. Ibid.
22. Ibid., pp. 183-84.
23. Ibid., p. 184.

working is a human activity. It must not abstract from the physiological limitations, the psychological makeup nor the social needs of the human being; nor may it ignore the social obligation human beings have to employ the full range of their talents and abilities for the sake of the common good. As we stated at the outset of this chapter, work must be a "place of responsibility." From this standpoint, the major failure of Taylor's method of job design is that it does not allow humans to work as humans. It eliminates the element of responsibility from work. By organizing work around the mechanical ideals of simplicity, uniformity, and repetition, scientific management makes use of "only the minimum in a man's repertory of behavior," as Herzberg points out, thus "amputating the rest of his capabilities."[24] The typically human components of work—intelligence, imaginative problem solving, informed decision-making, personal achievement—have been systematically deleted. In the Taylor-made job, human beings work like well-trained animals, or well-greased machines, but not as human beings. This is not only an ethical consideration, but practical as well. For numerous studies have indicated that when we do not work as humans, we do not work well.

Elton Mayo: The Hawthorne Experiment and the Discovery of the Human Dimension of Work

Despite initial resistance from various quarters, Taylorism spread throughout the Western industrial world during the first quarter of the twentieth century. The political realities of the time contributed in part to this rapid proliferation of scientific management. The First World War had put a tremendous demand on the industrial capacities of all involved nations. For the sake of the war effort, many of them turned to Taylor's works for advice on improving productivity. By the 1920s Taylorism—

24. Herzberg, *Nature of Man*, p. 36.

and its corollary in the form of Henry Ford's assembly line—became accepted as the most rational and efficient way to organize human labor. Virtually all forms of industrial and office work were subjected to incredibly detailed time and motion studies, and volumes of reference works containing the resulting data were published and made available to industrial engineers for application in job design. The appeal of scientific management even transcended the forbidding ideological barriers between East and West. In 1918 Lenin published an article in *Pravda* calling for the use of Taylor's principles in the new Soviet workplace.[25]

Industrial productivity during this period was everywhere on the rise. So was the general level of prosperity. When Henry Ford invented the assembly line for the production of the Model T in 1908, more cars were produced per man-hour of work than ever before. As a result, the cost of cars went down, and wages went up—up to an unprecedented five dollars a day by 1914 at the Ford factory. Between 1921 and 1929 the industrial output of the United States nearly doubled. But as prosperity rose, so did its human cost. The work touched by the spirit of Taylorism was invariably reduced to a matter of dull and monotonous routine. This led, quite understandably, to a new industrial problem: inefficiency due to boredom and fatigue. From the outset it was assumed, however, that if these problems had been created by Taylor's science, they could also be solved by Taylor's science. A new wave of studies in the 1920s was unleashed on the physiological factors of work pace, duration of work periods, frequency and duration of rest breaks, levels of illumination, temperature, humidity, and the like. Taylor had put the work routine on a firm scientific foundation; now the same had to be done for working conditions.

But the results of these new studies were destined to challenge the fundamental assumptions of Taylor's science of management. Following Taylor, one might expect the problems

25. V. I. Lenin, *Collected Works*, vol. 27 (Moscow: Progress Publishers, 1965), p. 259.

of boredom and fatigue to be solved by the scientific determination of the one right way to set the relevant variables (e.g., the work pace, the frequency and duration of rest breaks, the temperature, humidity, and level of illumination in the workplace, etc.). Indeed, this was the initial approach. However, while some progress was made in reducing the physiological problem of fatigue, the scientific approach foundered on the psychological problem of boredom. It was quickly discovered that the objective conditions of the work routine and working conditions had little to do with the amount of experienced boredom. The degree of boredom can vary, for example, while the work routine remains the same. One report made by the Industrial Fatigue Research Board in England pointed out that "the amount of monotony experienced probably depends more on the attitude of the operative towards his work. It is well known that the same industrial task has different subjective effects upon different individuals, and while some may find the work extremely monotonous and at times even intolerable, others find it comparatively pleasant, and prefer it to more varied occupations."[26]

Here Taylor's science encountered the mysterious workings of human subjectivity—for which Taylor had made little, if any, provision. The lack of a strong correlation between objective conditions and subjective experience demanded that a wider range of factors be taken into account in the study of work. In the Fourth Annual Report of the Industrial Fatigue Research Board, May Smith adroitly pointed out that a whole host of "human factors" were relevant to individual productivity: the attitudes of fellow workers towards authorities, emotional changes, physiological changes, as well as the social life of the factory. "The total reaction at any given moment will be a reaction to a composite situation which does not remain unchanged. The consciousness of one or the other factor of the composite sit-

26. H. M. Vernon, T. Bedford, and S. Wyatt, *Two Studies in Rest Pauses in Industry*, Industrial Fatigue Research Board, Report No. 25 (London: H. M. Stationery Office, 1924), p. 23.

uation varies from person to person and even from time to time in the same person."[27] If one takes the "mechanical point of view," Smith contended, "which looks upon the person as a kind of extension to a machine," the human dimension drops out of the picture. But the human dimension, which is in fact always present and operative, opens up "if one studies the worker as a human being and not only as a performer of a repetition process."[28]

These early intimations of the human dimension in work and the limitations of Taylor's approach were soon to be confirmed in an astounding series of studies conducted at the Hawthorne Works of Western Electric on the west side of Chicago between 1927 and 1932. These studies have become known in management literature as the famous "Hawthorne Experiment."

The Hawthorne Experiment took place in fifteen periods, measured in weeks. In April of 1927 five female relay assemblers were put in an experimental room, set off from the main assembly area by ten-foot-high partitions, and subjected to changes in their work routine—number of breaks, changes in schedule, and payment scheme.[29] Practically every change was accompanied by a boost in productivity; and the highest level of productivity was attained when the workers returned to the initial conditions! The research group that conducted the studies was forced to conclude that "the itemized changes experimentally imposed, although they could perhaps be used to account for minor differences between one period and another, yet could not be used to explain the major change—the continually increasing production."[30]

At this point Elton Mayo, Associate Professor of Industrial Research at Harvard University, was called in to interpret and explain the paradoxical test results. Rather than speculate on the basis of the test results alone, Mayo decided to delve

27. Ibid., p. 29.

28. Ibid., p. 30.

29. Elton Mayo, *The Human Problems of an Industrial Civilization* (Boston: Harvard Business School, 1933), pp. 53-63.

30. Ibid., p. 63

deeper into the issue of work and what it meant to the workers. Between the years of 1928 and 1930 over 21,000 employees at the Hawthorne Works were interviewed. Mayo found that the secret to increased productivity was not found in the method of relay assembly (which remained constant throughout), nor in the changes in the working conditions. Rather it was the change in human relations between management and workers. In the test situation the workers had a greater sense of freedom. They participated in determining their own working conditions. They were consulted before every experimental change; their comments were accepted and discussed. What mattered was not so much the content of the changes, but the fact that the workers participated in them. Increases in productivity through this kind of participation has become known in the literature as the "Hawthorne Effect." When the work group is involved in decision making, Mayo contends, "the group unquestionably develops a sense of participation in the critical determinations and becomes something of a social unity."[31] This sense of participation and cooperation speaks to the social and psychological needs of the workers, and they respond by working more diligently. Furthermore, the role of the supervisor had changed: "He took a personal interest in each girl and her achievement; he showed pride in the record of the group. He helped the group to feel that its duty was to set its own conditions of work. He helped the workers to find the 'freedom' of which they so frequently speak."[32]

With the Hawthorne Experiment, the physical and physiological factors involved in job design receded into the background, and the "human factors"—the psychological and social factors—stepped to the center of attention. Thus was born the "Human Relations" school of management theory and practice. Typically, the Human Relations approach pays little attention to the objective organization of work and working conditions. The key to productivity is in the social interaction of the work force.

31. Ibid., p. 69.
32. Ibid., pp. 68-69.

People come to the workplace not only with economic needs—the only needs Taylor officially recognized—but with psychological needs as well: needs for social acceptance, self-esteem, and a sense of control and autonomy. When the human relations at work are adjusted to meet those needs, people will find personal fulfillment at work and put forth greater effort, resulting in higher productivity. Happy people make good workers. After a hiatus in further development of management theory during the Depression and the Second World War, management turned increasingly to the science of psychology for insight into the complex and sometimes "irrational" motivations of human action and how they might be harnessed in the interests of the business enterprise.

Chris Argyris: Conflicts Between Organizational Structure and Human Self-Realization

The discovery of the human dimension of work in the Hawthorne Experiment had a profound effect on subsequent management theory. That effect might be characterized as a shift in disciplinary basis. Management in itself is not a single academic discipline. Rather, it makes use of a number of disciplines for its own purposes. In this respect it is like the study of medicine.[33] In medical school one studies chemistry, biology, anatomy, and other disciplines insofar as they relate to the cure of disease and the promotion of health. Likewise, management draws upon other disciplines insofar as they relate to organizing human effort for the achievement of institutional goals. After the Hawthorne Experiment, the disciplinary base of management shifted from physics to psychology, from the natural to the behavioral sciences.[34]

33. Cf. Drucker, *Management,* p. 17.

34. Others parts and schools of management theory were based on mathematics.

One of the first and most prominent management thinkers to draw upon this new disciplinary basis was Chris Argyris, Professor of Industrial Administration at Yale. In his classic study, *Personality and Organization,* he claimed that the use of the behavioral sciences "to understand human behavior in organizations has now come of age."[35] But to understand human behavior in organizations—"organizational behavior"—the behavioral sciences alone are not sufficient. They must be brought into contact with the theory of organizational structure. In *Personality and Organization* Argyris does just that. The initial results were, however, far from encouraging. What Argyris discovered in the course of his work was a basic—and in some respects inevitable—conflict between the formal structure of human organizations and the psychological needs of human individuals.

The core insight that Argyris culled from the psychological literature of his day was that human behavior must be understood in terms of a number of developmental continua. As people pass from infancy to adulthood they typically become less passive and more active, less dependent and more independent; they pass from being able to do a few things to being able to do many things, from having short-term interests to having long-term interests, from short time-perspectives to long time-perspectives, from being subordinates to being in charge, from having no self-awareness and control to having a great deal of self-awareness and control.[36] Movement along these lines represents psychological progress toward the "self-actualization" or "self-realization" of the adult human being. To become a mature human being is just to be active, independent, competent, self-aware, and autonomous, with long-term interests and time-perspectives. Lack of development represents psychological failure, which in turn calls forth various defense mechanisms in order to protect the integrity of the ego. Those who fail tend to

35. Chris Argyris, *Personality and Organization* (New York: Harper, 1957), p. 2.

36. Ibid., p. 54.

rationalize their failure, often become apathetic, cynical, and, in some cases, physically ill.

Formal organizational structure, Argyris contends, is based upon the assumption that in any organization both the quality and quantity of the product can be increased by focusing workers on limited fields of endeavor. Hence "task specialization": individuals within the organization must have highly focused and narrowly specified tasks. Such tasks can be easily mastered, and, as a result, individual productivity will increase. Because the work of the individual will be highly specialized, it must also be organized, supervised, directed, and controlled. Hence the "chain of command": authority and decision-making within an organization must proceed from the top to the bottom in hierarchical fashion. Furthermore, each organizational unit must have a "unity of function"—a singular purpose defined from the top down, formulated and administered by the supervisor of that unit, not the unit itself.

When we compare the developmental needs of the adult personality together with the structural demands of formal organizations, we can easily see how conflicts will arise between them. Because of the chain of command, employees will be rendered passive, dependent, and subordinate; the chain of command plus the unity of direction will deprive them of almost all self-control. And task specialization means that they will do few rather than many things, that their work interests will be short-term and their productive time-perspectives brief. Thus the organizational imperative of efficiency runs contrary to the human needs for psychological growth. "The basic impact of the formal organizational structure is to make the employees feel dependent, submissive, and passive, and to require them to use only a few of their less important abilities."[37] For this reason the general characteristics of formal organizations "are much more congruent with the needs of infants in our culture. In effect, therefore, organizations are willing to pay high wages and provide adequate seniority if

37. Ibid., p. 56.

mature adults will, for eight hours a day, behave in a less than mature manner."[38]

The inevitable experience of conflict, frustration, and psychological failure by employees will consequently set in motion a number of defense mechanisms. Negative attitudes and behavior will abound: "decreases in production and identification with the organization; increases in waste, errors, absenteeism, sickness, apathy and disinterest in work, and increase in importance of the material [financial] aspect of work."[39] Such consequences are "all understandable and predictable ways for relatively healthy employees to adapt to conflict, frustration and failure they experience as a result of the formal organization."[40]

Management, however, tends not to see the problem this way. Rather than interpreting the negative attitudes and behavior as a healthy response to the manifold violations of psychological maturity, management attributes the problem to intrinsic character traits of the employees. "They [managers] observe their employees while at work and they conclude: 1) *The employees* are lazy, 2) *The employees* are uninterested and apathetic, 3) *The employees* are money crazy, 4) *The employees* create error and waste."[41] The typical managerial attitude was summed up by an admirably candid corporate executive who told Argyris that "the majority of workers are good-natured slobs who want to be left alone in routine jobs."[42]

Assuming the problem is with the employees and not the organization itself, management typically makes two responses. One is to reinforce those features of the formal organization that created the problems in the first place. Because the employees are by nature disinclined to work, what is needed is *more* control, *more* direction, *more* supervision, and *more* pressure. But of course these measures serve only to create more passivity, de-

38. Ibid., p. 66.
39. Ibid., p. 123.
40. Ibid.
41. Ibid.
42. Ibid., p. 126.

pendency, subordination, and lack of autonomy on the part of the employees, which in turn aggravates the negative attitudes and produces more negative behavior. Management practices "tend to reinforce the problems caused by organization, thus increasing the very behavior these practices were supposed to decrease."[43]

The second response—usually following the dismal failure of the first—is to try to alter the employees' attitudes through the "human relations" approach advocated by Mayo. The negative attitudes are seen as signs that the employees are somehow psychologically unhealthy, weak, and immature. What they need is a pep talk. Bring in the human relations experts to motivate them, make them feel as though they are an important part of the organization or the free enterprise system even if, in fact, they are not. This attempt, however, is usually no more effective than the first. Employees see it, quite rightly, as a form of manipulation. They respond with suspicion and form informal sub-groups which work counter to the aims of the organization. Furthermore, because they know their true attitudes are now out-of-line with the official emphasis on happiness and commitment, they tend to become secretive. This secrecy creates, in turn, "executive isolation." Managers no longer know what is really going on with their employees, and the efforts of the organization become uncoordinated.

According to Argyris, the only way out of this vicious cycle is recognizing that negative behavior is not the result of human nature as such, but rather the conflict between psychologically healthy individuals and the structure of formal organizations. There is nothing intrinsically wrong with the employees. It is the organization that has to be changed. The solution lies in changing the structure of the jobs so that individual needs for psychological growth can be met within them. How can this be done? Argyris suggests two ways: job enrichment and participatory leadership.

Scientific management assumed that work could be made

43. Ibid., p. 162.

more efficient if it were simplified and made a matter of routine. Job simplification, however, was deeply resented by those whose work was thus reduced to the mind-numbing repetition of mechanical motions. Bad attitudes towards work and sloppy work habits resulted. The solution to the problem, Argyris contends, is not to hold the job constant and try to change the attitude of the employee through various motivational techniques, but to change the job. The job needs to be "enriched." That is, the number of activities in a particular job needs to be increased and the average duration of the job cycle lengthened. Particular attention, however, must be paid to the kind of activities added. No real solution to the problem will occur if only the number of specialized tasks is increased—say, putting twenty nuts on wheel lugs rather than five. Rather, a job is relevantly enriched only if the activities added draw upon important abilities, abilities which involve the exercise of the intellect and the will, thereby increasing the employee's independence and autonomy.

The first solution quite naturally leads to the second: participative leadership. If employees are to achieve autonomy and self-control on the job, they must be involved to some degree in the formation of policy and the setting of goals which directly affect their work. Employee participation in decision-making, however, can never be a matter of total self-determination, with no direction given by management. For the organization does not exist for the sake of fulfilling the employee's psychological needs alone. The needs of the organization must be fulfilled as well. Management then has the delicate task of simultaneously maximizing the fulfillment of both the employees and the organization's needs—needs which will always to some degree stand in tension with each other. "Effective leadership behavior," Argyris writes, "is 'fusing' the individual and the organization in such a way that both simultaneously obtain optimum self-actualization."[44]

This "fusion" remains an ideal, and is complicated by the fact that employees do not come to the organization in a pris-

44. Ibid., p. 211.

tine state. Their work attitudes have already been formed by traditional management practices. They expect to be passive and dependent on the job. They do not look for personal fulfillment at work, only a paycheck. They often resist greater participation in making decisions or assuming more responsibility for their own work. For this reason Argyris recommends what he calls "reality leadership." Reality leadership cannot assume that all adults want to act as adults on the job. It has to work on a case-by-case basis, employing a mix of traditional and progressive management approaches.

Frederick Herzberg: Human Needs, Motivation and Hygiene

The fundamental insight of the human relations school of management was that worker productivity depends largely upon worker attitude. That attitude, however, is the result of the relation between the work setting and a complex set of psychological variables which are only partially understood. Thus, a research program is indicated: which factors in the work setting elicit positive attitudes, which negative; and, once these correlations are established, which psychological theory can explain them? Presumably, if we had such a theory in hand we could not only explain these correlations, but predict and control them for the sake of higher productivity.

One of the most provocative and influential participants in this new research program was Frederick Herzberg. In the 1950s, Herzberg conducted interviews with over 200 engineers and accountants in Pittsburgh.[45] They were asked about factors in their work that made their jobs satisfying and which made their jobs dissatisfying. As it turned out, those factors that made

45. For a critique of Herzberg's methodology, see Edwin A. Locke, "The Nature and Causes of Job Satisfaction," in *Handbook of Industrial and Organizational Psychology,* ed. M. D. Dunnette (Chicago: Rand McNally, 1976).

for job satisfaction were not the same as those factors that made the job dissatisfying. The five major factors in job satisfaction were achievement, recognition, the work itself, responsibility, and advancement. Those factors most often cited as sources of job dissatisfaction were company policy and administration, supervision, salary, interpersonal relations, and working conditions. When compared, Herzberg noted, the lists of "satisfiers" and "dissatisfiers" display the following feature: the satisfiers pertain to the intrinsic character of the work itself, while the dissatisfiers concern extrinsic factors. Herzberg referred to the satisfiers as "motivators," and the dissatisfiers as "hygiene factors." When something goes wrong in the hygiene factors—say, excessive noise in the workplace—job dissatisfaction results. People are unhappy with their work. But when such a problem is cleared up, it does not follow that they will be satisfied with their work, only that they will not be dissatisfied. Job satisfaction requires not just the absence of negative factors, but the presence of positive factors—"motivators" like achievement, responsibility, advancement, and the like. The factors that lead to job satisfaction—and, thus, higher productivity—play very little role in job dissatisfaction, while the factors that contribute to job dissatisfaction rarely play a role in job satisfaction.[46] Taking care of problems in the hygienic factors—ensuring adequate salary, pleasant working conditions, and so forth—will prevent discontent, but it will not create a positive sense of satisfaction. That requires something else.

The error of traditional management in both theory and practice, according to Herzberg, is that it has concentrated almost exclusively on hygienic factors. It has assumed, quite mistakenly, that by taking care of these factors it would "unleash positive feelings and the return of increased creativity, productivity, lowered absenteeism and turnover, and all the other indices of manpower efficiency."[47] Not only does an exclusive focus on hygienic factors fail to achieve its intended effect, it

46. Herzberg, *Nature of Man*, p. 77.
47. Ibid., p. 169.

quite often produces the opposite effect. That is, it actually creates more job dissatisfaction. Why? Because worker expectations regarding hygienic factors are subject to the law of escalation. The measure that prevents dissatisfaction today will create dissatisfaction tomorrow. The pay raise may stop present complaints, but it will also raise expectations for future pay raises. "Hygiene acts like heroin," Herzberg observes, "it takes more and more to produce less and less effect."[48] When employees are led by management to focus on factors extrinsic to the work itself they will become "chronically dissatisfied."[49]

The exclusive focus on hygienic factors by traditional management exposes, Herzberg claims, a basic misunderstanding of human nature and what it is that motivates people to work. Herzberg sets out to correct this misunderstanding in his key work, *Work and the Nature of Man.* There he begins with the notion that human motivation to act must be understood according to needs. We do what we do in order to fulfill our needs. So far, a mere truism. But what must be realized, Herzberg claims, is that human beings have two distinct sets of needs: animal needs and more typically human needs, needs for "psychological growth."

Animal needs are attuned to the project of self-preservation. To survive, we need food, shelter, and protection from disease and violence. But human beings are more than animals. Mere physical survival is not enough. We also have certain higher potentials that need to be actualized. We need to achieve, to be recognized, to be responsible, and to express our individuality. While animal needs pertain to self-preservation, human needs pertain to self-actualization. In meeting the animal needs, one avoids pain; in meeting the human needs, one achieves happiness. So Herzberg invites us to "think about man twice: once about events that cause him pain and, secondly, about events that make him happy."[50]

Part of our motivation to work is, of course, the satisfac-

48. Ibid., p. 170.
49. Ibid., p. 81.
50. Ibid., p. 86.

tion of animal needs. We work in order to make a living, to make enough money to pay the bills. But this is not, or need not, be the only motivation to work. In fact, if work is only for the satisfaction of animal needs, no human fulfillment will be found in it. "Probably one of the most destructive misinterpretations of the American way of life has been to belittle, attenuate and degrade the concept of the worker's initiative and achievement as pursued for economic profit. Man does work for profit in order to avoid pain; but in a positive sense, he works to enjoy the excitement and meaning that achievement provides for his own psychological growth and thereby his happiness."[51]

Herzberg's "motivation-hygiene theory" of organizational behavior also has direct implications for job design. Like Argyris, Herzberg argued that enriched jobs would lead to both higher productivity and worker fulfillment. We need no longer assume that work is a matter of self-denial for the sake of extrinsic rewards. Properly designed, work can be of intrinsic value to the worker. If he or she finds responsibility, accomplishment, and recognition there, then the work itself will be satisfying, apart from monetary compensation. Because Taylor's scientific management created jobs where the higher needs of human beings could not be met, the emphasis inevitably fell upon providing motivation to work through extrinsic rewards, like wages and benefits. But we can now see that this approach was fundamentally wrong: scientifically simplified jobs create negative attitudes towards the work itself. The result is boredom, fatigue, carelessness, resentment, absenteeism, and incessant demands for higher wages and better fringe benefits as a compensation for lack of fulfillment on the job. The right solution to the problem, according to Herzberg, could only lie in the "humanization" of work. Jobs must be redesigned to allow for opportunities for achievement and recognition, for complexity and responsibility. Furthermore, they must provide opportunities for creativity, personal growth, and advancement.[52] Only when

51. Ibid., p. 174.
52. Ibid., pp. 177-78.

work becomes a matter of self-fulfillment rather than self-denial will people develop a positive attitude toward work. And only with a positive attitude toward work will people produce at the highest levels.

Douglas McGregor: Theory X, Theory Y, and Management by Integration

The idea of promoting productivity by satisfying human needs on the job also received much attention in the work of another prominent management theorist of the 1950s and 1960s, Douglas McGregor. After receiving his Ph.D. from Harvard in 1936, McGregor taught both psychology and industrial management at Harvard and MIT. In 1948 he became the president of Antioch College. Like Herzberg, McGregor faulted scientific management for organizing work in a way that runs contrary to human nature.[53] Like Herzberg, he suggested that management draw upon more sophisticated psychological insights into the structure of human motivation. For his own disciplinary base, McGregor used the needs-hierarchy theory of the humanistic psychologist Abraham Maslow, and recommended a management practice he called "management by integration."

One of the central tasks of management, McGregor claims, "is to organize human effort in the service of the economic objectives of the enterprise."[54] To carry out this task, a manager must be in a position to both predict and control the behavior of others. "Successful management," McGregor writes, "depends—not alone, but significantly—upon the ability to predict and control human behavior."[55] In spite of the apparent irrationality of human behavior revealed in the Hawthorne Experiment, McGregor maintained that human behavior

53. McGregor, *Enterprise*, p. 9.
54. Ibid., p. 3.
55. Ibid., p. 4.

is predictable. The accuracy of the predictions, however, will depend upon the accuracy of the theoretical assumptions about "human nature."[56] Human behavior appears irrational only against the background of unwarranted assumptions about what makes human beings tick. Here McGregor thought that management has much to learn from the social sciences, which have effectively challenged the more traditonal ideas about human motivation. The manager "can draw upon a reasonable and growing body of knowledge in the social sciences as an aid to achieving managerial objectives."[57]

The cluster of assumptions about human nature employed by the traditional approach to management McGregor calls "Theory X." Theory X assumes that "the average human being has an inherent dislike of work and will avoid it if he can."[58] Because of this inherent dislike of work, "most people must be coerced, controlled, directed, threatened with punishment to get them to put forth adequate effort toward the achievement of organizational objectives."[59] Furthermore, Theory X assumes that the average human being does not mind the authoritarian style of scientific management because he or she "prefers to be directed, wishes to avoid responsibility, has relatively little ambition, [and] wants security above all."[60] Theory X, then, assumes that the needs of the organization and the needs of the individual are at odds with each other.[61] Managerial control must be asserted through hierarchical authority and the imposition of executive will. Workers must be motivated by extrinsic rewards, so that they will do what they would rather not do (i.e., work). For this reason Theory X management usually focuses on issues outside the job itself: compensation, medical benefits, vacations, retirement plans, and the like. Ironically, it is by focusing on such issues that management unwittingly entices employees to buy

56. Ibid., p. 11.
57. Ibid., p. 3.
58. Ibid., p. 33.
59. Ibid., p. 34.
60. Ibid.
61. Ibid., p. 50.

into the same assumptions it has about human nature and work. "It is not surprising, therefore, that for many wage earners work is perceived as a form of punishment which is the price to be paid for various kinds of satisfaction away from the job."[62] The problems associated with Theory X assumptions and resulting management practices are by now familiar: the deep dissatisfaction with work and the upward push for extrinsic rewards.

Theory X, then, assumes that work can never be more than a disagreeable means to an agreeable end. By contrast, Theory Y assumes that "the average human being does not inherently dislike work. Depending upon controllable conditions, work may be a source of satisfaction."[63] Humans have more than just survival needs, to which work relates only as a means. A sizable number of other important human needs can be satisfied on the job. Therefore, work can be valued for its own sake, and not just for the sake of extrinsic rewards.

To make his case, McGregor draws upon the needs-hierarchy theory of Abraham Maslow. According to this theory, our most basic needs are physiological: food, rest, and shelter. Second, we need safety. Third, we have social needs: the need to belong, to be accepted, and to enjoy friendship. Fourth, there are ego needs: needs for self-esteem, confidence, achievement, competence, and recognition. Fifth and finally, there is the need for "self-actualization": the need for realizing one's own unique potential, for creativity and growth.

The idea of a hierarchy of human needs is complemented by two principles. First, as soon as one need, or level of needs, is satisfied, satisfaction is sought on the next higher level of needs. "Man is a wanting animal—as soon as one of his needs is satisfied, another appears in its place."[64] If, for example, the physiological needs for food and shelter are taken care of, then attention will turn to the need for safety and protection. If those needs are satisfied, then social needs will be the central concern.

62. Ibid., p. 40.
63. Ibid., p. 47.
64. Ibid., p. 36.

Second, satisfied needs do not function as motivators. Food cannot motivate a well-fed person to do something he or she is not inclined to do. That person can only be motivated by an appeal to some unsatisfied need.

On Maslow's needs-hierarchy theory, it turns out that the chief drawback to scientific management is not that it violates human nature, but that it no longer works in American society today. The routinization of work, the reduction of work to the level of the mindless repetition of prescribed mechanical motions, and the use of money as the sole source of motivation might have worked when both jobs and money were scarce. But given the motivation structure of human beings and the current social situation, it will no longer work. Physiological and safety needs are not at issue for most members of today's workforce. Given the state of the economy and the general level of education, jobs with adequate pay are not that hard to come by. Losing a job is not the ultimate tragedy, nor is quitting unthinkable—there is lateral job mobility, unemployment insurance, and a welfare system. Physiological and safety needs no longer function as strong motivators. Thus, to persist in the ways of scientific management is to violate the second principle of the needs hierarchy: satisfied needs no longer serve as motivators. McGregor's criticism of Taylor's scientific management is not that it is always inappropriate, but rather that it is inappropriate in today's society.[65]

In one sense, the problem with scientific management was that it was successful. "By making possible the satisfaction of lower-level needs, management has deprived itself of the ability to use the control devices on which the conventional assumptions of Theory X has taught it to rely: rewards, promises, incentives, or threats and other coercive devices."[66] Here Theory Y steps in where Theory X has made itself obsolete. For Theory Y assumes that "external control and the threat of punishment are not the only means of bringing about effort toward organiza-

65. Ibid., pp. 41-42.
66. Ibid.

tional objectives."[67] Work can be organized to provide intrinsic satisfaction for needs higher up the needs hierarchy. The possibility of accomplishment, recognition, responsibility, achievement, and personal growth will function as the new motivators on the Theory Y organization. Here human beings will commit themselves to the objectives of the organization because the achievement of those objectives will at the same time satisfy their own ego and self-actualization needs.

Theory Y assumptions about human nature thus lead, in today's social situation, to management on the basis of intrinsic rather than extrinsic rewards, to management by integration rather than coercion. Of course, the extrinsic rewards—like wages and benefits—must be present. But their very presence means that they will no longer function as motivators. Motivation will have to be drawn from intrinsic factors, factors associated with the work itself. Management will then operate through "the creation of conditions such that the members of the organization can achieve their own goals *best* by directing their efforts towards the success of the enterprise."[68] The needs of the individual and the needs of the organization are in fact compatible. The task of management is to integrate them, so that the realization of one is, at the same time, the realization of the other. In such a situation, authoritarian control will no longer be necessary, since "people will exercise self-direction and self-control in the achievement of organizational objectives to the degree that they are committed to those objectives."[69]

Management by integration has a number of implications for job design. Chief among them is that the divorce between the planning and the doing of work must be overcome. In Taylor's scientific management, management's task was to plan the work on the basis of "scientific principles" apart from any input or consultation with those who were to do the work.

67. Ibid., p. 47.
68. Ibid., p. 49.
69. Ibid., p. 56.

The work was defined and imposed from above; the ego and self-actualization needs of the worker were entirely ignored. "If the practices of 'scientific management' were deliberately calculated to thwart these needs—which, of course, they were not—they could hardly accomplish this purpose better than they do."[70] Management by integration, on the other hand, makes the worker a part of the job design process. The worker must be able to take ownership of his or her job within the overall scheme of the organization. "A position description is likely to become a straitjacket unless it is recognized to be a broad set of guidelines within which the individual literally makes his own job. The conception of an organization plan as a series of predetermined 'slots' into which individuals are selectively placed denies the whole idea of integration."[71] The objectives of a particular job should not be externally imposed, but mutually determined.[72] Of course, "it is far quicker to hand a subordinate a position description and inform him of his objectives for the coming period. If, however, the strategy is perceived as a way of managing which requires less policing of subordinates and which is accomplished by growth in managerial competence, the expenditure of time will be accepted and natural."[73]

Peter F. Drucker: Respect for Persons, Management by Objectives, and Responsible Work

For all its variety, management theory of the 1940s, 1950s, and 1960s was at least unified in its reaction to the shortcomings of the scientific management of Frederick Taylor. The chief oversight of scientific management was that it left the human factor out of the job design equation. As a direct result, jobs designed

70. Ibid., pp. 38-39.
71. Ibid., p. 67.
72. Ibid., p. 69.
73. Ibid., p. 76.

on the basis of Taylor's "scientific principles" produced negative reactions: apathy, resentment, anger, absenteeism, rate-setting, and grievances. Job designs which drew upon the laws of physics and the principles of mechanical engineering alone were ill-fitted to the human species. "On-the-job research has made it abundantly clear," writes Taylor's biographer, Sudhir Kakar, "that an exclusive preoccupation with revision of the technical system—the technology of the job, its physical and mechanical requirements—may have adverse affects on the social-psychological system of which the worker is also a part, and hence a negative influence on overall productivity."[74] After the Hawthorne Experiment, management turned to the so-called behavioral sciences of sociology and psychology for instruction in the dynamics of human motivation and for guidance in the appropriate design of jobs. To all appearances, management in both its theory and practice was becoming more enlightened, humane, and ethically sensitive.

Yet even after this shift, the scientific ideal of prediction and control remained firmly ensconced in managerial consciousness. The problem with scientific management is not that it attempts to control human behavior, but that it attempts to do so in ways that will no longer work. It must be abandoned on purely pragmatic grounds. Today's workers, McGregor notes, are much less dependent upon the employer than they were in Taylor's day. The tables have turned, and the employer is now just as dependent upon the employee as the employee is upon the employer.[75]

What is called for in this new situation, however, is not the rejection of control, but the development of new, more subtle methods of control. It is no longer a matter of getting people to do what they would rather not do through extrinsic rewards, but of motivating them through intrinsic rewards. The manager's task is to help employees "discover objectives consistent both with organizational requirements and with their own per-

74. Kakar, *Taylor*, p. 150.
75. McGregor, *Enterprise*, p. 25.

sonal needs."[76] The manager must learn to work with human nature, rather than against it. "We can improve our ability to control only if we recognize that control consists in selective adaption to human nature rather than in attempting to make human nature conform to our wishes."[77] This new approach—what McGregor calls "selective adaptation"[78]—requires sophisticated insight into human psychology. To manage well, the managers must be able to discern the unsatisfied needs of human individuals if they hope to harness those needs in jobs that benefit the company. If jobs can be designed to meet those needs, then people will perform on the job and higher productivity will be achieved, all other things being equal.

Something about this tack in management theory is attractive, even commendable. Jobs are now to be designed so that human beings can find personal fulfillment in them. Who can oppose this "humanization" of work? Yet there is something deeply disturbing about the way in which this new style of management—with its emphasis on indirect control via psychology—typically gets worked out. Peter Drucker, the ascendent management theorist of the last two decades, calls it "enlightened psychological despotism."[79] Drucker notes that the industrial psychology writers of today "use terms like 'self-fulfillment,' 'creativity,' and the 'whole man.' But what they talk and write about is control through psychological manipulation."[80] Management is no longer a matter of controlling people on the basis of their economic needs, but their psychological needs. By becoming the indispensable servant of the employees in their search for "self-fulfillment," the manager actually becomes their master. "Under this new psychological dispensation," Drucker writes, "persuasion replaces command. . . . But it is despotism nonetheless."[81]

76. Ibid., p. 152.
77. Ibid., p. 11.
78. Ibid., p. 31.
79. Drucker, *Management*, p. 243.
80. Ibid.
81. Ibid.

According to Drucker, the psychology-based approach to management ought to be rejected because it violates a basic ethical imperative: respect for other persons. "The work relationship has to be based on mutual respect."[82] Management by psychology has little, if any, respect for the personal integrity of the employee. Employees are assumed to be psychologically weak and needy people who require professional assistance from the manager for their self-actualization. In effect, the relationship between manager and employee gets converted into a relationship between client and therapist. Furthermore, the approach is ethically unacceptable because it is deceptive: it pretends that the purpose of work is to promote the psychological health of the employee, when in fact that is not true.

Second, the psychology-based approach is not only unethical, it is also unworkable simply because it requires omniscience on the part of the manager. The manager must have total command of the correct psychological theory (whichever one that is!) together with its applications to different individuals in different situations. But human beings make lousy gods, and the attempt to manage by psychological omniscience will inevitably lead to one blunder after another.[83]

Management must assume, Drucker maintains, that the motivation to work is already in place, that "there are at least a substantial number of people in the work force who want to achieve."[84] It is the task of management not to motivate people to work, but to make it possible for them to achieve at work while at the same time making their work effective in advancing the goals of the business. Although the task of management is conditioned by the motivational structure of human beings, the organization and direction of work must ultimately be set by organizational objectives rather than human psychology. Thus Drucker recommends "management by objective." Experience with human relations approach has shown that happy

82. Ibid., p. 244.
83. Ibid.
84. Ibid., p. 245.

workers do not necessarily make for more productive workers. It is possible to organize work so it satisfies psychological needs, and yet have the work itself remain ineffective. The humanization of work is a prerequisite, but not the goal of management. Human psychology sets the limits, but does not provide the substance of job design. Psychology can tell us how jobs should not be designed. Jobs should not be overly simplified, repetitious, or uniformly paced. Such jobs generally go against the grain of the human psyche. But psychology cannot tell us how jobs should be designed. It can rule out what is psychologically unfeasible, but it cannot specify what ought to be included. Neither can the scientific analysis of work, as practiced and promoted by Taylor, tell us how jobs should be designed. It can isolate the elements of work. It can identify the most efficient elements. It can eliminate the unnecessary elements. But it cannot instruct us in how the remaining elements ought to be put together.

Where, then, do we turn for guidance in the appropriate design of jobs? Drucker's answer is this: to the workers themselves. Workers must be made responsible for their own work.[85] And that means, among other things, that they must be involved in designing their own jobs. Not because such involvement will satisfy their ego need for control, making them happier and thus more productive—although it might—but because the workers possess a significant pool of knowledge and expertise in matters pertaining to their own jobs. They are often in the best position to determine exactly how the components of their work are best carried out. Contrary to the tendency of scientific management, which seeks to eliminate the knowledge and judgment of the workers, Drucker seeks to draw the workers' knowledge and judgment out in order to make their work effective. It is a matter, he writes, of making "use of the worker's knowledge and experience in the one area where he *is* the expert."[86]

To say that the worker must be made responsible is not to say that management must forfeit all authority, and that

85. Ibid., p. 267.
86. Ibid., p. 273.

workers have the final word in how all aspects of a corporation are run. But it does mean that organizations must be constructed "in which every man sees himself as a 'manager' and accepts for himself the full burden of what is basically managerial responsibility: responsibility for his own job and work group, for his contribution to the performance and results of the entire organization, and for the social task of the work community."[87]

To insist that the workers must be made responsible for their own work, and that organization ought to be structured accordingly, is, however, to challenge one of the basic principles of Taylor's scientific management: the strict division of labor between planning and doing. In the organization run by scientific management, management provides the brains, and labor the brawn. One plans the work; the other does the work. Drucker concedes that planning and doing are functionally distinct operations, but he denies that they should fall to different persons. "Planner and doer . . . need to be united in the same person. They cannot be divorced—or else planning will cease to be effective and will indeed become a threat to performance."[88] Taylor argued for the divorce between planning and doing by an appeal to the native ignorance of the workers. Yet he admitted—in a revealing slip of the pen—that "the development of a science to replace rule of thumb is in most cases by no means a formidable undertaking, and that it can be accomplished by ordinary, everyday men without any elaborate scientific training."[89]

The concept of responsible work and its corollary—the reintegration of planning and doing—have far-reaching implications for the relation between management and labor. No longer can that relation be construed as a variation on the relation between master and slave. Recognizing worker's knowledge and expertise gives them a measure of authority and a domain of responsibility in which to exercise that authority.

In order to carry out their work in a responsible and ef-

87. Ibid., p. 284.
88. Ibid., p. 271.
89. Taylor, *Principles*, p. 119.

fective manner, however, workers need three things, according to Drucker. They need to be able to draw upon the scientific and analytical studies of their field of work; they need regular feedback on their performance; and they need continuous learning. And this is precisely where management comes in. The primary task of management is to supply the workers with what they need in order to perform their tasks effectively. To rely on the expertise of the workers in their own domains of work is not to let each one wander off and do what is right in his or her own eyes. Granted, management is not omnicompetent; that is why it must rely on the expertise of the workers. But neither are the workers omnicompetent. To work effectively, they must be supported by the expertise of management. That expertise comes in the form of technical assistance, advice, information, communication, coordination with related elements of the organization, and guidance in making the work contribute to organizational objectives.

Because of the interdependence between labor and management, the traditional role of management within that organization must change. The "supervisor" must become the "assistant."[90] "The proper role of the supervisor is not supervision. It is knowledge, information, placing, training, teaching, standard-setting and guiding."[91] As an assistant to the workers, the manager is no longer in the position of the traditional supervisor—representing the interests of the company over and against the workers. Rather, through serving the workers in the performance of their tasks the manager at the same time advances the objectives of the organization.[92] If the workers want to achieve in their work, no conflict of interests in principle exists between the needs of the worker and the needs of the organization.

An example of how the symbiotic relation between labor and management can lead to effective production can be found in Zeiss Optical Works. Founded by Carl Zeiss in the

90. Drucker, *Management*, p. 281.
91. Ibid.
92. Ibid., p. 259.

nineteenth century, Zeiss has since set industry standards for excellence in the production of optical equipment. When Zeiss died in 1888, Ernst Abbe, a trained physicist, took charge of the company. Like his contemporary Frederick Taylor, Abbe thoroughly analyzed the processes involved in the production of optical glass and lenses. Unlike Taylor, however, he turned the actual design of the machines and manufacturing processes over to the workers themselves. They received technical assistance and advice from the scientists and engineers, but their jobs were not determined by the scientists and engineers. Abbe realized that the workers themselves possessed the kind of knowledge and expertise which made them the authorities on the final shape their work should take. "A craftsman is in control of his work" was not only his slogan, but his inviolable principle of job design.[93]

One need not turn to the long ago and far away, however, for examples of corporate excellence achieved through responsible work. IBM, Hewlitt-Packard, Herman Miller, Delta Airlines, and Preston Trucking—to name a few domestic corporations, plus the majority of Japanese corporations—are run on similar principles. The key, as Drucker puts it, is to see people as resources rather than problems, and to lead them rather than control them.

Robert Levering: The Ethics of Trust and the Politics of Fair Play in Great Workplaces

Although it is difficult to overestimate the popularity of Drucker's writings on management today, the temptation to manipulate employees on the basis of psychological insight is still with us. Tom Peters and Richard Waterman, for example, in their best-selling book *In Search of Excellence,* claim that one of the traits of outstanding companies is this: they have learned

93. Ibid., p. 304.

how to "take advantage" of human needs.[94] Companies run only on the traditional assumptions of Taylor's scientific management fail to excel because they have a faulty picture of human nature. They assume that human beings are "rational," that they make their decisions on the basis of economic utility alone. A more accurate, if humiliating, appraisal of human nature, however, would indicate that people are for the most part "irrational." They seek to fulfill conflicting needs. People need to "fit in"; at the same time they need to "stick out."[95] Furthermore, they fall for what is often inconsistent with their better judgment. They may assent to the evidence that their work is mediocre, and yet they are "suckers for a bit of praise."[96] "Man," claim Peters and Waterman, "is the ultimate study in paradox."[97] And excellent corporations have evidently learned how to capitalize on man's paradoxical nature.

Furthermore, excellent corporations have found that to elicit their employees' hard work and dedication to organizational objectives, it is not necessary that these paradoxical needs be actually satisfied. They only have to be satisfied in appearance. For example, people need to think of themselves as winners.[98] They need to be affirmed by others and to think of themselves as competent. Yet, "researchers studying motivation find that the prime factor is simply the self-perception among motivated individuals that they are doing well. Whether they are or not by any absolute standard doesn't seem to matter much."[99] The irrelevance of fact is also true for the human need for control. Various psychological studies "indicate that if people *think* they have even modest personal control over their destinies, they will persist at tasks."[100] Desired employee behavior can be

94. Thomas Peters and Robert H. Waterman Jr., *In Search of Excellence* (New York: Warner Books, 1982), pp. 60, 80.

95. Ibid., pp. 56ff.

96. Ibid., p. 54.

97. Ibid., p. 102.

98. Ibid.

99. Ibid., p. 58.

100. Ibid., p. 81.

elicited by an appeal to deep—and often inconsistent—needs. But the real satisfaction of those needs is not required. Illusory satisfaction will do. Since we are dealing with psychology, perception, not reality, is the issue. To praise an employee for a mediocre job may not be truthful, but it will get him or her to work harder the next time.

The issue of manipulating people on the job is a central concern in the latest work of Robert Levering on workplace quality. A labor reporter in the San Francisco area, Levering provides a fascinating account of what, from the employee's perspective, makes for excellence in companies. After co-authoring *The 100 Best Companies to Work for in America,* based on extensive interviews with employees, Levering selected twenty companies from that list for closer scrutiny. What was it that makes these companies so attractive to their employees? Why are their employees so enthusiastic about their work? The results of his investigations were recently published in a book entitled, appropriately enough, *A Great Place to Work.*

Levering initially assumed that the answers to his questions would lie in management policy. Perhaps he would be able to identify a set of traits common to all management policies of good places to work. But he soon discovered that if "companies are good workplaces, it is not because of any specific policies. Far more important than the specific policies is the nature of the *relationship* between the company and the employees."[101] Specific arrangements varied from one company to the other, but, he reports, "once I looked instead at the employee-employer *relationship,* I found it easy to characterize the essential quality of good workplaces. Just as love characterizes the attitude of both partners of a good marriage, *trust* characterizes the attitude of both sides of a good employment relationship."[102] Suggesting that "trust" captures the nature of the relationship between employees and employers in good workplaces was not a matter of

101. Robert Levering, *A Great Place to Work: What Makes Some Employers So Good—and Most So Bad* (New York: Random House, 1988), p. 22.

102. Ibid., p. 23.

wishful thinking or moral speculation by Levering. The theme of trust arose again and again in the many interviews he conducted on both sides of the relationship. "Employees at good workplaces constantly speak about how they 'believe,' 'have confidence in,' 'have faith in,' or simply 'trust' their employers. Similarly, managers at the same companies talked about how they 'trust,' 'can rely on,' and 'can depend on' their employees. There's an atmosphere of mutual trust that permeates good workplaces."[103]

This is not to say, however, that management policies are irrelevant. But however enlightened such policies may appear, they generally work only if they represent a natural extension of the undergirding relationship of trust and partnership between employer and employee. Job design policies sold to the employees as attempts to enrich their lives and make them happy, when in fact they are only schemes to boost productivity, are quickly recognized as disingenuous. They invite suspicion and destroy trust. Such is the fatal flaw of the human relations school of management, for "beneath the guise of making people feel better," Levering points out, "lurks the real goal: increasing productivity."[104]

An example of the importance of the fit between management policy and the ethics of trust is found in a tale of two insurance companies' experience with job enrichment. Both of these companies were large Midwestern insurance agencies. Both tried to improve clerical worker productivity through job enrichment. One met with resounding success; the other was forced to admit defeat. What made the difference? According to Levering's account, the successful company had a genuine trust in its employees and interest in their welfare. The other was only willing to pretend that it did if it would enhance productivity. Because the successful company trusted its employees and saw them as a resource, it involved them in every phase of redesigning their jobs—not to make them feel as if

103. Ibid.
104. Ibid., p. 101.

they had some control over their jobs, but to actually give them control over their jobs. The unsuccessful company, on the other hand, provided only token forms of participation. The new job design was in fact imposed from the top down—in the employee's "best interest" of course. Moreover, the underlying relationship of trust and goodwill in the successful company was demonstrated by the consistency of its policies. For instance, employees were assured that no one would lose his or her job as a result of the restructuring of work. Furthermore, any increase in productivity would be rewarded by a pay increase. The unsuccessful company neither guaranteed job security nor did it adjust pay to productivity. It treated these as separate matters, when in fact they all hang together. Third, and most important, says Levering, the unsuccessful agency "claimed that the principal objective of the job-enrichment program was to increase worker happiness. The company assumed that if the employees were happier with their jobs, they would be absent less often, stay with the company longer, and work harder."[105] In the successful agency "worker happiness was not on the agenda. Improved service was the primary objective, and increased productivity was secondary."[106] As it turned out, the successful agency, Northwestern Mutual, "was more successful at achieving worker happiness than was the Chicago insurance company, whose specific aim was to make the workers happy."[107] Why? First of all, because

> It wasn't really true that the primary objective of the Chicago job-enrichment effort was worker happiness, despite such claims. Only a naive fool would believe that a big company would spend thousands of dollars merely to help workers feel better about their jobs. The top management presumably bought the underlying thesis of all motivational management techniques—that self-actualized workers will be more highly motivated workers and will work harder. So job enrichment is

105. Ibid., p. 99.
106. Ibid., p. 60.
107. Ibid.

a means to higher productivity; it is not an end in and of itself."[108]

The workers, however, knew that they were being manipulated and resented it. "Northwestern, on the other hand, told people honestly from the outset what it intended to do—and why. It wanted people to work smarter, if not harder. It wanted them to engage their minds and share their knowledge and experience to help improve service. This straightforward approach helps explain why employees there felt better about the changes in their jobs."[109] Moreover, "Northwestern Mutual did *not* involve employees in redesigning their own jobs to raise their morale and level of motivation. They did it because it made sense. The company genuinely believed employees had significant contributions to make. And the employees' ideas did make a difference."[110]

Here the crucial difference in orientation emerges. Levering claims that "where trust exists, the employer believes the workers want to be productive and participate fully in the enterprise."[111] Note: it is not that the employer believes that the workers want to fulfill, actualize, or realize themselves, or in some other way use work as a means for the satisfaction of their personal needs. Rather, the employer assumes that they want to be productive, and that they want to apply their talents and abilities to some meaningful task. Management then need make no secret of its goals. Rather than viewing people as psychologically incomplete, grasping, or using work for the fulfillment of personal needs, it sees them as the locus and repository of talents and knowledge, as people with skill, imagination, and expertise. It sees them, in other words, as potential contributors. Trust on the part of management means "believing that there is usually someone close to the problem who is able to solve it, or someone who is close to an opportunity who is able to exploit

108. Ibid.
109. Ibid.
110. Ibid., p. 61.
111. Ibid., p. 24.

it," according to Hugh De Pree, past President and CEO of Herman Miller, the design leader in the office furniture industry.[112] In his forty years of business experience, he found that "people are usually anxious to perform and will do more than you expect if they have the information they need, understand the direction and constraints, and believe they have the freedom to fail."[113] The task of management, then, is not to pander to workers' psychological needs to get them to do something beneficial for the organization, but to give them a place and means to make their strengths effective for the organization.

We can now see how the ethics of trust will lead quite naturally to the politics of democratic justice. A company built on mistrust will rely on the raw exercise of power—or the more subtle techniques of control—in the pursuit of its organizational objectives. It will assume the political shape of a miniature tyranny. The freedoms its employees enjoy on the outside must be checked at the front door. On the other hand, a company built on the presumption of trust will resemble a democracy. Because it perceives people as a resource to be developed rather than a threat to be contained, this company will make the workers responsible for their own work. But to be responsible for their own work, the workers must possess certain freedoms—the freedom to have their say without fearing recrimination, the freedom to get information that relates to their work, and freedom from unfair or arbitrary treatment. Thus workers' freedom to pursue their work in a responsible way must be protected by the economic equivalant of the Bill of Rights—the right to free speech, the right to free press, and the right to due process.

In the great workplaces Levering examined, trust and respect for employees translated directly into a passion for openness and fair play. Management policies born of fear and suspicion tended to breed dictatorial regimes where management lords it over a body of sullen employees who have been reduced

112. Hugh De Pree, *Business as Unusual* (Zeeland, MI: Herman Miller, 1986), p. 3.

113. Ibid.

to the status of compliant oxen. Their gifts and abilities remain both unwelcome and untapped. Management policies flowing from a spirit of trust and respect, on the other hand, were able to create the political conditions under which human gifts could be freely developed and responsibly applied, where innovation was encouraged, and where bold efforts at problem-solving were rewarded. Financial records were made accessible to all, "town meetings" were held for freewheeling discussion of company policy from the chief executive on down to the custodial staff, lines of communications between the employees of all departments were opened; employees elected representatives on every decision-making body affecting them; employee compensation was tuned to profitability, and mechanisms were set in place for handling grievances in ways that would not jeopardize employment or promotion.

The Bottom Line: Must We Choose Between People and Profits?

Work is a social place where we can employ our gifts in service to others. God calls us to work because he wants us to love our neighbors in a concrete way. In fact, John Calvin contends, nothing pleases God more than when we apply ourselves diligently to our callings in the service of the human community.[114] The practical implication we drew from the Christian concept of work as calling was simple and direct: jobs ought to be designed so that we can in fact apply ourselves—our whole selves—to our calling. Not that our work on the job ought to take up all our time; for we have other callings to attend to as well. Only that our jobs ought to engage us as whole persons, as creatures with high-level capacities for thought, imagination, and responsible choice as well as motor abilities. Our jobs ought to be places where the whole person can respond to the call of God, where,

114. Calvin, *Harmony of the Evangelists*, p. 144.

as Dorothy Sayers put it, the job represents "the full expression of the worker's faculties, the thing in which he finds spiritual, mental, and bodily satisfaction, and the medium in which he offers himself to God."[115] In short, the job ought to be a place of responsibility.

Our account of the development of management theory led us to the same conclusion, shorn of the theological gloss. Of course our story was incomplete. A number of options were being explored at any one point in the development of management theory; and many of the past theories continue to represent live options today. One can still detect a lot of Taylor, and a mix of Mayo, Herzberg, and McGregor in the largely eclectic management styles of the work world today. But it is significant that the concept of responsible work arose within the course of pragmatic reflection upon managerial experience itself, receiving its most forceful articulation in the work of Peter Drucker. It was not imported.

Yet we can anticipate the first question that will come to the lips of those who actually run a business. In competitive times like these, can we afford to make ourselves vulnerable through trust? Can we risk making the workers responsible for their own work? Can we enter into a genuine relationship of partnership with our employees? Granted, people will take more satisfaction in their work if we do. But we are not, after all, running a social service agency. We must make a profit in order to survive. It is all well, and perhaps good, for theologians and humanistically-inclined management theorists to think about how jobs ought to be designed in the best of all possible worlds, but those of us in the business world are playing hardball with the big boys.

Even some theologians think that the ethical demands which follow from the Christian concept of work are, in some sense, unreasonable. Should we suggest, asks lay theologian Jacques Ellul, that the Christian employer "grant conditions of

115. Dorothy Sayers, *Creed or Chaos?* (New York: Harcourt, Brace, 1947), p. 53.

work which will satisfy his employees? In the competitive system of free enterprise changes or improvements of this kind might well drive him out of business. Perhaps the Christian employer ought to be prepared for this, but if it happened he would simply be contributing in the last analysis to a rise in unemployment."[116]

This worry, however, assumes that the concern for people and the need for profits are always at loggerheads; that humanizing work makes a company less competitive; that maximizing productivity means tight, top-down control; that maximizing efficiency means task specialization. Many empirical studies, however, suggest the contrary. The writers of the 1973 report to the Department of Health, Education, and Welfare entitled *Work in America* contend that "the redesign of work . . . *can* lower such business costs as absenteeism, tardiness, turnover, labor disputes, sabotage, and poor quality, all of which is to the advantage of employer and consumers. The evidence suggests that meeting the higher needs of workers can, perhaps, increase productivity from 5% to 40%."[117] Such evidence shows that "not only can work be redesigned to make it more satisfying but that significant increases in productivity can also be obtained."[118]

To show that nice guys don't always finish last, Levering points to a comparative study conducted by Patrick McVeigh, a stock analyst for Franklin Research and Development. Taking the seventy publicly owned companies from the list of Levering's earlier book, *The 100 Best Companies to Work For,* McVeigh compared their financial performance to Standard & Poor's 500. In terms of earnings per share, the best companies to work for were more than twice as profitable as Standard & Poor's 500; between the years of 1975 and 1984, the stock price of the best companies appreciated at nearly three times the rate of the 500. In another study of the publicly owned companies of the 100 best

116. Ellul, *Ethics,* p. 460.
117. *Work in America,* p. 27.
118. Ibid., p. 94.

list conducted for Dean Witter Reynolds, Theodore A. Brown and Thomas Van Dyck found that in the period from 1981 to 1985 the best companies earned 17.69 percent more in average compounded total return than the Standard & Poor 500. They concluded that "the evidence is strong that the companies that treat their workers well benefit on the bottom line."[119]

The flip side of this positive correlation between people and profits is the fact that when human limits are transgressed in the name of profits, productivity often goes down. What appears on paper to be the most efficient way to run business may not be the most effective, once human beings are plugged into the formulas. "Efficiency" can be terribly inefficient. Robert O. Snelling, president of one of the largest job search agencies in America, speaks of a case in his own business where less efficiency made for more effectiveness. "At one time in our company we were working our national marketing consultants very hard. Travel was up to 80 percent of their time, with most of them away from home every night. We had divorces, job turnover, poor productivity, and an identifiable lack of results." The solution to the problem was not to make the consultants work harder and travel more, but less. "We reduced travel to a maximum of 40 percent. Turnover is virtually gone, productivity is at an all-time high, and results are gratifying in every respect."[120]

This is but one instance of the rule that the long-term best interests of the company are often better served by treating employees with human decency and respect. The values associated with expediency, Robert Roy points out in his book, *Cultures of Management,* are "immediate and perceptible." The values associated with decency, on the other hand, are "diffuse and impalpable." Nevertheless, in the long run the "economics of decency yields the best return to the organization."[121] To realize

119. Levering, *Great Place to Work,* p. 260.

120. Robert O. Snelling, *The Right Job* (New York: Viking, 1987), p. 44.

121. Robert Roy, *The Cultures of Management* (Baltimore: Johns Hopkins University Press, 1977), p. 358.

this, Roy writes, and to take it to heart, is to know that "for the management of human organizations the Golden Rule is the best doctrine ever expounded."[122]

Live Options for Job Design: Restoring a Sense of Vocation to Work

Up to this point our treatment of the problem of the appropriate design of human work has been largely historical. Our story began with the systematic attempt by scientific management to eliminate responsibility from human work and place it entirely in the hands of a managerial elite. It ended with the growing recognition of employees as valuable resources, able to make contributions to the realization of organizational goals through the responsible application of their knowledge and expertise. With more responsibility for the planning, organizing, and controlling of work being given to the employees themselves, the role of manager has been reinterpreted accordingly: from supervisor to facilitator, from director to assistant, from driver to leader. "Indeed," comments John R. Schermerhorn, Professor of Management at the Southern University of Illinois at Carbondale, "managers are increasingly being expected to focus their attention on creating 'work environments' within which people can perform on their own initiative and with a minimum of outside control."[123]

It is time to sum up the positive results of our historical overview of the development of American management theory in a way that makes clear what are the contemporary options for the redesign of human work. We begin with a restatement of the normative implications of the Christian idea of vocation: work is to be a social place for the responsible exercise of a sig-

122. Ibid., p. 359.

123. John R. Schermerhorn, Jr., *Management for Productivity*, 3rd ed. (New York: John Wiley & Sons, 1989), p. 230.

nificant range of human talents and abilities in the service of one's neighbor. To this norm we add one comment on human existence: it is mutifaceted. Human beings are not one-dimensional. The created order of human life has numerous dimensions—physical, psychological, social, ethical, and political. The appropriate design of human work must seek to realize the norm of vocation in a way that addresses each of these dimensions of human existence as they pertain to the job. Scientific management violated the norm of vocation in two respects. First of all, it eliminated the element of responsibility from human work; second, it reduced human work to the repetition of simplified physical movements—something any well-designed machine could do. Thus it ignored, to its peril, the multifaceted character of human existence. The psychological reaction to the "scientific" organization of work as if human beings were machines was extremely negative.

What are the contemporary options for restoring a sense of vocation to work emptied of responsibility and talent? The most recent developments in management theory and practice are encouraging. Many companies, recognizing the need for making work a place where their employees can freely exercise a wide range of abilities, have restructured jobs accordingly. And management theorists have begun to capture these changes in new concepts of job design. In bringing this final chapter to a close, we will briefly review these concepts. Those of us responsible for the work of others may find these concepts helpful in bringing the structure of that work closer to the demands of the idea of vocation.

In the previous section of this chapter we argued that building more freedom and responsibility into jobs rarely harms productivity, and usually enhances it. But here we are not recommending these changes in job design on the basis of pragmatic considerations alone. Rather, we are recommending these changes because employees are entitled to such jobs. Created in the image of God, endowed with a variety of gifts, and called to exercise those gifts in the service of neighbor, they are *entitled* to a social place where they can pursue their calling. That is why

Pope John XXIII spoke of the appropriate design of human work as a matter of *justice*, not prudence.[124]

Contemporary management theorists often think of the structure of the content of a job as extending along two axes. The horizontal axis represents the range of tasks performed; the vertical axis represents the degree of freedom and responsibility in the performance of those tasks. Scientific management advocated a severe restriction of job content in both respects—the fewer tasks and less freedom, the better. The resulting jobs, however, in the words of a woman interviewed in Studs Terkel's *Working*, were "not big enough" for people.[125] They must be expanded through what is known as "horizontal" and "vertical loading." Horizontal loading expands the scope of tasks performed in a particular job. Common techniques of such loading are "job rotation" and "job enlargement." Job enlargement increases the number and variety of tasks involved in a job by adding tasks that come before and after a simplified task. Instead of performing just one task in the assembly of a computer keyboard, I might assemble the entire keyboard through an extended series of tasks. Job rotation does not actually involve the redesign of a particular job. Rather, it achieves task variety by rotating different people through a particular job on a regular basis. Mornings I might assemble keyboards; afternoons I might work on monitors.

Although horizontal loading represents a step in the right direction, it does not guarantee that a significant range of abilities will be employed on a job. It may only add to the sequence of mechanical motions. Nor does horizontal loading reintegrate the missing element of responsibility. It only increases the number of tasks. The responsible exercise of a significant range of talents and abilities comes with vertical loading, where the employee acquires a greater measure of freedom and responsibility for the planning, organizing, and quality control of his or her own work. Here higher-order skills are

124. Pope John XXIII, *Mater et Magistra*, sec. 82 and 83.
125. Studs Terkel, *Working* (New York: Pantheon Books, 1972), p. 521.

called forth and developed: information must be assimilated, tasks understood, problems solved, efforts coordinated, work planned, feedback assessed.

With the assumption of the traditional managerial functions of planning, organizing, and control, employees must also be in a position to coordinate their efforts with others working on directly related concerns. It is quite natural at this point to take the next step in the redesign of jobs and form "work groups" or "production teams." Work is, after all, a social effort. It involves the coordinated efforts of a number of people. As long as the planning, organizing, and control of work is conducted from the top down, it is possible for individuals to work in relative isolation—their efforts being orchestrated by the manager above them. But once the functions of planning, organizing, and control shift to the employee, coordination best occurs horizontally through the formation of work groups with a common task. Once the task and goals of the work group are established, that group can take over many of the prerogatives traditionally reserved for management. Carl Anderson, Professor of Management at the University of North Carolina at Chapel Hill, points out that such groups "should be able to decide how to do the work, the methods they will use, work pace, the priorities of jobs, and who will be assigned to what jobs."[126] In other words, once the group has a clear conception of its task, it plans, organizes, and controls its own work, adjusting its efforts in the light of continuous feedback.

The formation of work groups—now associated with the "socio-technical" approach to the design of work—not only brings human work closer to the norm of vocation, it has often given a dramatic boost to productivity as well. Many management theorists have argued that the socio-technical approach is the wave of the future because it best comports with new market demands for flexibility, rapid response, creative problem-solving, and direct client relationships. Moreover, it is designed to

126. Carl R. Anderson, *Management: Skills, Functions and Organization Performance* (Dubuque, IA: Wm. C. Brown, 1984), p. 536.

take advantage of the new opportunities afforded by technology. Take the experience of Shenandoah Life Insurance Company, for instance. It once took twenty-seven days and the separate attention of thirty-two clerks in three different departments to process a typical policy conversion in this company. But after organizing its clerks into groups of five to seven, allowing the groups to perform the functions of all three departments, and redesigning the computer system, the average time for processing a case was reduced to two days. Tektronix Inc. recently converted from an assembly line approach in its metals division to a team approach. One of the teams now produces as many pieces in three days as it took the assembly line to produce in fourteen days with twice as many people. Self-managing work groups have had such a good track record that a number of major American corporations are turning to them as they prepare for the future. At its new Saturn plant in Tennessee, General Motors intends to take the team approach as well, using autonomous work groups of six to fifteen people to produce the major automotive assembly units.[127]

Another form of cooperative work effort which raises the level of employee participation and responsibility is the "quality circle." Developed in concept by American management theorists decades ago and implemented by the Japanese with huge success after the Second World War, quality circles have made a recent comeback within American companies. A quality circle is a group of representatives from a particular production area or service division that meets together for an hour on a weekly or bi-weekly basis. Its task is to identify, rank, analyze, and solve work-related problems. Where such circles have been implemented, significant savings and improvements in productivity have often been noted, not to mention increased employee involvement and commitment to the goals of the enterprise. As with work groups, companies with quality circles treat employees as valuable resources rather than potential problems. This basic attitude of trust and respect seeks ways of giving em-

127. Schermerhorn, *Management*, pp. 242-43.

ployees more responsibility for their own work and a greater say in what they do.

Thus far we have discussed only the organization of "job content"—the specification of tasks to be performed on the job together with the degree of responsibility for those tasks. The other half of job design pertains to what is known as "job context"—the conditions under which the tasks of a job are performed. In our discussion of Levering's work on great workplaces we were already introduced to several important issues in the design of the job context. Great workplaces, Levering claims, are characterized by trust and fair play. Here he is referring to the ethical and political elements of the job context. What Levering found is that employees flourish in a context of trust and respect. In great workplaces there are tangible expressions of goodwill in open lines of communication and freedom of information. Furthermore, employees flourish where their rights are protected. Great workplaces make good on their commitments to fair play by setting up mechanisms of redress.

Another aspect of job context pertains to the relation between the employee's work life and non-work life. We recall that work is not all there is to life. In fact, work is not all there is to one's vocation. Because one of the chief tensions between demands of work and the requirements of non-work life comes down to time, the scheduling of work is an important element of the job context. Recently there has been a move away from the rigid nine-to-five work schedule. More flexibility is being built into jobs in order to make them more accommodating to the rest of an employee's life and commitments. Flextime, for instance, establishes certain core hours when all employees must be on the job—say nine to eleven and one to three. To them it adds three flexible two-hour modules: seven to nine, eleven to one, and three to five. Employees are then allowed to choose any two of these flexible two-hour components in order to make up an eight-hour day which best fits their daily routine. For instance, one could work from seven to three and get off work early to meet the kids at home after school, or one could work from nine to seven with a two-hour midday break for appointments and errands. Other companies have introduced a "4-40" schedule, where employees put in forty hours in four days, making every weekend a three-day affair.

With the advent of personal computers, modems, and fax machines it has also been possible to introduce "flexplace." Knowledge workers—people who manipulate data and information—no longer need to come into the office every day. They can work on their computers at home and "telecommute." As long as they reach certain levels of productivity, they can organize their work schedule and pace at will. This makes it possible to stay in touch with life at home, and yet work at the same time. Another innovation which has built in more flexibility is "job sharing"—where two people share the same full-time job. This allows many people to work and meet family obligations as well. One company, especially attuned to the life schedules of those with school-age children, has a job-sharing plan where parents can work from 9:30 to 2:30, at which point high-school students come in and work until 5:30.

Each of the new concepts in job design we have reviewed represents some improvement in the structure of human work. Some call for an increase in the level of freedom and responsibility; some provide for an expansion of the range of skills and abilities; some make work more amenable to employees' nonwork life. It doesn't follow, however, that all of them ought to be implemented in every business situation. Flextime will not work in some companies; the 4-40 schedule will not work in others. Moreover, not every employee can handle a marked increase in responsibility. For some that would only produce a great deal of anxiety; others have enough responsibilities outside of work. Management has learned that specific programs are just that—specific. One now reads of the "contingency" approach to management. This approach realizes that what works in one situation will not necessarily work in all situations. It recommends that managers proceed on a case-by-case basis, drawing on a full range of options as the need may be. The contingency approach represents, I think, the better part of wisdom. What makes a particular managerial solution work in one situation often depends on a number of variables which will change from one situation to the next. But it doesn't follow from the contingency approach that "anything goes." In all situations the aim of the appropriate design of human work remains the same: making a job the kind of place where a vocation can be pursued.

Bibliography

Adeney, Bernard. "Work: Necessity, Vocation and Strategy." *Radix* 15 (January/February 1984): 13-15.

Agrell, Goeran. *Work, Toil, and Sustenance: An Examination of the View of Work in the New Testament, Taking into Consideration Views Found in Old Testament, Intertestamental, and Early Rabbinic Writings.* Lund: Verbum, Hakan Ohlssons, 1976.

Alber, Antone. "Job Enrichment for Profit." *Fundamental Readings in Modern Management.* 2nd ed. Dubuque, IA: Wm. C. Brown, 1983.

Alexander, John F. "Kingdom Work: Why We Must Begin Thinking About Our Jobs in a Christian Way." *The Other Side* (August 1979): 10-14.

Almen, Louis T. *The Doctrine of Vocation in Luther and Calvin.* Princeton: Princeton Theological Seminary Press, 1955.

Althaus, Paul. *The Ethics of Martin Luther.* Philadelphia: Fortress, 1972.

Anderson, Carl R. *Management: Skills, Functions and Organization Performance.* Dubuque, IA: Wm. C. Brown, 1984.

Anderson, Nels. *Dimensions of Work: The Sociology of a Work Culture.* New York: David McKay, 1964.

Anthony, P. D. *The Ideology of Work.* London: Tavistock Publications, 1977.

Antonides, Harry. *Industrial Democracy, Illusion and Promise.* Toronto: Christian Labour Association of Canada, 1980.

———. "A Christian Perspective on Work and Labour Relations." *The Guide* 35, 5-7 (July/October 1987).

Arendt, Hannah. *The Human Condition.* Chicago: University of Chicago Press, 1958.

Argyris, Chris. *Personality and Organization.* New York: Harper, 1957.

———. "Is Capitalism the Culprit?" *Organizational Dynamics* (Spring 1978): 21-37.

Aristotle. *Nicomachean Ethics.* Indianapolis: Hackett, 1985

———. *Politics.* Oxford: Oxford University Press, 1958.

Aronowitz, Stanley. *False Promises: The Shaping of American Working Class Consciousness.* New York: McGraw-Hill, 1973.

Attwood, David. *The Spade and the Thistle: The Place of Work Today.* Bramcote, Notts.: Grove Books, 1980.

St. Augustine. *The City of God.* Garden City, NY: Doubleday, 1958.

———. "On the Morals of the Catholic Church." Vol. 4 of *The Nicene and Post-Nicene Fathers.* Grand Rapids: Eerdmans, 1956.

———. *On the Trinity.* Vol. 3 of *Nicene and Post-Nicene Fathers of the Christian Church.* Phillip Schaff, ed. New York: The Christian Literature Co., 1886-1890.

———. "On the Work of Monks." Vol. 16 of *The Fathers of the Church,* Roy J. Defarrari, ed. New York: Fathers of the Church, 1952.

Bacon, Leonard, ed. *Select and Practical Writings of Richard Baxter.* New Haven: Durrie and Peck, 1955.

Bainton, Roland. *Here I Stand: A Life of Martin Luther.* New York: Abingdon, 1950.

———. "Calvin, Beza, and the Protestant Work Ethic." *The Reformed Journal* 32 (April 1982): 18-21.

Barnette, Henlee H. *Christian Calling and Vocation.* Grand Rapids: Baker Book House, 1965.

Barrett, Lois. "Make Your Labor Christian." *The Other Side* (March/April 1976): 53-57.

Barth, Karl. "Vocation," *Church Dogmatics.* III, 4, 52, pt. 2. Edinburgh: T. & T. Clark, 1961.

———. *The Priority of Labor.* New York: Paulist Press, 1982.

Baum, Gregory. *Work and Religion.* New York: Seabury, 1980.

Baxardall, Rosalyn, et al. *America's Working Women.* New York: Random House, 1976.

Bayne, Paul. *Exposition of Ephesians.* Reprint. Evansville: Sovereign Grace, 1953.

Beach, Waldo. *The Christian Life.* Richmond: CLC Press, 1966.

Beardslee, William A. *Human Achievement and Divine Vocation in the Message of Paul.* London: SCM Press, 1961.

Beer, Michael and Driscoll, James. "Strategies for Change." *Improving Life at Work.* J. Richard Hackman and J. Lloyd Suttle, eds. Santa Monica, CA: Goodyear, 1977.

Bellah, Robert N., et al. *Habits of the Heart: Individualism and Commitment in American Life.* New York: Harper & Row, 1986.

Bendix, Reinhard. *Work and Authority in Industry: Ideologies of Management in the Course of Industrialization.* Berkeley: University of California Press, 1974.

Berch, Bettina. *The Endless Day: The Political Economy of Women and Work.* New York: Harcourt Brace Jovanovich, 1982.

Bernbaum, John A., and Steer, Simon M. *Why Work? Careers and Employment in Biblical Perspective.* Grand Rapids: Baker Book House, 1986.

Bernstein, Harry and Joanne. *Industrial Democracy in Twelve Countries.* Department of Labor, Monograph No. 2, 1979.

Bernstein, Paul. "Necessary Elements for Effective Worker Participation in Decision Making." *Journal of Economic Issues* 10 (1976): 490-552.

———. *Workplace Democratization: Its Internal Dynamics.* New Brunswick, NJ: Transactions Books, 1980.

Bert, Ivar, et al. *Managers and Work Reform.* New York: Free Press, 1978.

Bieber, I. "Disorders of the Work Function." In *Dynamics of Work and Marriage,* Vol. 16 of *Science and Psychoanalysis.* J. H. Masserman, ed. New York: Grune & Stratton, 1970.

Billing, Einar. *Our Calling.* Trans. Conrad Bergendoff. Philadelphia: Fortress, 1964.

Bizer, Roland Theodore. *Luther and Calvin on Vocation.* B.D. Thesis, Eden Theological Seminary, 1961.

Blackler, F. H. M., and Brown, C. A. "Job Redesign and Social Change: Case Studies at Volvo." In *Changes in Working Life.* K. D. Duncan, M. M. Gruneberg, and D. Wallis, eds. New York: John Wiley & Sons, 1980.

Blauner, Robert. "Work Satisfaction and Industrial Trends in Modern Society." In *Labor and Trade Unionism: An Interdisciplinary Reader.* Walter Galenson and S. M. Lipset, eds. New York: John Wiley & Sons, 1960.

Bleakley, David. *In Place of Work . . . The Sufficient Society.* London: SCM Press, 1981.

"The Blue-Collar Blues." *Newsweek,* 17 May 1971, 80-82, 86.

Blumberg, P. *Industrial Democracy: The Sociology of Participation.* New York: Schocken, 1969.

Board, Stephan. "The Changing Character of Work." *Christianity Today* (August 1972): 26-29.

Boggs, Wade H. *All Ye Who Labor: A Christian Interpretation of Daily Work.* Richmond, VA: John Knox Press, 1961.

Bolles, Richard. *The New Quick Job-Hunting Map.* Berkeley: Ten Speed Press, 1985.

———. *What Color is Your Parachute?* Berkeley: Ten Speed Press, 1989.

Bonhoeffer, Dietrich. "Vocation." In *Ethics.* New York: Macmillan, 1964.

Boone, Louis, and Bowen, Donald. *The Great Writings in Management and Organizational Behavior.* Tulsa, OK: Petroleum Publishing Co., 1980.

Borne, Etienne, and Henry, Francois. *A Philosophy of Work.* London: Sheed and Ward, 1938.

Bose, Keith W. "Searching for Meaning in Work: The Loss of Purpose." *Washington Post,* 6 February 1972.

Boulding, Kenneth. "In Praise of Inefficiency." *AGB Reports* 20 (January 1978).

Bourg, Carroll J. "Work and/or Job in Advanced Industrialized Societies." *Soundings* (Spring 1974): 113-25.

Bower, Marvin. *The Will to Manage.* New York: McGraw-Hill, 1966.

Bradley, John David. *Christian Career Planning: Finding the Place God Has for You.* Portland, OR: Multnomah Press, 1977.

Braverman, Harry. *Labor and Monopoly Capital: The Degradation of Work in the Twentieth Century.* New York: Monthly Review Press, 1974.

Bray, John S. "The Value of Works in the Theology of Calvin and Beza." *Sixteenth Century Journal* 4 (October 1973): 77-86.

Breakwell. *The Quiet Rebel: How to Survive as a Woman and Businessperson.* New York: Grove Press, 1986.

Breen, T. H. "The Non-Existent Controversy: Puritan and Anglican Attitudes on Work and Wealth 1600-1640." *Church History* 35 (1966): 273-87.

Brody, David. *Workers in Industrial America: Essays on the Twentieth Century Struggle.* Oxford: Oxford University Press, 1980.

Brunner, Emil. *The Divine Imperative.* New York: Macmillan, 1937.

———. *Christianity and Civilization.* New York: Scribner's Sons, 1949.

Bruno, Gordiano. *The Expulsion of the Triumphant Beast.* Arthur D. Imerti, trans. New Brunswick, NJ: Rutgers University Press, 1964.

Buckley, Jack. "Calvin's View of Work." *Radix* 15 (January/February 1984): 8-12, 28.

Calhoun, Robert Lowry. *God and the Common Life.* New York and London: Scribner's Sons, 1935.

Calvin, John. *Sermons of M. John Calvin upon the Epistle of Saint Paul to the Galatians.* London: Lucas Harison and George Bishop, 1574.

———. *A Commentary on the Harmony of the Evangelists.* William Pringle, trans. Grand Rapids: Eerdmans, 1949.

———. *The Institutes of the Christian Religion.* Philadelphia: Westminster, 1960.

———. *Sermons on the Epistle to the Ephesians.* Edinburgh: Banner of Truth Trust, 1973.

Carnoy, Martin, and Shearer, Derek. *Economic Democracy.* Armonk, NY: M. E. Sharpe, 1980.

Carter, Michael. *Into Work.* Baltimore: Penguin, 1966.
Case, Thomas. *Two Sermons Lately Preached.* London, 1642.
Catherwood, Fred. *On the Job: The Christian 9 to 5.* Grand Rapids: Zondervan, 1983.
Cawdrey, Robert. *A Table Alphabeticall of English Wordes.* 1604. Reprint. New York: W. J. Johnson, 1970.
Chafe, William. *The American Woman: Her Changing Social, Economic, and Political Roles.* New York: Oxford University Press, 1972.
Charnock, Stephen. *Discourses upon the Existence and Attributes of God,* 1680 Reprint. New York: Robert Carter and Bros., 1873.
Chenu, Marie Dominique. *The Theology of Work: An Exploration.* Lilian Soiron, trans. Chicago: Henry Regnery, 1966.
Chew, Peter T. "Why Do We Need to Work?" *The National Observer,* 5 July 1971.
Clark, Martin E. *Choosing Your Career: The Christian's Decision Manual.* Grand Rapids: Baker Book House, 1981.
Coles, Robert. "On the Meaning of Work." *The Atlantic* (October 1971): 103-4.
Connell, Father Francis. *Business and the Liberal Arts.* Jamaica and New York: St. John's University Press, 1962.
Coontz, Stephanie, and Henderson, Peta, eds. *Women's Work, Men's Property: The Origins of Gender and Class.* London: Verso, 1986.
Cooper, C. M. and Clarke, J. A. *Employment, Economics, and Technology: The Impact of Technological Change in the Labour Market.* New York: St. Martin's Press, 1982.
Corlett, E. N. "Problems of Work Organization Under Conditions of Technological Change." *Changes in Working Life.* K. D. Duncan, M. M. Gruneberg, and D. Wallis, eds. New York: John Wiley & Sons, 1980.
Cotton, John. "The Christian Calling." *The Puritans.* Vol 1. Perry Miller and Theodore Johnson, eds. New York: Harper & Row, 1963.
Creedman, Nancy and Michael. "Angst, the Curse of the Working Class." *Human Behavior* (November/December 1972).
Dahl, Gordon J. "Work, Play and Worship: Toward a New Moral Economy." *Leisure Today* (November/December 1974): 38-40.
Davies, Margery. *Women's Place is at the Typewriter.* Philadelphia: Temple University Press, 1982.
Davis, Louis E. "Toward a Theory of Job Design." *Journal of Industrial Engineering* 8 (1957): 305-9.
———. *Job Satisfaction Research: The Post-Industrial View.* Los Angeles: Institute of Industrial Relations, University of California, 1971.

Davis, Louis E. and Canter, R. R. "Job Design Research." *Journal of Industrial Engineering* 7 (1956): 275-82.

Davis, Louis E., and Taylor, J. C. *The Design of Jobs.* Baltimore: Penguin, 1972.

Davis, Louis E., and Werling, R. "Job Design Factors." *Occupational Psychology* 24 (1960).

de Grazia, Sebastion. *Of Time, Work, and Leisure.* Garden City, NY: Doubleday Anchor, 1962.

DeKoster, Lester. *Work, the Meaning of Your Life: A Christian Perspective.* Grand Rapids: Christian's Library Press, 1982.

De Pree, Hugh. *Business as Unusual.* Zeeland, MI: Herman Miller, 1988.

De Pree, Max. "The Process of Work." *The Reformed Journal* 29 (May 1979): 9-13.

———. *Leadership is an Art.* New York: Doubleday, 1989.

Deutscher, M. "Adult Work and Developmental Models." *American Journal of Orthopsychiatry* 38 (1968): 882-92.

Diehl, William E. *Christianity and Real Life.* Philadelphia: Fortress, 1976.

———. *Thank God, It's Monday.* Philadelphia: Fortress, 1976.

———. *In Search of Faithfulness.* Philadelphia: Fortress, 1987.

Douglas, Jane Dempsey. "Calvin's Relation to Social and Economic Change." *Church and Society* 74 (March/April 1984): 74-78.

Douglas, Richard M. "Talent and Vocation in Humanist and Protestant Thought." *Action and Conviction in Early Modern Europe.* Theodore K. Kabb and Jerrold E. Seigel, eds. Princeton: Princeton University Press, 1969.

Drellich, M. "The Interrelationships of Work and Play." In *Dynamics of Work and Marriage.* Vol. 16 of *Science and Psychoanalysis.* J. H. Masserman, ed. New York: Grune & Stratton, 1970.

Drucker, Peter F. *The Practice of Management.* New York: Harper & Row, 1973.

———. *Management: Tasks, Responsibilities, Practices.* New York: Harper & Row, 1974.

Eisenstadt, S. N., ed. *The Protestant Ethic and Modernization.* New York: Basic Books, 1968.

Ekstein, R. "Play and Work." *Journal of Humanist Psychology* 3 (1963): 20-31.

Eller, Vernard. "A Voice on Vocation." *Reformed Journal* 29 (May 1979): 16-20.

Ellul, Jacques. "Work and Calling." *Katallagete* 4 (Fall/Winter 1972): 8-16.

———. *The Ethics of Freedom.* Grand Rapids: Eerdmans, 1976.

Elster, Jon. "Self-Realization in Work and Politics: The Marxist Conception of the Good Life." In *The Main Debate.* Tibor R. Machan, ed. New York: Random House, 1987.

Elton, Mayo. *The Social Problems of an Industrial Civilization.* Boston: Division of Research, Graduate School of Business Administration, Harvard University, 1945.

Engnell, Ivan. "Some Biblical Attitudes to Work. 1. Work in the Old Testament." *Svensk Exegetisk Arsbok* 26 (1961).

Eusebius. *Proof of the Gospel (Demonstrata Evangelica).* Grand Rapids: Baker Book House, 1981.

Farnsworth, Kirk E., and Lawhead, Wendell H. *Life-Planning: A Christian Approach to Careers.* Downers Grove, IL: InterVarsity, 1981.

Faunce, William A. "Automation and the Automobile Worker." *Social Problems* 6 (1958): 68-78.

Fein, Mitchell. *Motivation for Work.* New York: American Institute of Industrial Engineers, 1971.

Ficino, Marsilio. *Platonica Theologica.* 3 Vols. Raymond Marcel, ed. Paris, 1964-70.

Field, David, and Stephenson, Elspeth. *Just the Job.* London: Inter-Varsity, 1978.

Filsinger, Howard George. *The Age of Technology and the Calvinist Doctrine of Work.* Thesis (S.T.M.) British Columbia: Union College, 1968.

Flippo, Edwin B. *Management: A Behavioural Approach.* Boston: Allyn and Bacon, 1970.

Ford, Robert N. "The Third Revolution in Work." *Bell Telephone Magazine* (March/April 1971): 24-25.

Forrell, George W. *Faith Active in Love.* New York: American Press, 1954.

———. "Work and the Christian Calling." *The Lutheran Quarterly* 8 (May 1956).

Forrell, George W., and Lazareth, William H., eds. *Work as Praise.* Philadelphia: Fortress, 1979.

Forrester, William Roxburgh. *Christian Vocation.* New York: Scribner's Sons, 1953.

Fox, Mary Frank, and Hesse-Biber, Sharlene. *Women at Work.* Palo Alto, CA: Mayfield, 1984.

Freud, Sigmund. *Beyond the Pleasure Principle.* New York: W. W. Norton, 1961.

———. *Civilization and Its Discontents.* New York: W. W. Norton, 1961.

Friedmann, Eugene A., and Havighurst, Robert J. *The Meaning of Work and Retirement.* Chicago: University of Chicago Press, 1954.

Friedmann, Georges. *Industrial Society.* New York: Free Press, 1955.

Garson, Barbara. *All the Livelong Day: The Meaning and Demeaning of Routine Work.* Middlesex: Penguin, 1972.

Gartner, Bertil. "Work in the New Testament." *Svensk Exegetisk Arsbote* 26 (1961).

Gataker, Thomas. "Sermon." In *Capitalism and the Reformation.* M. J. Kitch, ed. London: Longman & Green, 1967.

Geoghegan, Arthur T. *The Attitudes Towards Labor in Early Christianity and Ancient Culture.* Washington, D.C.: Catholic University of America Press, 1945.

George, Charles H., and George, Katherine. *The Protestant Mind of the English Reformation.* Princeton: Princeton University Press, 1961.

George, C. S., Jr. *The History of Management Thought.* Englewood Cliffs, NJ: Prentice-Hall, 1968.

Gershuny, J. I. *The New Service Economy: The Transformation of Employment in Industrial Society.* New York: Praeger, 1983.

Gibbs, Mark. *Christians With Secular Power.* Philadelphia: Fortress, 1976.

Gibson, Mary. *Workers' Rights.* Totowa, NJ: Rowman & Allanheld, 1983.

Gilbert, James. *Work Without Salvation.* Baltimore: Johns Hopkins University Press, 1977.

Gill, David. "Jacques Ellul on the Ethics of Work." *Radix* 15 (January/February 1984): 4-7, 28.

Gillet, Richard W. "The Reshaping of Work: A Challenge to the Churches." *The Christian Century* (5-12 January 1983): 10-13.

———. *The Human Enterprise: A Christian Perspective on Work.* Kansas City, MO: Leaven, 1985.

Ginzberg, Eli. "Work: The Eye of the Hurricane." *Humanitas* 7 (Fall 1971): 227-42.

Glenn, Evelyn, and Feldberg, Roslyn. "Proletarianization of Clerical Work: Technology and Organizational Control in the Office." In *Case Studies on the Labor Process.* A. Zimbalist, ed. New York: Basic Books, 1972.

———. "Degraded and Deskilled: The Proletarianization of Clerical Work." *Social Problems* 25 (1977): 52-64.

Glueck, William F. *Management.* Hillsdale, IL: Dryden, 1977.

Gordon, David M., et. al. *Segmented Work, Divided Workers.* Cambridge: Cambridge University Press, 1982.

Gorney, R. "Work and Love Revisited." In *Proceedings of the Fourth World Congress of Psychiatry,* 1966, pp. 2542-44.

Gorz, Andre. *Farewell to the Working Class.* Boston: South End Press, 1982.

———, ed. *The Division of Labor: The Labor Process and Class Struggle in Modern Capitalism.* Sussex: Harvester Press, 1978.

Grant, Robert M. "Work and Occupations." In *Early Christianity and Society: Seven Studies.* New York: Harper & Row, 1977.

Green, James R. *World of the Worker: Labor in Twentieth-Century America.* 2nd ed. New York: Hill & Wang, 1980.

Green, Robert W., ed. *Protestantism, Capitalism, and Social Science: The Weber Thesis Controversy.* 2nd ed. Lexington, MA: Heath, 1973.

Green, Thomas F. *Work, Leisure and the American Schools.* New York: Random House, 1968.

Gregory, Dwight T. "The Protestant Work Ethic Today." *The Asbury Seminarian* 25 (October 1971): 20-39.

Guest, Robert. "Quality of Work life—Learning from Tarrytown." *Harvard Business Review* (July / August 1979): 76-87.

Gunn, Christopher Eaton. *Workers' Self-Management in the United States.* Ithaca, NY: Cornell University Press, 1984.

Gutman, Herbert C. *Work, Culture and Society in Industrializing America: Essays in America's Working Class and Social History.* New York: Random House, 1977.

Gurnall, William. *The Christian in Complete Armor.* London: Banner of Truth Trust, 1969.

Gyllenhammer, Pehr G. "How Volvo Adapts Work to People." In *Fundamental Readings in Modern Management.* 2nd ed. Samuel Certo, Daniel Brenenstuhl, and Kenneth Newgren, eds. Dubuque, IA: Wm. C. Brown, 1983.

Hackman, J. R. "Changing Views of Motivation in Work Groups." In *Changes in Working Life.* K. D. Duncan, M. M. Gruneberg, and D. Wallis, eds. New York: John Wiley & Sons, 1980.

Hall, Cameron Parter. *The Christian at his Daily Work.* New York: National Council of Churches of Christ, 1951.

Haraszti, Miklos. *A Worker in a Worker's State.* Baltimore: Penguin, 1977.

Hardy, Lee. *The Christian and Career Choice.* Grand Rapids: CRC Publications, 1985.

———. "Nice Compliments." A review of *Not Just a Job* by Judith Allen Shelly and *Getting a Job* by Michael Pountney. *The Reformed Journal* 36 (April 1986): 29-32.

———. "Our Work: God's Providence." *The Banner* (5 October 1987): 6-7.

———. "Christians at Work." A review of *Work and Leisure in Christian Perspective* by Leland Ryken. *The Reformed Journal* 39 (September 1989): 23-26.

Hatterer, L. "Work Identity." *American Journal of Psychiatry* 122 (1966): 1284-86.

Haywood, Carol Lois. "Does Our Theology of Work Need Reworking?" *Currents in Theology and Missions* 8 (October 1981): 298-301.

Hazelton, Roger. *God's Way with Man.* New York: Abingdon, 1956.

Heiges, Donald R. *The Christian's Calling.* Philadelphia: Fortress, 1984.

Heinecken, Martin J. "Luther and the 'Orders of Creation' in Relation to a Doctrine of Work and Vocation." *The Lutheran Quarterly* 4 (November 1952): 393-413.

Heisler, W. J., and Houck, John W. *A Matter of Dignity: Inquiries into the Humanization of Work.* Notre Dame: University of Notre Dame Press, 1977.

Heller, Agnes. *Renaissance Man.* London: Routledge, Kegan and Paul, 1978.

Hendrick, Ives. "Work and the Pleasure Principle." *Psychoanalytic Quarterly* 12 (1943): 311-29.

Hengel, Martin. *Property and Riches in the Early Church: Aspects of a Social History of Christianity.* Philadelphia: Fortress, 1974.

Henry, Carl F. "The Ailing World of Work." *Christianity Today* (January 1970): 22-23.

Herzberg, Frederick. *Work and the Nature of Man.* Cleveland: World, 1966.

———. "One More Time: How Do You Motivate Employees?" *Harvard Business Review* (January/February 1968): 53-62.

———. *The Managerial Choice: To be Efficient and to be Human.* Homewood, IL: Dow Jones-Irwin, 1976.

Herzberg, F., and Snyderman, B. *The Motivation to Work.* 2nd ed. New York: John Wiley, 1959.

Hess, H. "A Psychiatric Critique of *Work in America.*" *Journal of Occupational Medicine* 16 (November 1974).

Hiblers, A. "Nieuwe Visie op Arbied en Beroep: Calvijn." *Een goddelijk Beroep.* Goes: Oosterbaan & Le Cointre, 1962.

Hiltner, Seward. "Needed: A New Theology of Work." *Theology Today* (October 1974): 243-47.

Hinrichs, John R. "Psychology of Men at Work." *Annual Review of Psychology* 21 (1970): 519-54.

Hogben, Rowland. *Vocation.* London: Inter-Varsity, 1959.

Holden, Mark. *Called by the Gospel.* Minneapolis: Augsburg, 1983.

Holdsworth, C. J. "The Blessings of Work: The Cistercian View." *Studies in Church History* 10 (1973): 59-76.

Holl, Karl. "The History of the Word Vocation (Beruf)." *Review and Expositor* 55 (April 1958): 126-54.

Holland, John L. *Making Vocational Choices: A Theory of Careers.* Englewood Cliffs, NJ: Prentice Hall, 1973.

Holloway, James Y., and Campbell, Will D., eds. *Callings!* New York: Paulist Press, 1974.

Holmes, Arthur. "Wanted: A Christian Work Ethic for Today." *The Reformed Journal* 28 (October 1978): 17-20.

Houck, John W., and Williams, Oliver F. *Co-Creation and Capitalism: John Paul II's Laborem Exercens.* Lanham, MD: University Press of America, 1983.

———, eds. *The Judeo-Christian Vision and the Modern Corporation.* Notre Dame: University of Notre Dame Press, 1982.

Husslein, Joseph. *Bible and Labor.* New York: Macmillan, 1924.

Industrial Fatigue Research Board. *Two Studies in Rest Pauses in Industry.* Report No. 25. London: H. M. Stationery Office, 1924.

Iso-Ahola, Seppo E. *The Social Psychology of Leisure and Recreation.* Dubuque, IA: Wm. C. Brown, 1980.

Jacard, Pierre. *Histoire Sociale du Travail.* Paris: Payot, 1960.

Jahoda, M. "Notes on Work." *Psychoanalysis: A General Psychology.* R. Loewenstein, ed. New York: International Universities Press, 1966.

———. "The Psychological Meanings of Unemployment." *New Society* (6 September 1979): 492-95.

Janson, Robert. "Work Redesign: A Result-Oriented Strategy that Works." *Advanced Management Journal* (Winter 1979).

Jaques, Elliot. *Work, Creativity, and Social Justice.* New York: International Universities Press, 1970.

Jenkins, Clive, and Sherman, Barrie. *The Collapse of Work.* New York: Methuen, 1978.

John XXIII. *Mater et Magistra.* Boston: St. Paul Editions.

John Paul II. *On Human Work: Laborem Exercens.* Washington, DC: United States Catholic Conference, 1981.

———. "Work: A Path of Liberation." *Origins* 16 (17 July 1986): 166-68.

Johnston, Robert K. "Work: Its Relationship to Play." In *The Christian at Play.* Grand Rapids: Eerdmans, 1983.

Jolley, Steve. "Don't Ask Me What I 'Do.'" *Christianity Today* (5 September 1986): 14.

Jones, Barry. *Sleepers, Wake! Technology and the Future of Work.* New York: Oxford, 1982.

Kahn, Robert L. "The Meaning of Work: Interpretation and Proposals for Measurement." In *The Human Meaning of Social Change.* A. A. Campbell and P. E. Converse, eds. New York: Basic Books, 1972.

———. "On the Meaning of Work." *Journal of Occupational Medicine* 16 (November 1974).

Kaiser, Edwin G. *Theology of Work.* Westminster, MD: Newman Press, 1966.

Kakar, Sudhir. *Frederick Taylor: A Study in Personality and Innovation.* Cambridge, MA: MIT Press, 1970.

Kaplan, Glenn. *The Big Time: How Success Really Works in 14 Top Business Careers.* New York: Congdon and Weed, 1982.

Keiser, Jack. *Men at Work.* London: Epworth, 1978.

Kessler-Harris, Alice. *Out to Work: A History of Wage Earning in the U. S.* Oxford: Oxford University Press, 1982.

Killeen, S. M. *The Philosophy of Labour According to Thomas Aquinas.* Washington, DC: Catholic University Press, 1939.

Klauser, Alfred P. *Christ on Your Job.* St. Louis: Concordia, 1957.

Klein, L. *New Forms of Work Organization.* Cambridge: Cambridge University Press, 1976.

Kobobel, Janet. *But Can She Type? Overcoming Stereotypes in the Workplace.* Downers Grove, IL: InterVarsity, 1986.

Kranzberg, Melvin, and Gies, Joseph. *By the Sweat of Thy Brow: Work in the Western World.* New York: G. P. Putman's Sons, 1975.

Kraus, Elliot. *The Sociology of Occupations.* Boston: Little Brown, 1971.

Kreps, Juanita M. *Women and the American Economy—A Look at the 1980's.* Englewood Cliffs, NJ: Prentice Hall, 1976.

Kuhn, Harold B. "The Christian Mind and the Work Ethic." *The Asbury Seminarian* 25 (April 1971): 3-5.

Kuhne, R. J. *Co-Determination in Business.* New York: Praeger, 1980.

Küng, Hans, and Kasper, Walter, ed. *The Plurality of Ministries.* New York: Herder and Herder, 1972.

Kuyper, Abraham. *Christianity and Class Struggle.* Grand Rapids: Piet Hein, 1950.

LaBier, Douglas. *Modern Madness: The Emotional Fallout of Success.* Menlo Park, CA: Addison Wesley, 1986.

Landes, David S. *The Unbound Prometheus: Technological Change and Industrial Development in Western Europe from 1750 to the Present.* Cambridge: Cambridge University Press, 1969.

Lantos, Barbara. "Work and the Instinct." *International Journal of Psychoanalysis* 24 (1943): 114-19.

———. "Metaphysical Considerations on the Concept of Work." *International Journal of Psychoanalysis* 33 (1952): 439-43.

Lasson, Kenneth. *The Workers.* New York: Bantam Books, 1972.

Latta, G. W. *Profit Sharing, Employee Stock Ownership, Savings, and Asset Formation Plans in the Western World.* Philadelphia: University of Pennsylvania Press, 1979.

Lawler, E. E. III. "Job Design and Employee Motivation." *Personnel Psychology* 22 (4 November 1969): 426-35.

———. "Motivation: Closing the Gap Between Theory and Practice." In *Changes in Working Life.* K. D. Duncan, M. M. Gruneberg, and D. Wallis, eds. New York: John Wiley & Sons, 1980.

Lawrence, C. H. *Medieval Monasticism.* London: Longman, 1984.

Leacock, Eleanor, et al., eds. *Women's Work: Development of the Division of Labor by Gender.* South Hadley, MA: Bergin & Garvey, 1986.

Leavitt, H. J. *Readings in Managerial Psychology.* Chicago: University of Chicago Press, 1964.

Leavitt, Harold, and Whisler, Thomas. "Management in the 1980s." *Harvard Business Review* (1985): 41-48.

Lenin, V. I. *Collected Works.* Vol. 27. Moscow: Progress Publishers, 1965.

Leo XIII. *Rerum Novarum.* Boston: St. Paul Editions.

Lesieur, F. G., ed. *The Scanlon Plan.* New York: John Wiley, 1958.

Levenstein, Aron. *Why People Work: Changing Incentives in a Troubled World.* New York: Crowell-Collier, 1962.

Levering, Robert. *A Great Place to Work: What Makes Some Employers So Good—and Most So Bad.* New York: Random House, 1988.

Levinson, Harry. "Various Approaches to Understanding Man at Work." *Archives of Environmental Health* 22 (May 1971): 612-18.

Lindenfield, Frank, and Rothschild-Whitt, Joyce, eds. *Workplace Democracy and Social Change.* Boston: Extending Horizons Books, Porter Sargent, 1982.

Little, David. "Max Weber Revisited: The 'Protestant Ethic' and the Puritan Experience of Order." *Harvard Theological Review* 59 (1966): 415-28.

Locke, Edwin A. "The Nature and Causes of Job Satisfaction." In *Handbook of Industrial and Organizational Psychology.* M. D. Dunnette, ed. New York: Rand McNally, 1976.

———, et al. "The Relative Effectiveness of Four Methods of Motivating Employee Performance." In *Changes in Working Life.* K. D. Duncan, M. M. Gruneberg, and D. Wallis, eds. New York: John Wiley & Sons, 1980.

Lohse, Bernard. *Mönchtum und Reformation: Luther's Auseinandersetzung mit dem Münchideal des Mittelalters.* Göttingen: VandenHoeck & Ruprecht, 1963.

Luther, Martin. *Werke Kritische Gesamtausgabe,* Weimar: Hermann Böhlaus, 1883.

———. *Luther's Works.* St. Louis: Concordia, 1958.

Lüthy, Herbert. "Variations on a Theme by Max Weber." In *International Calvinism: 1541-1715.* Menna Prestwich, ed. Oxford: Oxford University Press, 1985.

McCarthy, Colman. "Superworkers in the Rat Race: What Makes Them Run?" *Los Angeles Times*, 26 March 1972.

McClelland, D. *The Achieving Society*. Princeton, NJ: Van Nostrand, 1961.

McGregor, Douglas. *The Human Side of Enterprise*. New York: McGraw-Hill, 1960.

Machlowitz, M. "Workaholics." *Across the Board* 14 (October 1977): 30-37.

McLean, Alan. "Work as a Four Letter Word." *Journal of Occupational Medicine*. (October 1970).

———, ed. *To Work is Human: Mental Health and the Business Community*. New York: Macmillan, 1970.

McNeill, John Thomas. "Calvin's Vocational Idealism and the Disciplined Community." In *Unitive Protestantism*. Richmond, VA: John Knox Press, 1964.

Marcson, S., ed. *Automation, Alienation, and Anomie*. New York: Harper & Row, 1970.

Marcuse, Herbert. *Eros and Civilization*. Boston: Beacon, 1955.

Mares, William, and Simmons, John. *Working Together: Participation from Shopfloor to Boardroom*. New York: Alfred A. Knopf, 1982.

Marshall, Paul. "The Calling: Secularization and Economics in the Seventeenth Century." Unpublished paper delivered at the annual meeting of the Canadian Political Science Association, May 1978.

———. "Work and Vocation." *The Reformed Journal* 30 (September 1980): 16-20.

———. "Calling, Work and Rest." In *Christian Faith and Practice in the Modern World*. Mark Noll and David Wells, eds. Grand Rapids: Eerdmans, 1988.

———. "The Shape of the Modern Work Ethic." In *Work in Canada*. J. Peters, J. Redekop, and J. Jenkins, eds. Waterloo, Ont.: Wilfrid Laurier University Press, n.d.

Marshall, Paul, et al. *Labour of Love: Essays on Work*. Toronto: Wedge Publishing Foundation, 1980.

Marx, Karl. *Karl Marx: Selected Writings*. David McLellan, ed. Oxford: Oxford University Press, 1977.

Maslow, A. H. *Motivation and Personality*. New York: Harper & Row, 1954.

Mather, Cotton. "A Christian at His Calling." In *Puritanism and the American Experience*. Michael McGiffert, ed. Reading, MA: Addison-Wesley, 1969.

Mattox, Robert. *The Christian Employee*. Plainfield, NJ: Logos International, 1978.

Mattson, Ralph, and Miller, Arthur. *Finding a Job You Can Love.* Nashville: Thomas Nelson, 1982.

Mayo, Elton. *The Human Problems of an Industrial Civilization.* Boston: Harvard Business School, 1933.

Medical Research Council. *Report of Investigation of Certain Industries.* Report 27. London: H. M. Stationery Office, 1924.

Meilander, Gilbert. *Friendship: A Study in Theological Ethics.* Notre Dame: University of Notre Dame Press, 1981.

Meloon, Walter. "Labor and Rest." *Applied Christianity* (September 1974): 24-28.

Menninger, Karl. "Work as a Sublimation." *Bulletin of the Menninger Clinic* 6 (1942): 170-82.

Merton, Robert K. "Social Structure and Anomie." In *Social Theory and Social Structure.* Glencoe, IL: Free Press, 1957.

Michaelson, R. S. "Changes in the Puritan Concept of Calling or Vocation." *New England Quarterly* 26 (September 1953).

Milkman, Ruth. *Gender at Work: The Dynamics of Job Segregation by Sex During World War II.* Urbana, IL: University of Illinois Press, 1987.

Miller, Alexander. *Christian Faith and My Job.* New York: Association Press, 1959.

Miller, Delbert C., and Form, William H. *Industrial Sociology: The Sociology of Work Organizations.* New York: Harper & Row, 1951.

Million, Elmer G. *Your Faith and Your Life Work.* New York: Friendship Press, 1960.

Mills, C. Wright. *White Collar.* New York: Oxford University Press, 1971.

Minear, Paul S. *To Die and to Live: Christ's Resurrection and Christian Vocation.* New York: Seabury, 1977.

Mitchell, Robert M. *Calvin's and the Puritan's View of the Protestant Ethic.* Washington, DC: University Press of America, 1979.

Moltman, Jürgen. "The Ethic of Calvinism." In *The Experiment of Hope.* Philadelphia: Fortress, 1975.

———, ed. *Recht auf Arbeit—Sinn der Arbeit.* Munich: Kaiser, 1979.

Moran, Pamela J. *The Christian Job Hunter.* Ann Arbor: Servant Books, 1984.

Morse, Nancy C., and Weiss, Robert S. "The Function and Meaning of Work and the Job." *American Sociological Review* 20 (April 1955): 191-98.

Mosse, Claud. *The Ancient World at Work.* London: Chatto and Windus, 1969.

Nadworney, Milton J. *Scientific Management and the Unions.* Cambridge, MA: Harvard University Press, 1955.

Neff, Walter S. "Psychoanalytic Conceptions of the Meaning of Work." *Psychiatry* 24 (November 1965): 324-33.

Nelson, John Oliver, ed. *Work and Vocation: A Christian Discussion.* New York: Harper, 1954.

Nickelhoff, Andrew, ed. *Extending Workplace Democracy: An Overview of Participatory Decision-making Plans for Unionists.* 2nd ed. Labor Studies Center Institute of Labor and Industrial Relations, University of Michigan, 1982.

Nicol, Rev. Dr. Iain G. "Vocation and the People of God." *Scottish Journal of Theology* 33 (1980): 361-73.

Niedner, Frederick A. "Putting on One's Neighbor." *Cresset* 46 (May 1983): 12-17.

Nosow, Sigmund, and Form, William H., eds. *Man, Work, and Society.* New York: Basic Books, 1962.

Nouwen, Henri J. M. *Out of Solitude.* Notre Dame: Ave Maria Press, 1974.

Oates, W. *Confessions of a Workaholic.* New York: World, 1971.

Oberndork, C. "The Psychopathology of Work." *Bulletin of the Menninger Clinic* 15 (1951): 77-84.

Ogilvie, David. *Confessions of an Advertising Man.* New York: Atheneum, 1963.

Olson, Richard. *A Job or a Vocation.* Nashville: Nelson Publishers, 1973.

Orzack, Louis H. "Work as a 'Central Life Interest' of Professionals." *Social Problems* 7 (1959): 125-32.

Osborne, William. *Man's Responsibility: An Ecumenical Study.* New York: Philosophical Library, 1968.

O'Toole, James. *Energy and Social Change.* Cambridge, MA: MIT Press, 1976.

———. "The Uneven Record of Employee Ownership." *Harvard Business Review* (November/December 1979): 185-97.

Ouchi, William. *Theory Z.* New York: Avon, 1981.

Palm, Goeran. *The Flight from Work.* Cambridge: Cambridge University Press, 1977.

Paul VI. *Populorum Progressio.* Boston: St. Paul Editions.

Peabody, Larry. *Secular Work is Full-Time Service.* Fort Washington, PA: Christian Literature Crusade, 1974.

Peifer, Claude J. "The Relevance of the Monastic Tradition to the Problem of Work and Leisure." *American Benedictine Review* 28 (December 1977): 373-96.

Penn, R. et al. "Job and Organization Characteristics as They Pertain to Job Satisfaction and Work Motivation." In *Changes in Working Life.* K. D. Duncan, M. M. Gruneberg, and D. Wallis, eds. New York: John Wiley & Sons, 1980.

Pennington, M. Basil. *Called: New Thinking on Christian Vocation.* New York: Seabury, 1983.

Perkins, William. "A Treatise of the Vocations or Callings of Men." In *The Work of William Perkins.* I. Breward, ed. Abingdon, Berks.: Courteney Press, 1970.

Peters, Thomas, and Waterman, Robert H., Jr. *In Search of Excellence.* New York: Warner Books, 1982.

Peterson, Donald J. "Flextime in the United States: The Lessons of Experience." In *Fundamentals of Management.* 4th ed. James Donnelly, Jr., James Gibson, and John Ivancevich, eds. Plano, TX: Business Publications, 1981.

Pico Della Mirandolla, Giovanni. *Oration on the Dignity of Man.* Chicago: Henry Regnery, 1956.

Pieper, Josef. *Leisure: The Basis of Culture.* Alexander Dru, trans. New York: Random House, 1963.

Pius XI. *Quadragessimo Anno.* Boston: St. Paul Editions.

Plato. *Plato's Republic.* G. M. A. Grube, trans. Indianapolis: Hackett, 1974.

———. "Phaedo." In *Five Dialogues.* G. M. A. Grube, trans. Indianapolis: Hackett, 1981.

Pollard, Sidney. "Factory Discipline in the Industrial Revolution." *Economic History Review* 16 (1963): 254-71.

Pooley, Roger. "The Puritan Doctrine of Calling." *Christian Graduate* 26 (1973): 22-24.

Pountney, Michael. *Getting a Job.* Downers Grove, IL: InterVarsity, 1984.

Prynne, William. *Histrio-Mastix* (1633). Reprint. New York: Johnson Reprint, 1972.

Raines, John C., and Day-Lower, Donna C. *Modern Work and Human Meaning.* Philadelphia: Westminster, 1986.

Reeck, Darrell. *Ethics for the Professions.* Minneapolis: Augsburg, 1982.

Reik, Theodore. "What is the Meaning of Work to Man?" An Interview with Theodore Reik in *The Why Report.* Lucy Freeman and Martin Theodore, eds. New York: Pocket Books, 1965.

Reisman, David. "The Themes of Work and Play in the Structure of Freud's Thought." *Psychiatry* 13 (1950): 1-17.

Ribicoff, Abraham. "The Alienation of the American Worker." *Saturday Review,* 22 April 1972, 29-33.

Richardson, Alan. *The Biblical Doctrine of Work.* London: Student Christian Movement Press, 1952.

Riddel, Jim. *Career Decision Making.* Nashville: Broadman Press, 1979.

Riesman, D., with Glazer, N., and Denny, R. *The Lonely Crowd.* New Haven, CT: Yale University Press, 1950.

Robinson, John. *Works I.* Boston: Doctrinal Tract and Book Society, 1851.

Rodgers, Daniel T. *The Work Ethic in Industrial America.* University of Chicago Press, 1978.

Rosen, Corey. *Employee Ownership in America.* Oakland, CA: National Center for Employee Ownership, 1981.

Rosow, J., ed. *The Worker and the Job.* Englewood Cliffs, NJ: Prentice Hall, 1974.

Roy, Robert. *The Cultures of Management.* Baltimore: Johns Hopkins University Press, 1977.

Rubin, Lilian B. *Worlds of Pain: Life in the Working Class Family.* New York: Basic Books, 1977.

Rush, Myron. *Management: A Biblical Approach.* Wheaton, IL: Victor Books, 1983.

Ryken, Leland. "Puritan Work Ethic: The Dignity of Life's Labors." *Christianity Today* (October 1979): 14-18.

———. *Work and Leisure in Christian Perspective.* Portland, OR: Multnomah Press, 1988.

Sabel, Charles F. *Work and Politics: The Division of Labor in Industry.* Cambridge: Cambridge University Press, 1982.

Sanderson, Robert. "Sermon in St. Paul's Church on I Cor. 7:24" (1621). In *The English Sermon.* Vol. 1. M. S. Smith, ed. Cheddle: Carcanet Press, 1979.

Savary, Louis M. *Man, His World, and His Work.* New York: Paulist Press, 1967.

Sayers, Dorothy. "Why Work?" In *Creed or Chaos.* New York: Harcourt, Brace, 1947.

Scanzoni, John. "The Christian View of Work." *Applied Christianity* (September 1974): 16-23.

Schein, E. H. *Organizational Psychology.* 2nd ed. Englewood Cliffs, NJ: Prentice Hall, 1970.

Schermerhorn, John R., Jr. *Management for Productivity.* 3rd ed. New York: John Wiley & Sons, 1989.

Schlosser, Felix. *Forms of Christian Life.* Milwaukee: Bruce Publishing Company, 1969.

Schrank, Robert. *Ten Thousand Working Days.* Cambridge, MA: MIT Press, 1978.

Schumacker, E. F. *Small is Beautiful.* New York: Harper & Row, 1973.

Scotchmer, Paul. "The Christian Meaning of Work." *New Oxford Review* 47 (May 1980): 12-18.

Scott, Donald I. *The Psychology of Work.* London: Duckworth, 1970.

Scott, Thomas. "Vox Dei." In *Works.* New York: Da Capo. Reprint. 1973.

See, Ruth Douglas. *The Protestant Doctrine of Vocation in the Presbyterian Thought of Nineteenth-Century America.* Unpublished thesis for the School of Education, New York University, 1952.

Seeman, Melvin. "On the Personal Consequences of Alienation in Work." *American Sociological Review* 32 (1967): 273-85.

Seerveld, Calvin. *Christian Workers, Unite!* Toronto: Christian Labour Association of Canada, 1964.

Segundo, Juan Luis. "The Hermeneutical Circle, Third Sample Attempt: Weber on Calvinism and Capitalism." In *Liberation of Theology.* Maryknoll, NY: Orbis Books, 1976.

Shaikan, Harley. *Work Transformed.* New York: Holt Rinehart, 1984.

Shepard, Jon M. "Functional Specialization and Work Attitudes." *Industrial Relations* 8 (May 1969): 185-94.

———."Functional Specialization, Alienation and Job Satisfaction." *Industrial and Labor Relations Review* 23 (January 1970): 207-19.

———. *Automation and Alienation: A Study of Office and Factory Workers.* MIT Press, 1971.

Sherman, Douglas Richard. "Towards a Christian Theology of Work." Unpublished thesis presented to the faculty of the Department of Systematic Theology, Dallas Theological Seminary. April, 1984.

Shetty, Y. K. "Is There a Best Way to Organize a Business Enterprise?" *Advanced Management Journal* (April 1973).

Simon, Yves R. *Work, Society, and Culture.* New York: Fordham University Press, 1971.

Sloan, Alfred P., Jr. *My Years With General Motors.* Garden City, NY: Doubleday, 1964.

Smith, Charles Ryder. *The Bible Doctrine of Wealth and Work.* London: Epworth Press, 1924.

Smith, Gary S. "The Spirit of Capitalism Revisited: Calvinists and the Industrial Revolution." *Journal of Presbyterian History* 59 (Winter 1981): 481-97.

Snelling, Robert O. *The Right Job.* New York: Viking, 1987.

Soelle, Dorothee, with Shirley A. Cloyes. *To Work and To Love: A Theology of Creation.* Philadelphia: Fortress, 1984.

Solmsen, Friedrich. "Greek Ideas about Leisure." In *The Wingspread Lectures in the Humanities.* Racine, WI: The Johnson Foundation, 1966.

Spenner, Kenneth. "Temporal Changes in Work Content." *American Sociological Review* (1979): 965-75.

———."Deciphering Prometheus: Temporal Change in the Skill Level of Work." *American Sociological Review* (1983): 824-37.

Steele, Richard. *The Tradesman's Calling.* London, 1684.

Steere, Douglas V. *Work and Contemplation.* New York: Harper & Bros., 1957.

Still, W. *Rhythm of Rest and Work.* Aberdeen: Gilcomston South Church, 1985.

Stokes, B. *Worker Participation: Productivity and the Quality of Worklife.* Washington: Worldwatch Institute, 1978.

Stolz, Barbara. *Still Struggling: America's Low-Income Working Women Confronting the 1980's.* Lexington, MA: Lexington Books, 1985.

Stott, John R. W. "Reclaiming the Biblical Doctrine of Work." *Christianity Today* (May 1979): 36-37.

———. "Creative by Creation: Our Need for Work." *Christianity Today* (June 1979): 32-33.

———. "Work and Unemployment." In *Involvement: Being a Responsible Christian in a Non-Christian Society.* Old Tappan, NJ: F. H. Revell, 1985.

Strauss, George. "Managerial Practices." In *Improving Life at Work.* J. Richard Hackman and J. Lloyd Suttle, eds. Santa Monica, CA: Goodyear, 1977.

Striner, Herbert E. *1984 and Beyond: The World of Work.* Staff Paper. (Washington, DC: W. E. Upjohn Institute for Employment Research, 1967).

Stuchi, Lorenz. "In Praise of Laziness." *Parks & Recreation* (August 1973): 17-35.

Stuermann, Walter Earl. *The Divine Destroyer: A Theology of Good and Evil.* Philadelphia: Westminster, 1967.

Suttle, J. Lloyd. "Improving Life at Work—Problems & Prospects." In *Improving Life at Work.* J. Richard Hackman and J. Lloyd Suttle, eds. Santa Monica, CA: Goodyear, 1977.

Swados, Harvey. On the Line. Boston: Little Brown, 1957.

Swinnock. "A Christian Man's Calling." In *Works.* Volume I. Edinburgh: James Nichol, 1868.

Symons, W. *Work and Vocation.* London: SCM Press, 1946.

Tausky, Curt. *Meaning of Work Among Blue Collar Men.* Paper presented to the annual meeting of the American Sociological Association in San Francisco, 1968.

Tawney, R. H. *Religion and the Rise of Capitalism.* New York: Harcourt, Brace & Co., 1926.

Taylor, Frederick W. *The Principles of Scientific Management.* New York: Harper & Bros., 1911.

Terkel, Studs. *Working.* New York: Pantheon, 1972.

Theissen, Gerd. *Sociology of Early Palestinian Christianity.* Philadelphia: Fortress, 1978.

Thompson, Donald B. "Enrichment in Action Convinces Skeptics." *Industry Week* (14 February 1972): 36-43.

Thompson, E. P. "Time, Work and Industrial Capitalism." *Past and Present* 38 (1967): 56-97.

Thompson, Paul. *The Nature of Work: An Introduction to Debates on the Labour Process.* New York: Macmillan, 1983.

Thrall, Margaret. "Christian Vocation Today." *Theology* 59 (March 1976): 84-89.

Tilgher, Adriano. "Work Through the Ages." In *Man, Work, and Society.* S. Nosow and W. Form, eds. New York: Basic Books, 1962.

———. *Work: What It Has Meant to Men Through the Ages.* New York: Arno Press, 1977.

Tjosvold, Dean. *Working Together to Get Things Done.* Lexington, MA: Lexington Books, 1986.

Todd, John Murray, ed. *Work: Christian Thought and Practice: A Symposium.* Baltimore: Helicon Press, 1960.

Toffler, Alvin. "Decoding the New Rules." In *Fundamental Readings in Modern Management.* 2nd ed. Dubuque, Iowa: Wm. C. Brown, 1983.

Torrance, T. F. *Royal Priesthood.* Edinburgh: Oliver and Boyd, 1955.

Trevor-Roper, Hugh Redwald. *Religion, the Reformation, and Social Change.* London: Macmillan, 1967.

Troeltsch, Ernst. *Protestantism and Progress: A Historical Study of the Relation of Protestantism to the Modern World.* W. Montgomery, trans. New York: Putnam's, 1912.

———. *The Social Teaching of the Christian Churches.* Volumes 1 and 2. London: George Allen and Unwin, 1931.

Trueblood, David Elton. *Your Other Vocation.* New York: Harper & Bros., 1952.

Urwick, Lyndall Fownes. *Scientific Principles and Organization.* New York: American Management Association, 1938.

Urwick, Lyndall F., and Brech, E. F. L. *The Making of Scientific Management.* London: Sir Isaac Pitman and Sons, 1952.

Vanderkloet, Edward. *Industrial Conflict: A Christian Perspective.* Toronto: Christian Labour Association of Canada, 1976.

———, ed. *A Christian Union in Labour's Wasteland.* Toronto: Wedge Publishing Foundation, 1978.

———, et al. *Beyond the Adversary System: Essays on Industrial Relations.* Toronto: Christian Labour Association of Canada, 1976.

Vanek, J., ed. *Self-Management.* Baltimore: Penguin, 1975.

Van Wyke, Millie. *You're Hired! Insights for Christian Women Who Work Outside the Home.* Grand Rapids: Baker Book House, 1984.

Veblen, Thorstein. *The Theory of the Leisure Class.* New York: Modern Library, 1934.

Volf, Miroslav. "On Human Work: An Examination of the Key Ideas of the Encyclical Laborem Exercens." *Scottish Journal of Theology* 37 (1984): 67-79.

———. "Arbeit und Charisma." *Zeitschrift für Evangelische Ethik* 31, 4 (1987): 411-33.

Vos, Melvin. "To Take Life Leisurely." *The Reformed Journal* 29 (May 1979): 14-16.

———. *Seven Days a Week: Faith in Action.* Philadelphia: Fortress, 1985.

Vroom, Victor H. *Work and Motivation.* New York: John Wiley, 1964.

Walker, E. R., and Guest, R. H. *The Man on the Assembly Line.* Cambridge, MA: Harvard University Press.

Wall, T. D. "Group Work Redesign in Context: A Two-Phase Model." In *Changes in Working Life.* K. D. Duncan, M. M. Gruneberg, and D. Wallis, eds. New York: John Wiley & Sons, 1980.

Wallace, Ronald S. *Calvin's Doctrine of the Christian Life.* Edinburgh: Oliver and Boyd, 1959.

Walter, J. A. *A Long Way From Home.* London: Paternoster, 1980.

Ward, Patricia, and Stout, Martha. *Christian Women at Work.* Grand Rapids: Zondervan, 1981.

Weber, Max. *The Protestant Ethic and the Spirit of Capitalism: The Relationships Between Religion and the Economic and Social Life in Modern Culture.* Talcott Parsons, trans. New York: Scribner's Sons, 1958.

White, Jerry, and White, Mary. *Your Job: Survival or Satisfaction?* Grand Rapids: Zondervan, 1977.

Whyte, William H., Jr. *Organization Man.* Garden City, NY: Anchor, 1957.

Widick, B. J., ed. *Auto Work and Its Discontents.* Baltimore: Johns Hopkins University Press, 1976.

Wiener, Norbert. *The Human Use of Human Beings.* Boston: Houghton Mifflin, 1950.

Wilensky, Harold. "Work as a Social Problem." In *Social Problems: A Modern Approach.* Howard S. Becker, ed. New York: John Wiley, 1966.

Wilson, A. T. M. "The Manager and His World." *Industrial Management Review* (Fall 1961).

Wingren, Gustaf. *Luther on Vocation.* Carl C. Rasmussen, trans. St. Louis: Concordia, 1957.

———. "The Concept of Vocation—Its Basis and Its Problems." *Lutheran World* 15, 2 (1968): 87-99.

Winick, Charles. "Atonie: the Psychology of the Unemployed and the Marginal Worker." In *The Frontiers of Management Psychology.* George Fish, ed. New York: Harper & Row, 1964.

Wolfbein, Seymour. *Work in American Society.* Glenview, IL: Scott Foresman, 1971.

Wollard, A. G. B. "'Self-Actualization' and the Christian Doctrine of Work: A Theological Critique of the Ideas of Frederick Herzberg." *Church Quarterly* 3 (January 1971): 225-31.

Wolterstorff, Nicholas. "More on Vocation." *Reformed Journal* 29 (May 1979): 20-23.

Work in America. Report of a task force to the Secretary of Health, Education, and Welfare. Cambridge, MA: MIT Press, 1973.

"Work, Theology of." In *The New Catholic Encyclopedia.* Volume XIV. New York: McGraw-Hill, 1967, pp. 1015-17.

Wrege, C. D.; Stotky, A. M.; and Cooke, A. M. "The Story Behind F. W. Taylor's Principles of Scientific Management." *Academy of Management Review* (1978): 736-49.

Yankelovich, D. "The Meaning of Work." In *The Worker and the Job.* J. Rosow, ed. Englewood Cliffs, NJ: Prentice Hall, 1974.

———. "The Work Ethic is Underemployed." *Psychology Today* (May 1982): 5-8.

Zargoric, Sam. "Searching for Meaning in Work: Rebellion and Reform." *The Washington Post,* 6 February 1972.

Zehring, John William. *Making Your Life Count: Finding Fulfillment Beyond Your Job.* Valley Forge, PA: Judson Press, 1980.

Zimbalist, Andrew, ed. *Case Studies on the Labor Process.* New York: Monthly Review Press, 1979.

Zwerdling, Daniel. *Workplace Democracy.* New York: Harper & Row, 1980.

Zwingli, Ulrich. "Of the Education of the Youth." In *Zwingli and Bullinger: Selected Translations.* Geoffrey W. Bromiley, trans. Philadelphia: Westminster 1953.

* * *

Index of Names

Althaus, Paul, 51, 54
Aquinas, St. Thomas, 17, 18, 19, 55
Arendt, Hannah, 9, 10, 14n.17, 25, 26n.51
Argyris, Chris, 145-151
Aristotle, 7-15, 26, 56, 57
Augustine, Saint, 17, 19, 57, 95, 120

Barth, Karl, 86, 93, 98, 113
Bellah, Robert N., xiv, xv
Benedict, Saint, 20, 23
Bonhoeffer, Dietrich, 127
Brunner, Emil, 50n.13, 92, 103, 106, 125, 126-127

Calvin, John, xvi, 50n.14, 52n.18, 54-63, 65, 66n.47, 90, 98, 120, 121, 174

Drucker, Peter, 84, 138, 139, 145n.33, 162-167, 175

Ellul, Jacques, 103-106, 126, 175

Freud, Sigmund, 38-43

Herzberg, Frederick, 137, 140, 151-155, 175

Jesus, 52, 53, 54, 55, 63, 74, 75, 81, 99, 136
John XXIII, 69, 74, 75, 94, 127
John Paul II, 68, 70, 71, 72, 74, 75

Leo XIII, 67, 68, 73
Levering, Robert, 169-174, 176, 183
Luther, Martin, 44, 45-54, 59, 63, 64, 65, 67, 82, 105, 112, 120

McGregor, Douglas, 138, 155-160, 161, 162, 175
Marx, Karl, 29-37, 38, 39, 68
Maslow, Abraham, 157
Mayo, Elton, 140, 143, 149, 175

Paul, Saint, 62, 65, 80, 81, 95, 102
Paul VI, 69, 71, 76

Pius XI, 63n.44, 68, 69, 73
Plato, 11, 14, 15, 16

Taylor, Frederick Winslow, 129-140, 141, 142, 154, 159, 160, 161, 165, 167, 175

Terkel, Studs, 5, 32, 33, 38
Tilger, Adriano, 7, 14, 23, 34, 64

Weber, Max, xviii
Wingren, Gustaf, 48, 49, 50n.14, 54, 65, 112

* * *

Index of Subjects

Activity, free productive, 28, 29, 30, 32, 34; practical, 9, 11; productive, 8, 27, 28, 29, 30, 39

Body, 7, 8, 16, 17; and contemplation, 13; discipline of, 45; needs of, 9, 13, 14; pleasures of, 11, 40; relation to soul, 14, 15

Calling, biblical concept of, 80-81; general, 80, 119; particular, 80-81, 119
Capitalism, 33-36, 68
Communism, 34-38
Contemplation, 14, 57; of God, 18-19, 26, 45; and the active life, 27, 30, 119
Cultural mandate, 71

Flexplace, 184
Flextime, 183

Gifts, 66, 85, 91, 122; as concerns, 91-92; discovery of, 85-88; and God's will, 92; as interests, 91
God, grace of, 20; providence of, 47-48, 72-73; Reformed idea of, 57; Renaissance idea of, 27; union with, 19-20
Gods, 12, 13, 40; philosophical idea of, 27
Gospel, counsels of, 24-25; precepts of, 24-25; response to, 52

Hawthorne effect, 144
Hawthorne experiment, 143-145, 155, 161

Individualism, xiv-xv, xvii
Indulgences, 22
Industrial Revolution, 128

Job, content, 183; context, 183; dissatisfaction, 152-153; enlargment, 180; enrichment, 150, 154, 170-172; rotation, 180; satisfaction, 98, 152, 159, simplification, 150
Job design, 123, 127, 174-175, 178-185; and justice, 180;

socio-technical approach to, 181-182

Labor, aliented, 31, 37; division of, 31-32, 37, 64; manual, 23
Labor laws, 37
Labor relations, 134
Lay brothers, 24, 26
Lay patrons, 22, 23
Leisure, xv, 17, 19, 24, 39
Life, active, 18-19, 26-27, 53, 56, 58, 75, 119; contemplative, 11-14, 17-19, 23, 25, 53, 55-58, 75, 119; monastic, 19, 48; mixed, 119; philosophical, 13; practical, 12-13, 26; productive, 12, 18; religious, 26; spiritual, 20
Loading, horizontal, 180; vertical, 180-181

Management, as a discipline, 145; contingency approach to, 184; human relations approach to, 144-145, 149, 170; by integration, 159, 160; by objective, 163; and manipulation, 162, 167-169; participatory, 150; role of, 166, 178; and trust, 169-172
Monastery, 19, 45, 50
Monasticism, 19-26; Calvin's criticism of, 54-58; Luther's criticism of, 48-54; Reformed, 119-121
Monastic vows, 22, 25, 50, 120

Obligations, social, 61, 63, 69, 70, 80, 94, 98, 122
Organizations, behavior within, 146; structure of, 147

Pleasure, pursuit of, 11, 39, 42

Quality circles, 182-183

Retirement, 6

Salvation, 17, 20, 22, 23, 49
Scientific management, 131-136, 149, 154, 160, 178, 180; criticism of, 138-139, 155, 159, 165, 179; impact of, 141; labor's reaction to, 135-136
Self-deception, 89
Self-knowledge, 86-88
Self-sufficiency, 13-14
Slaves, 10, 14, 26, 65
Slavery, 9-11
Social Question, 68, 70, 76
Social reform, 65-67, 75-76, 105-107, 107-111
Society, structure of, 60-61, 62, 73, 75, 85; hierarchical structure of, 14, 46, 64
Soul, 11, 12, 20; Aristotle's concept of, 15; Plato's concept of, 15-16; relation to body, 14-15
Spiritual disciplines, 20, 26
Stations, 46-47, 51; Calvinist attitude toward, 64-67
Suffering, religious, 52, 53

Technology, 30, 40, 43, 125, 161
Theory X, 156
Theory Y, 157-159

Unemployment, 5-6, 7
Union movement, 37

Vocation, biblical idea of, 80; con-

cept of, 45, 82; broad concept of, 82, 100, 111-113, 122; Calvinist concept of, 54-63; Catholic concept of, 67-76; and God's providence, 83; Luther's concept of, 45-48, 51-53; narrow concept of, 112-113
Vocational choice, principles of, 81, 84, 93; problems of, 79-93
Vocational counseling, 88
Vocational integration, 113, 118, 122

Work, as ascetic discipline, 23-24; and civilization, 40-43; contemporary attitude toward, 4-6; de-vocationalization of, 103, 136-137; dissatisfaction with, 157; as essential activity, 28; and God's providence, 47-48; Greek attitude toward, 6-16; Freudian concept of, 38-43; human factors of, 142; idolatry of, 117; Marxist concept of, 29-37; medieval attitude toward, 16-26, 45, 50; motivation to, 137, 145, 153-154, 161, 163; as necessary, 7-9, 10, 27, 41, 42; productive, 11, 17, 25; Renaissance attitude toward, 26-29; religious dignity of, 58-59; and responsibility, 151, 164-165, 167, 175, 178, 184; social organization of, xvii, 124-125; and vocation, 100-107, 125-128; volunteer, 101-102, 104
Workaholism, 114-118
Work groups, 181